Clicker Training: Colt Starting the Natural Horse

Disclaimer of Liability:
Equine training can be a hazardous activity, which may subject participants to possible serious injury to you or your horse. Leslie Pavlich and her associates will not assume any liability for your activities. This, book provides general information, instruction and techniques that may not be suitable for everyone. No warranty is given regarding the suitability of this information, the instructions, and techniques to you or other individuals acting under your instructions.

Copyright © 2008 Leslie Pavlich
All rights reserved.
ISBN: 1-4196-8475-2
ISBN-13: 978-1419684753

LESLIE PAVLICH
Edited by Jeanne Johnson
Photography by Sandra Mings
www.clickhorse.info

CLICKER TRAINING: COLT STARTING THE NATURAL HORSE

2008

Clicker Training: Colt Starting the Natural Horse

FORWARD FROM THE EDITOR	xix
INTRODUCTION	xxi
CHAPTER 1 UNDERSTANDING CLICKER TRAINING	**1**
A GOOD EXAMPLE OF HORSE BEHAVIOR DURING CLICKER TRAINING	7
CLICKER TRAINING HISTORY	9
CHAPTER 2 GETTING STARTED	**15**
UNDERSTANDING HORSES	15
MY FIRST EXPIERIENCE WITH CLICKER TRAINING	16
ITEMS YOU WILL NEED	16
HOW HORSES REACT DIFFERENTLY TO TARGETING	18
LOCATION	20
TARGETING TASK	20
MAKING A NEW BELIEVER	23
IS CLICKER TRAINING BRIBERY	25
HAND FEEDING BEFORE CLICKER TRAINING	25
HAND FEEDING WITH CLICKER TRAINING	26
TURNING HEAD AWAY TASK	28
BEING GOOD WITH HORSES	29
GUIDELINES TO REMEMBER	30
CLICKER GAMES	31
CHAPTER 3 CUES	**39**
PHASING OUT CLICKER TRAINING WITH CHAINING	40
SHOW ME WHAT YOU KNOW	41
ANOTHER EXPLANATION	42
ANTICIPATION VERSES OFFERING BEHAVIORS	42
OFFERING BEHAVIORS	43

GETTING THE SAME RESULTS WITH
DIFFERENT METHODS DOESN'T MEAN THAT
   IT'S SAME THING   44
IF YOUR YOUNG HORSE OR YOUNG FOAL IS NOT
   HALTER BROKE   46
FACILITY   48

CHAPTER 4 GETTING TO KNOW YOUR HORSE OR COLT   49
YES, THEY WILL KICK YOU   50
DISENGAGEMENT OF HINDQUARTERS
AT LIBERTY   52
ADDING A CUE TO IT   55
MISTAKES CAN HAPPEN   57
FIXED, VARIABLE REINFORCEMENT
   SCHEDULE, AND CHAINING   57

CHAPTER 5 TOUCHING YOUR HORSE   59
TOUCHING YOUR HORSE FOR THE FIRST TIME   59
FREEDOM GAMES   62
FREEDOM GAMES WITH OLDER HORSES   65
WALKING ON A BRIDGE TASK   67
MORE SLICKERS AND FLAGS   70
PLASTIC BAG TASK   71
SOFT FLAGS   71
TARPS AND SLICKERS   72

CHAPTER 6 THE HALTER   75
PUTTING HAND OVER NECK   75
SIMULATE PUTTING THE HALTER ON   77
PUTTING HALTER ON   79
PRESSURE WITH HALTER   84
THE LEAD   85
DISENGAGEMENT WITH HALTER, AND LEAD   86
CHANGING HALTERS TO A WEB HALTER   87
MORE ABOUT COMING FORWARD WITH
   PRESSURE   88

BACKING WITH HALTER	89
ADDING A CUE TO BACKING	90
COMBINING BACKING AND COMING FORWARD	91
ANOTHER EXERCISE	92
MORE FREEDOM GAMES TARGETING OBJECTS	94

CHAPTER 7 EXPANDING ON TOUCHING YOUR HORSE — 97

STROKING YOUR HORSE WITH AN EXTENSION STICK	97
STROKING WITH OUR HANDS	101
PHASING OUT FOR TOUCHING YOUR HORSE WITH YOUR HAND	104
INTRODUCING THE BRUSH AND BRUSHING YOUR HORSE	104
TOUCHING THE BACK SECTION OF YOUR HORSE WITH YOUR HAND	104

CHAPTER 8 CRUCIAL TASKS — 107

SHOW ME WHAT YOU KNOW CHECKLIST	107
DISENGAGEMENT OF HIND QUARTERS FROM THE LEFT SIDE	107
BACKING	110
MOVING THE FOREQUARTERS OVER FROM THE LEFT SIDE	111
MOVING OVER WITH YOUR STICK	113
PRACTICING DISENGAGEMENT WITH YOUR CUES	114
BACKING WITH A CUE	115
COMBINING BACKING AND COMING FORWARD	117

CHAPTER 9 MAINTANANCE — 119

TONGUE CLICK SECONDARY CLICK	119
VACCINATIONS	119

CHAPTER 10 FEET — 123

GETTING STARTED WITH THE FRONT FEET	124

CLEANING OUT THE FRONT FEET	127
STRADDLING THE FRONT FEET	128
TRIMMING YOUR HORSES FRONT FOOT	129
RASPING THE FRONT FEET	130
SHOES FOR THE FRONT FEET	130
GETTING STARTED WITH THE BACK FEET	131
ADDING A CUE TO RESTING THE FOOT	134
PICKING UP THE HIND FOOT	135
HAVING YOUR HORSE HELP YOU PICK UP THE FOOT	136
CLEANING OUT THE BACK FEET	138
STRADDLING THE BACK FOOT	138
RASPING THE BACK FEET	139
TRIMMING THE BACK FEET	140

CHAPTER 11 ROUND PENNING — 143

DOMINANT HORSES	143
ROUND PEN WORK	145
ROUND PENNING TASK	148
ADDING A CUE TO IT	150
DISENGAGEMENT OF HINDQUARTERS FOR STOPPING	151
GOING THE OTHER DIRECTION	153
MIXING IT UP	154
ADDING THE HALTER AND LEAD	154
LUNGING WITH HALTER AND LEAD WITH NO ROUND PEN	155
WORKING AT LIBERTY WITH A ROPE IN A ROUND PEN	157

CHAPTER 12 CONTINUATION OF FREEDOM GAMES — 161

TOUCHING YOUR HORSE WITH A CLOTH OR TOWEL	161
STANDING ON TOP OF BLANKETS, JACKETS, AND TARPS	164
WAVING AROUND A JACKET	167

STANDING ON JACKET TASK	168
TARP	168
TOUCHING WITH THE SADDLE PAD	172
RUBBING THE SADDLE PAD ON THEIR LEGS	173
LAYING THE PAD ON YOUR HORSES BACK	174
WALKING WITH THE PAD ON	175
HAVING THE PAD FALL OFF YOUR HORSE	175
TOUCHING YOUR HORSE WITH A JACKET, SLICKER AND TARP	176
KILLER PLASTIC BAGS	177
TOUCHING YOUR HORSE WITH A PLASTIC BAG	177
TOUCHING THE BELLY AND LEGS WITH ALL THE OBJECTS	187
JACKET	179
TOUCHING WITH A TARP	179
HAVING BLANKET, SLICKERS AND TARPS FALL OFF WHILE TROTTING	181

CHAPTER 13 TRAILERING — 183

IMAGE'S LIFE THREATENING ORDEAL	183
PICKING THE RIGHT TRAILER	185
HAVING YOUR HORSE FOLLOW YOU THROUGH A GATE	185
HAVING YOUR HORSE WALK WITH YOU	186
HAVING YOUR HORSE WALK THROUGH A GATE FIRST	187
INTRODUCTION TO THE TRAILER	190
GOING INTO THE TRAILER	191
LOADING INTO THE TRAILER WITH ALL FOUR FEET	193
EXAMPLE OF LOADING IN A STOCK TRAILER	195
SCARED TO LOAD	196
DOMINANCE ISSUE	198
DOMINANCE TRAILER TASK	199

CHAPTER 14 FACE MUZZLE AND EARS — 201

TOUCHING THE EARS	201

HAVING YOUR HORSE TOUCH YOUR HAND WITH THEIR EAR	202
CLIPPING EARS	204
TOOTHBRUSH TASK	205
TOUCHING EARS WITH THE TOOTHBRUSH	207
PHASING OUT THE CLICK ON THEIR FACE ON ONE SIDE	208
WORKING WITH CLIPPERS ON THE FACE	208

CHAPTER 15 HEAD DOWN AND STANDING STILL — 211

HEAD DOWN TASKS	212
STANDING STILL TASK	214
WHEN IS THE BEST TIME TO START YOUR HORSE?	216

CHAPTER 16 LATERAL FLEXION — 219

ADDING A CUE TO LATERAL FLEXION	221

CHAPTER 17 SADDLING — 227

PREPARING FOR THE SADDLE WITH ROPES	227
INTRODUCING THE SADDLE PAD	229
INTRODUCING THE SADDLE WITHOUT THE PAD	230
TIGHTEN CINCH OF THE SADDLE	233
WALKING YOUR HORSE WITH THE PAD AND SADDLE ON	236
PHASING OUT THE CLICKS FOR SADDLING	237
GETTING YOUR HORSE USED TO SADDLE NOISES	238
TROTTING IN A ROUND PEN OR SMALL AREA	241
CLICKING FOR YOUR HORSE NOT PULLING ON THE LEAD AT A TROT	242
CANTERING ON-LINE IN AN OPEN SPACE WITH OR WITHOUT THE LEADS ON GROUND	244

CHAPTER 18 LINE DRIVING YOUR HORSE — 247

GETTING YOUR HORSE USED TO THE ROPES	247

BACKING WITH DRIVING REINS	255
CHAPTER 19 RIDING	**259**
GETTING READY TO RIDE	259
BEFORE YOU START TO RIDE CHECKLIST	259
FIRST RIDE BAREBACK	259
LAYING ON YOUR HORSES BACK	262
TIME TO GET ON	263
FEEDING WHILE SITTING ON YOUR HORSE	264
MOUNTING YOUR HORSE FROM THE GROUND WITH A SADDLE	266
WALKING FORWARD WHILE MOUNTED WITH THE SADDLE	267
CHAPTER 20 FLEXING WHILE RIDING	**273**
TURNING	273
FLEXING TO A STOP USING PRESSURE IN THE ROUND PEN	275
WALKING STRAIGHT FOR LONGER PERIODS	276
USING YOUR LEGS TO TURN	277
WALKING AND TURNING UNTIL A STOP	278
CHAPTER 21 TROTTING	**281**
TROTTING FOR THE FIRST TIME	281
EMERGENCY STOP FROM THE TROT	283
UNDER PRESSURE RIDING	284
BACKING WHILE MOUNTED	284
CHAPTER 22 ADVANCING	**287**
SIDEPASSING	287
SIDE PASSING ON-GROUND	288
SIDE PASSING IN THE SADDLE	289
TURNING EXERCISE WITH LEGS	290
CANTERING	292
EMERGENCY STOP AT THE CANTER	295
BITS	295
INTRODUCTION TO THE SNAFFLE BIT, OR	

RETRAINING FOR THE BIT	296
WORKING WITH THE BIT AND THE HEADSTALL	297
STARTING TO USE THE BIT ON GROUND	298
USING YOUR BIT WHILE MOUNTED	299
HERD BOUND HORSES	300
HERD BOUND HORSES WHILE RIDING	301
HONEY THE HERD BOUND HORSE	302
RIDING A YOUNG HORSE ON THE TRAIL	305
IN CLOSING	306

I Would Like To Thank My Husband Frank, My Mom Sandy, Jeanne J, Laura C, Yvonne T And All The Horses.

FORWARD FROM THE EDITOR

Every once in a while, someone comes into your life and makes a difference. Leslie is that person for me. Not just me, but also my horses. I have learned more about horse psychology from her in the 11 years I have known her. If you are reading this book, you and your horse are about to be among those blessed to make a connection with her. Like so many that have climbed that mountain to ask the wise old sage about the meaning of life, Leslie now sits at the top of the mountain ready to explain the true meaning of the horse/human relationship. This book and the concept of Clicker Training will give you a form of communication with your horse that can go beyond anything you ever dared to dream. To watch Leslie dance with Cheyenne is truly inspiring. It's as if they are telepathically communicating the steps. I was amazed and in awe that a horse could be taught the intricate move that I was seeing right in front of me. When you discover how easy and fun it is to train your horse with the "Clicker" you will find there are no limits to what you can do with your horse.

Thanks Leslie for helping my horses and me to have a better relationship, and for writing this book so others may have the same opportunity. *Jeanne J*

INTRODUCTION

I was raised with horses and I took my first trot on a horse when I was 3. When I was 5 I was bucked off almost everyday by a Shetland Pony named Peanuts, but that didn't bother me, I got back on again and again. I started my first colt when I was 14. A Morgan horse named Gallant. In my teens I showed horses, and even show jumped. I guess I was always fascinated with horses, and how to work with them.

I went to equine school for a year, worked with Natural Horsemanship for 10 years, and continued to train the entire time. When I started with Clicker Training, I had a breeding farm full of horses, and a few clients. I was sure ready for something new and different, but no one else was as ready. They didn't want to know about this new type of training, and most everybody thought I was half- crazy. Alone, with not much to do other than train my own horses, I went to the web for support. I found the support I was seeking, but mostly I ended up helping others online with Clicker Training. I had prior experience with horses, which helped with advice, but unfortunately, writing e-mails took most of my time. After writing over 100 pages of help to others, I decided to write for myself. I am not a writer and knew nothing about writing a book. I was even amazed that anyone could understand my e-mails. Punctuation was never a strong point. The only thing that I could do was type fast. Most of the words were misspelled and incomplete sentences, but I did get it down. Everybody thought I lost my mind training horses with a box and food. How could I write a book about it? Why would I want to? I just felt I needed to do something. I was very serious about working with Clicker Training. I felt that it was easier and safer for the horse and me. My clients didn't agree so I lost most of them. They just couldn't understand how I could use food as a reward. I had to work with no pay, but did have some savings that I could use. I had an opportunity to work on this new project with no limitations. Four years on a project with no pay is stressful, but you have to make sacrifices to try something new.

After about 4 years of writing, my book was three-quarters finished. People were starting to figure out I was serious about this type of training method. I started to get my clients back with much curiosity. I am sure everyone thought I would give it up, and that I would find out that it doesn't work. Four years would have been a long time to put into something that didn't work. Then others started to give it a try. It worked and now I have more faithful clients than ever before. My success shows in their horses, and I am still just as excited about Clicker Training as the day I started with it.

This book is the result of over 4 years working with 50 different horses with Clicker Training. This book was also originally intended for just me. I needed a program for myself that I could stick to, so my training would go smoother. I work with many different ages of horses. I would be working on more finished colts, then 6 months later I was back to just weanlings. I wrote a manual that I went by to get me back on track, and to keep me consistent. Since Clicker Training is so new and so different to anything else that I used before, I needed my own training manual. You may forget the interesting moments and forget why you do the things you do. If you write those special moments down, you can capture those feelings forever. Consistency is your greatest asset with training a horse. A horse can stay consistent, but the human tends to forget. I needed to know what worked best for the weanlings and the older horses.

CHAPTER 1
UNDERSTANDING CLICKER TRAINING

When I was about 14, I started show jumping my horse Jack. I was fortunate enough to have an Olympic jumping instructor for awhile. We went to a show in Durango Colorado about 50 miles from where we lived. This show was elaborate. More elaborate than I think anyone had seen in Durango. The jumps where very colorful and decorated with many plants. We didn't have those kinds of jumps in my small town. When Jack took one look at the arena his eyes got huge and he tensed up. When we approached the first jump, Jack stopped dead in his tracks just before he got to the jump. I knew I had three tries to get him over each jump. On the second try he stopped just before the jump again. I remember thinking "It's going to be one of those days." I was so embarrassed. On the third try he jumped it beautifully. Jack did it all again on the second jump. By this time I was hot and sweaty. It took all of my focus to try again. I was getting even more embarrassed. It took me three tries for Jack to get enough confidence to jump every jump. I thought I would never get through the course. It took us about 20 minutes to complete. I was horrified. When it was over I looked up and everybody in the stands stood up and clapped. I asked my mom, "Why are they clapping? That was so horrible!" She said, "They are clapping for you. You tried so hard and you made it. That was incredible!" I was shocked that my efforts were being rewarded. I never got a standing ovation before, even when winning a blue ribbon. I still remember that moment, even though it was so many years ago. That moment was life changing for me.

That sums up what Clicker Training is all about, but your horse gets that feeling. The blue ribbon would be the food, and the click was the clapping. I was there because of the hopes of a blue ribbon, but the clapping is what I remember, because I was getting rewarded for my hard work. I did place in the class, but I have forgotten all about that.

When I started with Clicker Training, I had about 10 horses in training. They were all about the same level, and most of them were not even halter broke yet. My end goal was to figure out if I could use Clicker Training to shorten my training time and make it safer for me and the horses. There was not much instruction at the time, so I had to play a little bit of a guessing game on how to use it. I was excited everyday just knowing how fast I could get horses to do certain things, and how easy and safe it was. I learned mostly by trial and error, and I also had to get rid of some of my bad habits. I made a lot of mistakes. My horses ended up teaching me most of what I know about Clicker Training. Horses are really your best teachers.

This book is about the program that I developed with horses, and adding Clicker Training to my own training program. The tasks are in order of how I start a colt. I have been using Clicker Training for over 6 years, and I am here to tell you that **it does work**! Before I started Clicker Training I tried to work with the horse's natural instincts, but there was something missing. I knew I was not making the complete connection that I needed. All of the horses reacted in the same way to this new training program, and what worked I continued with. I learned a great deal from those 10 horses, more than the many others that I had started in the past. I wrote down everything that happened daily, and compared notes. Writing the day's work down was one of the best things that I did to have a log on the successes and failures of the day. Those horses paved a path to what I use today. I made many mistakes, and it took more than one horse to tell me what I needed to be doing. Every horse that I worked with, I learned from. There are some tasks that really make a difference, and other tasks you don't have to do. You have to bend to the individual horse, but if it works with one, try it with others. They basically think the same, but with different personalities, likes, dislikes, and attitudes.

I was working with a very difficult horse, a horse that had never been touched. I have worked with many horses that had never been touched before and most were easy to work with. About 1 out of 100 are extreme in difficulty, and this particular horse was that one. This book was inspired by that one horse.

CLICKER TRAINING: COLT STARTING THE NATURAL HORSE

There is no way that I can gauge how difficult or easy your horse is. If you go with difficult, you won't miss any tasks. I have skipped some tasks, because the horses were easy, and I only ended up getting into more trouble down the road. If you have an easygoing horse, they will go through the tasks fast and in just a few days. You cannot skip crucial training tasks, because if you do, it can be tragic. Do your homework. It is for your horse, the horse you plan on keeping for their entire lifetime. No one wants to sell their horse because they were considered un-trainable or just plain unmanageable. It's not the horse, but the human, and the way they teach. Since I have been using Clicker Training, I can say that it works on all horses.

It is very easy to understand what Clicker Training is. The problem that we have is there are no set programs available. You can add it to any training program that you like, but you will have 2 training programs. The unlearned task program, (*Clicker Training*) and the learned task program (which is usually *Negative Reinforcement*). *Clicker Training* is working with the mind more than the body, and it will change how your horse perceives you. The understanding of what your horse has been taught becomes clearer to him. Clicker Training is rewarding your horse for specific things that they have done. The clicker is a small hand held plastic box that makes a noise when pressed. It tells the horse "yes, that is correct." We need to communicate to a horse in a clear, unmistakable manner, what they did right, not what they did wrong. I can recognize something that my horse is doing, and mark the behavior with my clicker (the yes signal) and reinforce it with food, so the click (the yes signal) has value. The food is the horse's paycheck for getting it right. It is what motivates the horse. Every time the box is clicked, I give some food. If there were no reward, the horse would not be interested in trying to get me to click the box. You can't make a horse be interested in work without motivation. The food can be anything that your horse likes, such as hay, grain, candy, apples, carrots, and sugar. All horses are different on their food selections. It is up to you to figure out what works best. Some horses would do anything for just a small piece of hay, while others make sure you do some searching to find out what kind of food they are interested in.

So far, we have learned that the click of the box is what tells the horse that what they did was correct, and we give them some food to motivate them to try again. When a horse understands that the click means something desirable, and something good to eat, I call that *"Bridge Trained."* When you click the box, you have plenty of time to get the food out because the horse has figured out that what they were doing at the time of the click was the right thing, not when the food was given. A horse will immediately stop what they are doing, and wait for you to give them their favorite treat. If they want that treat again, they need to repeat what they just learned when the click was given. I call this the start of *"Offering Behaviors."*

When you first start with Clicker Training your horse will be very motivated to do what you have clicked for. They become workaholics. The confusing part is, if you don't have a program to help you, you might feel overwhelmed, but you will discover the intelligence of your horse, and it will amaze you. Some people don't think that horses are intelligent enough to be asked what they would like to do, and learn from it. They think that you have to tell a horse what to do all the time. That includes the learning process. During the learning process, the horse should 'think,' and do the task on their own.

I have to set up each situation so the horse succeeds. Once a behavior is learned, I need to back it up with something that is sensible to maintain it. Clicking and feeding for the same task over and over again doesn't make much sense. The horse would end up like a spoiled child, working less and less, due to boredom. We have things that we have learned, and we have to do things that we don't like, but we know how, so it becomes a responsibility. After a task is learned you can set it up to be a responsibility, and maintain it. The advantage of Clicker Training is that I know the horse truly understands, because I set the horse up to show me that they can do the task.

When there is a problem with a horse, we don't always know if the problem is fear, confusion, illness, pain, or just lack of respect. We can take away confusion and fear, because we set our horse up for the success of the task, and the task was performed by the horse's choice. Eliminating illness or injury is a priority. After that all we have left are respect issues. It is not fair to work on respect issues when the horse is confused about the task. So we first can go back to Clicker Training for a double check, then we can work on respect. Some horses have built in respect for humans, and others just love to take advantage of every situation. I know all of us have met someone in our lifetime that has taken advantage of our kindness. It's just natural to test to see what they can get away with. We will always treat the next person with the same kindness in the beginning, because that is what is fair. If that person takes advantage of that kindness, they will be dealt with accordingly. Same goes with the horse. I don't treat all horses as if they are going to take advantage of each situation. They are all given the opportunity to learn. It is up to them how they work with what they have learned later on. I can always take care of respect issues when they know better.

Horses are not vocal, as we are. They use body language to communicate. So do we, but we are more in tune to our voices than our body language. We add a huge amount of body language to our voices, but we seem to forget how our body moves with our voices. It's like watching someone who can't dance to the beat. All their movements seem to be a little off, and it looks a little funny. If we move our body in a different way than we are speaking, it changes the whole meaning of the word that was spoken. If our body has a jerking motion when we are trying to say something soft, it doesn't make much sense. How you move your body is a huge reflection of what you are saying. Horses do the same thing. They are talking with their minds and their bodies. We just can't hear it. I bet you could tell if someone was angry, or happy, just by looking at how they move. It is the same for a horse.

We would all love for our horses to just say it in words when they don't understand. They can't, so we have to read their body language. We have to watch what they do to figure out what they are telling us. When you go to a baseball game, the pitcher and the catcher have their own language just before the big pitch is released. They can tell each other what ball to pitch. They use signals and body language to achieve their goals. There are no mistakes between the two of them. We are just the opposite team trying to figure out what kind of pitch they will be throwing next. It is a big mystery about horses, and what they really think of us. Clicker Training can take some of the mystery out of training and make it more clear between the two of us. We both agree on the task, and it is fun for the horse and us.

What kind of things can we click for, and what do you want your horse to do? I train horses to turn, stop, back, stand still, etc. Clicker Training works great with anything that you would like to teach your horse. There are 2 different types of training: Clicker Training which is *positive reinforcement,* and *negative reinforcement,* which is the use of pressure. Basically, positive reinforcement means something different to everyone. Some people think that it is petting your horse when they do something right. I believe just petting a horse is for comfort. They don't really know exactly what they did right. Petting and stroking your horse is a wonderful thing that we all do, and should be done, but there is nothing specific to tell the horse exactly what he has done, so repeating what they were petted for is nonexistent. When a horse increases the behavior at their own free will, for the click and then for the reward, that is *Positive Reinforcement.*

Negative reinforcement is a painful or unpleasant stimulus that a horse can avoid by changing their behavior (the use of pressure). A good example is pulling on the reins to slow a horse down. The pull slows the horse down. When the horse slows down, you release the pressure so your horse can learn. The horse avoided the pressure by slowing down. We all use this everyday in our training, and we cannot get along without it, but in reality we are causing something unpleasant so the horse will avoid it, not enjoy it. When you use only negative reinforcement your horse will only give you minimal effort to get rid of the pressure. I want my horses to want to work without fear and the unpleasantness of it. I want them to learn because it is fun, and interesting. Negative Reinforcement doesn't mean that it is bad, it is just the name that they gave it.

With Clicker Training you can get very specific to the task. I can tell my horses that if the speed of the trot was correct, or if I am proud of them for standing still. You can even teach them to hold their foot in exact position for trimming. You will have this new language between the two of you that is unmistakable, and the horse will become calmer and more trusting over time.

My colt, Kiowa, was a good example of getting specific. He learned that when I clicked, he would freeze where he was, and he would get his favorite treat. I was asking him to get on top of a small bridge that I had

CLICKER TRAINING: COLT STARTING THE NATURAL HORSE

made. He was doing great until the last foot. When he was bringing the foot up in the air I clicked, hoping to get my timing right. He hung his foot in the air, and froze to collect the food. He had all three feet on the bridge, but he left the last foot hanging in the air waiting for more instruction. My husband happened to be watching, laughing with amazement at how specific Clicker Training can be.

A GOOD EXAMPLE OF HORSE BEHAVIOR DURING CLICKER TRAINING

If I have something in my hand, let's say an empty small water bottle, and I want my horse to touch it with their nose, I would take the water bottle, and put it in a position so my horse could look at it. When my horse looks at it, I would click and then feed my horse. I would repeat this same exercise a few times. My horse will be thinking about the food at this point, not the bottle. My goal is to get my horse to touch the bottle with their nose. I will hold it out to see if my horse will touch it without my help. My horse most likely will go straight to the food source for more food. They smell it, so they attempt to mug you. I use a pouch that can be zipped up, so I can't be mugged. Mugging fails, so they have to figure something else out. Some will paw or continue mugging. They are hunting for an answer to this puzzle. They will be thinking, "How do I get this food?" which is what you want. If you physically bring the bottle to their nose, and click when it touches their nose, then feed them some food, their mind will start to think more of what worked. If I hold the bottle out again without bringing it to their nose, my horse will 'think,' look at the bottle, and touch their nose to it. Click as soon as their nose touches the bottle, then feed. Hold the bottle out again, so my horse will bring their nose to it all on their own. The mugging didn't work, but touching their nose to the bottle does, and when they touch it, I would click, then feed. Then I can raise the bottle high, and my horse should follow it. I can move it around and my horse should follow it and touch it with their nose. It's a very simple concept. The problem is that people think horses are not that smart. It can take on the average about 5 minutes for a horse to offer touching the bottle. This is using positive reinforcement to the fullest. 'Thinking' of what to do by the horse increases the behavior.

I am sure you are wondering what a water bottle has to do with training a horse. The water bottle is what we call a *'Target.'* The horse has to focus on something, so we give them an object to touch with their nose. Target training is one of the most useful tools to have with Clicker Training. The target can be anything from a water bottle to a plunger. I use a broken broom handle with a t-post topper on it. You can ask a horse to follow the target from point A to point B. You can ask your horse to look at something without having to cause pressure. It is a wonderful aid for getting your point across. You can move a horse from stall to stall without them even being halter broke, and it was the horses idea. You can teach them to get on bridges, go in trailers, and walk up to scary objects. The target becomes something safe to look at.

I use Clicker Training for unlearned tasks. It gets your horse excited about the tasks. You can't feed your horse forever for the same tasks. It will get dull, and boring. When a task is learned, I back it up with *negative reinforcement*. It is like our first day at school, we know the first day is going to be easy, they can't ask us to take a test because we don't even know what is on the test. The teacher has to show us what to do. But in about a week or so we have to take a test or a pop quiz. It is required to test what we have learned. The one problem that I do see with teaching with negative reinforcement is that the horse can mistake it as punishment or even abuse because our timing was off. In the learning process there really should be a reward system for the horse in order for the horse to want to do the task

When Clicker Training is used, the subject is always given the opportunity to succeed. That means that the trainer always succeeds as well. This creates a more positive shift in thinking for both teacher and learner. This really is the key. Your horse will look at the human differently. They won't have the same attitude of, "do I have to," but more of "I can do that I know how." This changes your relationship with your horse, which in turn changes everything else about your horse. This doesn't mean your horse will always get it right or that they won't spook or have bad moments. You cannot rewire a horse's instincts, but you can do everything you can to try to work in their world, and help them work in yours. It is a constant getting along that the both of you have to try to achieve.

CLICKER TRAINING: COLT STARTING THE NATURAL HORSE

CLICKER TRAINING HISTORY

I have been asked many times about Clicker Training history. I do think that it is important to know, and understand where something comes from, and who figured it all out first, and why. The History amazed me. I was training horses for many years before I really understood positive reinforcement. The understanding of the beginning of Clicker Training made me want to continue with it even more.

Clicker Training was invented back in the 1940's. First studied by E.L Thorndike, and then studied by B.F Skinner at Harvard University. B.F Skinner named it Operant Conditioning. Operant Condition Method is the process of changing behavior by rewarding a subject each time an action is performed until the subject animal associated the action with pleasure or distress. This is generally done with no restraints. The subject (horse) is free to do what they choose. An example of Operant Conditioning is if a horse was rubbing on an apple tree, and an apple fell, they most likely would try it again, and the process of rubbing would be increased for the tasty apple.

In 1944, during World War II Skinner gained funding for a project called Project Pigeon. The theory was to train pigeons to guide bombs. How did Skinner train the pigeons to do this? He arranged a box so that food was presented to food-deprived pigeons automatically every fifteen seconds. What Skinner discovered was that the pigeons where acting very odd just before the food was released. They each did something a little different, and continued to repeat the action just before the food was released. Some pigeons would turn around, and some would jump up and down, and others would scratch. The pigeons felt they were being rewarded for their actions

You might call this "Superstitious" behavior. If the pigeons turned around, and the food appeared, they would repeat the turning, so more food would come out. Even though the food was coming out every fifteen seconds no matter what the actions of the pigeons. Soon Skinner found out he could mark a certain behavior by using the food to reinforce the behavior. Skinner's goal was to get the pigeons to peck a target 300 times. To do this the food only came out when the pigeon pecked, not if they spun around, or scratched. Working intently, he did train pigeons to keep pecking a target that would hold missiles on a target. The pigeons pecked reliably, even when falling rapidly, and working with warlike noise all around them. The Pigeon Project was never used because of the invention of radar, but they learned a tremendous amount about animal behavior.

There are a few key people that helped create Clicker Training: Marian Kruse Breland-Bailey, Keller Breland and Bob Bailey.

Marian Kruse was a straight A student in high school, and the valedictorian of her class. Marian headed for college at the University of Minnesota to major in Latin and minor in Greek. Needing a science, she chose psychology. As a straight A student she was recommended for a special psychology class to be taught by B.F. Skinner. As a woman in a field dominated by men, she worked closely with B.F. Skinner and others. She soon changed her major to Psychology. Marian began a long association with B.F. Skinner from this early exposure.

Keller Breland, who later became Marian's husband, was also a student of B. F. Skinner's at the University of Minnesota. Marian and Keller were both asked to work on the Pigeon Project. With what they learned from the Pigeon Project Marian and Keller began to train a variety of animals with the new technology. In 1943 they formed their own company, and named it Animal Behavior Enterprises or ABE. Their goal was to train an animal to do anything within the animal's psychological capabilities. They used Operant Conditioning for this training, and called it "Bridge Conditioning." They would use a whistle, a flashlight, a noisemaker, or any sound to tell the animal what they did was right.

Marian became one of the first psychologists to utilize Operant Conditioning commercially. Marian and Keller first tried to get into dog training, but were met with rejection. As Marian describes, "We knew there were so many dogs in the country, and people always wanted to get them trained. We thought this would be a cinch. We'd tell people about this new humane way of training, and they'd be talking to us by the thousands, but nobody listened to us."

CLICKER TRAINING: COLT STARTING THE NATURAL HORSE

The Breland's began to train animals for show. They had much success with animal shows, as the public largely had not seen trained animals at the time. By the 1950's, ABE had trained animals for use in shows and fairs across the U.S. They were the first to have trained dolphins and bird shows. Marian also pioneered and trained animals for use in commercials. The most noted was Buck Bunny, which ran for 20 years. In 1955 the Brelands opened the IQ ZOO, featuring animals performing skits, such as playing baseball, playing musical instruments, and dancing to music. Many famous people came to learn from Marian, including such notables as Walt Disney, and Marlin Perkins. Keller was hired by Marineland to develop a training program for their marine mammals. Keller devised a system of marine mammal training that is still used today.

In 1960 Keller and Marian both where hired to teach their training skills to Navy personnel for use with dolphins. At that time Bob Bailey was the Navy's first Director of Training. All three were able to work together studying dolphin communication. During WWII they trained dolphins to attach mines to warships, and crows to carry listening devices deep behind enemy lines. Bob Bailey went on to become a pioneer in the use of dolphins in open ocean work. With the help of ABE, Marian and Keller trained over 6000 different animals using Operant Conditioning.

Marian and Keller trained many domestic animals and wild animals. They were the leaders of modern scientific animal training. Psychologists, animal trainers, and behaviorists came from all over the world to learn. They taught many animal trainers who later moved on to the Bush Gardens and Sea World. Marian became one of the best known animal behaviorists.

In 1961 the Brelands published an article called, "The Misbehavior of Organisms," about some of the problems they were having with instinctive behavior. This was a break through for them with Operant Conditioning. This brought about taking the instinct of the animal and using it to your advantage. You can't change the animal's instinct through training. There were many different animals that were using their instincts in their training process that could not be overridden, no matter what the reinforcement. Marian talked about a raccoon that they were trying to train to put a coin into a coin bank. The raccoon would wash the coin before he put it into the bank. Raccoons instinctively wash their food before they eat it. They could not stop what was natural to the raccoon.

Keller Breland died in 1965, leaving Marian, and 3 children, so Bob Bailey took over as ABE's director. Marian married Bob Bailey in 1978. Bob had 6 children (three sets of twins) of his own living with him at the time of their marriage.

By the mid-nineties the Internet was becoming a great way to teach. Many more people were getting information about Marian's work. Dog training was changing through a trainer named Karen Pryor. Karen Pryor had extensive work with training dolphins, and is the author of a wonderful book named, "Lads Before the Wind," about her experiences with training dolphins. She later wrote the book, "Don't Shoot the Dog," which was about a new approach to training animals. Slowly word spread about this new type of training, even though psychologists had known about it for years. Soon dog trainers were recommending this book to others. Dog trainers were having successes that they had never experienced before. Soon classes were being offered on Operant Conditioning. The Internet allowed chat groups to talk about their successes with this training method now being called *Clicker Training*.

With this new audience hungry for training and instruction, Marian and Bob began offering more classes using chickens. In 1997 they traveled coast to coast teaching mostly animal trainers. They pulled a small trailer loaded with their chickens and equipment.

Bob Bailey explains, "Why train chickens? Chicken models can dramatically shorten the time it takes to teach the scientific fundamentals and the basic mechanical and timing skills needed for efficient training. With chickens, it goes swiftly, depending on the trainer's skill. Behaviors happen swiftly because chickens learn and move quickly. We compress the days required to train most animals into minutes of chicken training." *(Bailey 2003).*

CLICKER TRAINING: COLT STARTING THE NATURAL HORSE

Marian Baily died in 2001 at the age of 81.

Bob Baily still offers summer seminars at the University of Arkansas in Little Rock, Arkansas.

CHAPTER 2
GETTING STARTED

UNDERSTANDING HORSES

I always wondered why my horses play in the pasture the way they do. They bite each other to the hide, kick until they were almost knocked down, and go back for more. I feel that physical pain will do nothing to help your horse suppress bad behaviors. It only sparks the "game" in a horse. If you use force to stop a horse from doing something, even though you feel your timing is perfect, you are postponing real learning. You are just challenging your horse for battle.

Some of them really love this type of work. They will fight you till the end. My colt King taught me this. King likes to bother the lead mare in his pasture. He will run up to her and try to get as close to her as possible until she charges him and bites him. Sometimes she will bite him till his hide comes off. He runs away in a sprint. In a few seconds, he comes back for more. She chases him around the pasture with her ears back, and teeth bared trying to bite him. You can tell he is having a good time playing with her. It doesn't matter how much she bites him, and how much it hurts to be bit. It is a game. He can take the pain for the fun of getting to her in this way. It gives him power.

I don't want to act like another horse. I sure don't want to take the hide off of them to get them to do what I want, but we need to have an understanding of how they function naturally, and use that to our advantage. I see no use in using any type of pain or force to **teach** a horse. It will only exhaust you physically and mentally, and your horse will always win the battle. We have to remember the word "**Teach**." After a horse has learned a task, and I am sure that there is a clear understanding, I will use *Negative Reinforcement* to maintain the task. <u>Horses are looking for a leader, and a good leader is one who can teach</u>

<u>in a clear manner, but maintain what is taught.</u> There has to be some type of discipline to maintain what they have learned. Most horses are very happy to do what is asked, if they know how. We only suppress bad behaviors through punishment and fear. To get to the heart of a horse, Positive Reinforcement (Clicker Training) is the way to go.

MY FIRST EXPIERIENCE WITH CLICKER TRAINING

I had an 8-month-old half-Arabian colt named Zipper that was sold, and the owner was coming in less than a week to pick him up. I managed to work with Zipper a little, and we were doing well, but I knew he had a lack of confidence. He seemed to be scared of everything. I was working with him in the halter, but had not taken him out of the pen yet. He had very little training outside. I didn't want to see him get scared or confused. Zipper needed confidence. I introduced target training to him, and he took to it right away. His attitude changed over night. I was able to walk him out of the pen with the help of the target, and right into the trailer. He was a completely different horse. Everyone around the farm asked me what I did to Zipper. He seemed so mellow now. The owner came to pick him up a few days later. He was very happy that he made the right purchase, and he could not believe how calm his new colt was. I asked Zipper to walk into his trailer, which the little guy had never seen before, and he walked up into it without any problems. The little colt was calm and cool, and nothing seemed to scare him. Well, I was sold. To see the difference in Zipper was amazing to me. I was determined to continue using this type of training method.

ITEMS YOU WILL NEED

The first items you will need to get started will be the following:

A clicker, fanny pack or pouch full of grain or treats, and some sort of a target.

Clicker

Some people like to use words such as "Good." You can really use any type of noise you like, but the noise has to be like nothing else. I was in a pet store, and wanted to check out a clicker that I found. I clicked it a few times and liked the sound. It was the only one I could find, and I needed another one. My husband went to the back of the store to ask for help finding more clickers. The lady said, "They are all the way in the front of the store. Were you the one clicking a minute ago?" She could hear my clicks from the front of the store, and this was a huge store. The communication was clear to her. I was fascinated by the sound travel, and with its unique sound, she knew exactly what it was. I want to give my horses that unmistakable communication. I like to use a clicker because it has a sound that a horse cannot mistake. There is also something about it being very quick and precise. I do use a tongue click later on in my horse training and we will talk about that later.

Fanny Pack

I use a fanny pack that holds a heaping scoop of grain. I don't like fanny packs to be too small, or you will always run out of grain too soon. Once you run out of grain your session should be over.

Have your fanny pack on with grain in it whenever you see your horse. You are a Clicker Trainer now, and your horse will be ready to work every time he sees you. This is a commitment you have to make. Your horse will expect you to be with it, and as a leader that makes a deal, you must follow through with it, especially in the beginning. This will let your horse know that you can be consistent. It is very hard to tell your horse, "Oh, no, not today." You have to be committed to it, because this type of communication is so strong your horse will make sure you follow through with it.

For example, if you had some one to talk to and they didn't speak English and your life depended on that one person, communication would be very important. If you could get them to speak English, and it ended abruptly you would get very frustrated that the English-speaking friend just stopped talking your language. It would be devastating to you. No more clear communication. How would you feel? What would you do? Start yelling! So will your horse, and it can get ugly.

If you stay committed to Clicker Training, it will give your horse more confidence in you. Later on you will start phasing out the clicker. I do teach certain tasks to horses to help them out because they are in need, and it works very well, but not as good if you were on a set program. If they were on a set program, they would do even better. But I can get great results with just certain tasks. If you are nervous about trying Clicker Training, work with just one horse, and continue with another horse the same way you have been. This is a great challenge. You will start seeing a big difference in your clicker trained horse and they will soon be passing up your other horses. If you only have one horse and you are not sure about it, get online. There is loads of information on the web to help you. It can take just a few minutes for your horse to start understanding that the click means food, but for them to understand that their actions are being rewarded, it could take some time, depending on the horse.

Target

For my target, I use a cut off broom handle with a T-Post topper on one end of it. The target is about 2 feet long. I take my T-post topper off and put it on the end of a longer target when I need the length. You can use anything you like as a target.

HOW HORSES REACT DIFFERENTLY TO TARGETING

You will meet two different types of horses with Clicker Training. The ones that can catch on in about 5 minutes, and others that take days to just target on a consistent basis. I meet more horses that catch on in 5 minutes.

Boltus, a Welsh pony that was in for basic training, learned how to target in about 30 seconds, and he was solid on it. He acted like this was what he was waiting for all his life. Another horse in for training named Devon, was a great horse, but needed some help. Devon seemed to have a very high opinion of himself. He was not a bad horse, he just needed some direction. He could not target on a consistent basis. It took 3 days of working 3 to 4 sessions a day for Devon to target consistently.

CLICKER TRAINING: COLT STARTING THE NATURAL HORSE

I don't believe that he was dumb, just strong willed. I was determined, so we did the same thing every day. I had him in for training for a very short amount of time, about 9 days. And at the end of the 9th day we accomplished half of what I would expect of another horse in 1 day. What it did do was break down the thought process of Devon wanting to do the opposite of what I wanted, and he also found that something worked for him. This seemed to flow over to his riding automatically.

My colt King was one of those really over eager horses. When we started, I thought he was going to hyperventilate. He was so excited that he could do something and was given his favorite food, all he wanted was to work and eat as fast as he could. I couldn't work fast enough for him. So what I did was work shorter sessions (about 2 minutes) and when I clicked, I would feed a huge hand full of grain. His mouth was full all the time. This went on for only a few days. He soon slowed down and started to think. The more tasks that I added to the training, the slower he became. Soon the food was no big deal. He got it all the time and there was no need to think that this was a one-time thing. The first time he had to really think was such a great moving moment. He just thought of what he was doing. He had a look in his eyes like he was thinking and he slowed down. When the behavior was learned, we moved on and added more things to think about. This is called *"Chaining."* Piggy backing behaviors together to make one task, once the behavior has been piggybacked, you don't have to click for the first behavior any more, it has been learned, and the task becomes larger. **Reinforcing the last behavior in a chain acts to reinforce the entire chain.**

When I first start a horse with Clicker Training, I usually only work them for 5 minutes, and get away from them if they are very enthusiastic. All they want to do is work, work, work. It can drive you mad. For the ones that are not so eager, I have to be consistent and do the same task over and over until they get with the program. With a horse like King, who is a munching maniac, you better step up to the plate and join in. I have many times continually clicked, and my horse is still working faster than I can click. Some of these horses will just amaze you. The horses that are a bit slower fascinate me. These horses are the type of horse that are a bit strong willed. I love it when those horses finally say to me, "You mean if I do this, you will reward me?"

Then there are horses like Image. She is a great horse, but she does not show much emotion. She will do the task if she knows it. And is not very treat motivated, but task motivated. She has to be in the right mood for the food. It is my job to accomplish that for her. I have many times had to just put the food in her lips in the hope that she would eat it. She is the type of horse that we would all love to own. She only wants to hear the click, and she is ready to move on. She only wants to do the right thing, but is hard on herself when she is confused. We easily phased out most of the food to a good pat, but I always offer her food when she does something new to keep her interested.

LOCATION

You need to have a stall, or a pen to put your horse in. If you do not have a pen, a halter would work just fine. I prefer to have my horse in a pen, and for me to stand outside the pen. In the beginning horses will have different reactions to being given food, and we do want to be safe.

TARGETING TASK

Objective: Have your horse touch the target with their nose.

Stand outside the stall.

Present the target to your horse through the fence. Most likely they will just look at it.

CLICKER TRAINING: COLT STARTING THE NATURAL HORSE

Targeting outside the stall.

Click when they look at the target.

Pull your food out of the pouch.

Extend your arm out straight, and open your hand flat, and allow your horse to eat the food.

Present the target again. This time bring it to their nose, click, and feed every time their nose touches the target.

Repeat the same 4 more times.

This time hold the target out so your horse can see it. Don't bring the target to your horses' nose. Present it to your horse in a way that it will be very easy for them to touch it. I usually place it about 6 inches in front of their face, and let them touch it. When they touch the target on their own, click and feed.

Repeat the same for 4 more times.

As soon as they understand that touching the target gets the click, then the food, you can start moving it around so they follow it. Remember you have plenty of time to feed them. The click gives you time to get the food. The click is the '**yes**,' and the food is the reward for remembering what they did when you clicked.

Soon you can raise the target high, and they will raise their head high to touch it. Take it low and they will follow it. Click when their nose touches it. You now have control of their head. Practice this for a few sessions. In the beginning, your sessions should be very short for an enthusiastic horse, about 5 minutes. You might go longer for a horse that is slower. Your horse will let you know what works for them. If the session is going well I will do very short sessions before I lose their attention span.

If your horse is touching the target on his own, and has figured out that touching the target means reward, you can start to practice walking down the rail having your horse follow, and touching the target. Only click when their nose touches the target then feed. Start *"Chaining"* right away before your horse gets bored. Chaining is piggy backing tasks together to make one task. The last task is what you click for.

Ask them to touch the target. When they do, click and feed.

Walk about 2 feet with the target in front of your horse's face so they will follow it. Stop, then hold the target so your horse can touch it, then click and feed.

Walk about 4 feet with the target in front of your horses face so they will follow it, stop, then hold the target so your horse touch it, then click and feed.

Keep the steps moving up and up, until they follow it with ease. If your horse does not follow, that might tell you that you should end your session. It is hard for a horse to concentrate on one thing for too long. Take a break and come back later. This task could take a few sessions, so be prepared to spend some time on it.

CLICKER TRAINING: COLT STARTING THE NATURAL HORSE

MAKING A NEW BELIEVER

When I first started in Clicker Training, my friend Jeanne came to see me. We went camping and horseback riding. When we were ready to go home, my dad's horse, Joe, would not load in the trailer. It had rained the night before, and the flies seemed to have doubled in numbers. The flies were biting him, and he was in a rage trying to get them off. I had already gone through two bottles of fly spray, and I was out. It was a dark trailer, and Joe was not about to go in.

I used this as a test for my skills. I have a few choices of methods to get him in the trailer:

I could use comfort and discomfort, which would mean working him outside the trailer. When he faced the trailer he would receive comfort. This would work, but would take some time. It was 100 degrees out with very high humidity, and I was hot and close to a heat stroke before we started. Getting Joe busy was out of the question. Asking this horse to go for a lunge until the safe place was in the trailer would be hazardous to the health of both of us, and he was already hot and sweaty.

Tapping him until he walked forward, and quitting when he tried just made a game for him and he blew up more and pulled on me, and it was getting physical fast. I think the blow up had something to do with the flies. This solution was also not a good idea. He was not going in that trailer and he meant it.

Force. This is not in my vocabulary and would never be a consideration! You can always find a better solution!

Bribery! I had his favorite food bowl, and filled it with some good grain. That was not working either. It was not enough to get him to go in. He ate and backed up.

Clicker Training! Joe was *Bridge Trained*, and did know what the click meant. I had worked with him on a biting problem earlier with great results. I had my clicker, and my target. I used the food bowl to give him grain after I clicked. I clicked for him targeting to get him started, then I clicked for him walking up to the trailer while targeting. He seemed to get calmer. Every time he would try on his own, I would click and feed. This got his attention. I didn't ask him to go forward, I just guided him. He started wanting to go into the trailer. When he gave me a try, I clicked. This was a communication that he understood, and he calmed down. He stepped his two front feet into the trailer. I kept clicking and feeding, and he was offering me more. He was having a really hard time lifting his back legs. He would get a painful look on his face when he lifted his back foot. I could now tell this was also a pain issue. His back had been a little sore earlier in the day, and picking up his back legs was becoming a problem for him. He was hurting. He had no other signs of pain when fighting the trailer loading earlier. It was a combination of being a little sore, not liking the trailer, the heat, and the flies. Joe didn't want to stop. He was determined he was going to get in this trailer. He tried all by himself, and jumped in.

The whole process took 10 minutes for him to load, and we all survived without heat stroke. As soon as I figured out that it was pain related, I wanted to back him up, and move the trailer to a hill so he would not have to step up, but he didn't give me that chance. He went in all on his own. I couldn't believe it. As soon as I changed to Clicker Training he immediately started to try for me.

I also calmed down because I knew I didn't have to get physical, and that relaxed me also. We started talking together, and Joe felt that I would listen. He told me he was hurting, and that is why he could not go into the trailer. I had to show him that his efforts were being noticed. The only other way he felt he could tell me he was hurting and scared was to act out.

Positive Reinforcement training is so strong a horse will do things for you even when flies are biting them, they are scared, or even in pain. Jeanne could not believe it. She saw the huge difference when I switched to Clicker Training. She was so impressed by this that when she got home, she changed her training program.

CLICKER TRAINING: COLT STARTING THE NATURAL HORSE

IS CLICKER TRAINING BRIBERY?

We all know that we can't bribe a horse with food. At some point most horse owners have put some food in the trailer, and said, "Go in, there's food in the trailer." That only works if the horse was going to go in anyway. It's a good idea to have some food in the trailer to make it a more positive experience, but you are not going to have a horse go into a trailer just because there is food in it. If they are scared, they want to feel safe. There is no meaning to the food but that it tastes good, and it only works when they are relaxed. Bribery doesn't have much merit because they have done nothing for it. When a horse is excited they usually won't eat, they are surviving. A bribe is given *before* the request response; a reward *follows* a response. They only get the food if they go in. Clicker Trainers give them rewards for their effort and they understand they need to try again to get another reward, which shifts their thought process from scared to something that they worked for. It puts meaning to the task and allows your horse to focus on the task, not the fear. I like to only work with a horse when they are calm. It is my job to put the horse in an environment where they can stay calm. If your horse is acting up, and seems to be mindlessly snorting and running around, I would say it is not the time to work your horse, unless you are ready to fail, or you are looking for a fight. You can wait until your horse calms down, then it becomes a good time for your horse to learn.

HAND FEEDING BEFORE CLICKER TRAINING

We have all, and still do, give our horses food. Our horses get grain in their feed bowl, or get good quality hay. The horse exhibits behaviors with the presentation of the food. They put their ears back, stomp, throw their head in the air, or fight with other horses for the best spot. We usually ignore these behaviors because we have to feed them. Of course, we sometimes give them grain when they are exhibiting a bad behavior, because we are in too much of a hurry to notice. Most of us don't pay enough attention to these behaviors. We believe it is just a part of being a horse. If we do feed from our hand, most horses bite, mug, or do things that are undesirable to get the food. Most of the time we give in to it, not aware what we have just taught our horse. They will only remember what they were doing at the time they were given the food, or they might be fixated on something else and they believe that a certain behavior works. Most likely it is reaching for the food. So if they reach for the food, and you feed, this is what they think they are supposed to do. You have just taught them how to mug you. If their ears were back before you have given the food, you just might have taught them to put their ears back. When you feed from the hand without Clicker Training, the horse only repeats the behavior that they were thinking about at the time the food was given, which could be aggressive behavior. You can give your horse food in the hopes that the connection was made for what you want, but you cannot get specific. Clicker Training makes it so much easier, because you mark a specific behavior, then they get the reward.

HAND FEEDING WITH CLICKER TRAINING

Always try to feed with your hand flat. I like to feed their daily grain rations in my sessions. In the beginning, I give a big hand full of grain so they can get their fill. This will keep them busy, but I have to make the sessions short, so they don't get too much grain. I usually will give it to them in nickel size portions later on. It also depends on the type of food you use. If they like the grain too much you can switch to something less desirable, like pellets, or even hay. You can go back to the good stuff later on when you need more of their attention. Sometimes pasture horses just need to be in a stall for a while to get a little bored, and have them craving some attention. I don't like to clicker train with a really hungry horse. It is always best if their tummy is a little full. Your horse will tell you what works best.

Always try to feed with your arm stretched away from you. Stretch your arm out as far as you can, and let them find the food. You can teach "Head Away Task" (see Turning Head Away Task in Chapter 2) to help you, if there is a real problem. If they want to smell you first, just let them, but don't let them bite. You can move your body to discourage this. They may go for your arm first. They tend to forget that you are not part of the food program at this point. I just like to wiggle my arm to discourage this. They will figure out the food is in your hand only.

CLICKER TRAINING: COLT STARTING THE NATURAL HORSE

Always try to feed with your arm stretched away from you.

I have a few that bite a big chunk of grain, and they use their teeth. We have to teach them how to take food politely. Some lick and suck up the food. I prefer licking. If they use their teeth, they could bite your hand. They only do what you teach them. I like to wiggle my hand until they use their tongue or lips to take the food. They don't have to bite the grain to eat it, and some horses don't understand that until it is taught to them. Soon they will get more polite. If it is a real problem, you can click for them being polite. Most biting is not by accident. They are either taught to bite or they bite because they are frustrated. I have had my hand accidentally sucked up into their mouth, and they will not bite it. Horses sometimes use their mouths for communication when we brush them, or scratch them. Their instinct tells them to scratch us too, and some people mistake this as biting. I always say, "If your horse was going to bite you, you would know it.

Image is a funny horse. She cannot stand carrots. I had been working some other horses that loved carrots, and the carrots were accidentally mixed up in my grain bag for Image's session. I took some food out to feed Image. She ate the grain, and spit out all the carrot pieces, one by one, with not one tooth mark on them. She knew it was a carrot, and she didn't want them.

TURNING HEAD AWAY TASK

This is a task for having a horse turn their head away from you. I like this task because it reduces your horse mugging you, and it also helps with feeding your horse away from you, and not at the food pouch. This is a great task for the over enthusiastic horse.

Objective: To get your horse to turn their head away on their own.

If your horse happens to look away from you, click your clicker, and feed. If you cannot get your horse to look away have an assistant get your horse's attention by making some noise in the direction you want your horse to turn his head.

When your horse looks away from you, click.

Pull your food out of the pouch.

Extend your arm out straight in the direction your horse was looking.

Open your hand flat, and allow your horse to eat the food.

If your horse is mugging your hand, extend your arm out to the side. Your horse has to find the food away from your body. It's important to wait until your horse moves their head the full length of your arm.

Wait for your horse to look away again. Then click and feed.

Repeat 5 more times, or until you feel it is solid. It shouldn't take long. Your horse must offer you head away for the click, before you go to the other side.

Go to the other side of your horse.

Stand at their shoulder, and wait for your horse to look away, click, and feed. This side will be harder because your horse will be fixated on the previous side. Wait for your horse to turn their head away. You might need an assistant to help you.

Repeat the same.

Horses do what they know, and if this works, in their mind they will tend to keep away from you a little more. Go back to this exercise from time to time for help, or if your horse mistakes coming to you for the food.

BEING GOOD WITH HORSES

In training horses, it is not how good you are with horses, it is our desire to be good. I have spent most of my life trying to be better with horses. I am a very highly energized person, which doesn't mix with horses very well. I have overcome this with a long history of learning what not to do. If you have the will to be good at something, you will not fail. There is no failure in trying to be the best you can. The best thing that I ever did was to learn to listen to my horses. They really will tell you everything you need to know. When I get a new student that knows nothing about horses, they will ask me, "Do you think I can do this?" My answer to that always is, "Of course, if you try." Most people don't try hard enough. They think a horse should be a car, and do exactly what it is told. When good riders ride, it looks so smooth, like changing gears in a luxury car, but what people forget to think about is it takes a good rider many years of working very hard to get to that point, and they are still learning. Newcomers think they will achieve the same thing in a few lessons. Then when they get frustrated, they blame the horse.

I sold a mare to a really nice couple. They wanted lessons with the mare. The mare was kid safe, and a good trail horse. She was not perfect, but still a good horse. She was dominant with other horses, but loved people. The new owner took one lesson, and quit because she said she had a friend that was going to help her. There was great concern that her friend was going to take over. About a year later she called and said she could not get any bit to fit the mare, and needed some help. She informed me that she was using a shank bit, and the mare was throwing her head. I told her what bit to use. I told my family that the mare could take care of herself, she was just that kind of a horse. She was a dominant mare, and wouldn't let any horse mistreat her, so why would she let a human. The next call that I received was to tell me that they were selling the mare, because she kicks at people. I know that was not the same mare that I sold her. They did something to her, and the mare took care of it. I owned the mare for 5 years, and she had a heart of gold. I have had many novices ride her on trails, and she took care of them like her own foals. I was shocked and saddened that they mistreated her so. You have to take lessons and work at it, or you just might have the horse tell you that you did something wrong. The lady was just too lazy to work at it.

GUIDELINES TO REMEMBER

Clicker Training is rewarding your horse for specific things that they have done. The clicker is a small hand held plastic box that makes a clicking noise when pressed. When this box is pressed, it tells the horse "YES, that is correct." We need to communicate to a horse in a clear unmistakable manner what they did right, not what they did wrong.

Click when the desired behavior occurs, then feed. You do not have to rush for the food. The click tells the horse that the behavior was correct.

Extend arm out for feeding. Feed away from your body.

Your horse is never off the job. Horses like to know exactly what is going to happen at all times. Always have a pouch with food, and clicker ready anytime you are in contact with your horse. Assume they will always be ready to work. Take advantage of this. There will be no step made without complete understanding. This will bond your relationship. Your horse will become more relaxed, and take new things easier. This is the game. In general ignore the bad, and reward the good.

Do not get angry or impatient. It is better to wait for it to happen. Listen to your horse, they are always right. They will tell you how they are feeling through their body language. Remember to relax. If you are relaxed, your horse will be relaxed.

If you are confused, ask a question. There is no such thing as a stupid question, and there are plenty of Internet sites where you can learn from others trying the same techniques. There are no real mistakes if you are learning. You cannot do anything wrong, and neither can your horse. If you don't think you can make a mistake, you won't recognize one when you do.

If you desire a better relationship with your horse, you just have succeeded with Clicker Training. Have faith in your horse and yourself. You can do this! You can teach your horse to do anything!

Allow your horse to make his own choices. To do that you have to be a good teacher.

CLICKER GAMES

I wrote Clicker Games so you can get a feel of what a horse goes through when first introduced to Clicker Training.

Welcome to the Clicker Games for communication. I am Leslie's announcer, pleased to meet you all. Our first contestant is King. King is a yearling American Quarter Horse Cremello colt that likes taking naps in the hot sand, and chasing Easter, the lead mare, for fun. In general he has a love for people, and he's a swell guy. King has been handled previously, but is a little pushy. Pushy could be another word for trying to communicate, but no one is listening. King would also like to talk to Leslie, but there seems to be a language barrier.

Trainer, Leslie Pavlich, has over 20 years experience working with horses, and would also like to talk to King.

"Ready contestants? Time to have some fun."

King is brought in from the pasture. Leslie is leading him in the same old way. No real communication yet. Where is King's mind? Let's ask King. "Duh," nothing yet. Leslie is prepared with her pouch of food, her clicker, and her target. "King how are we doing?" "Ah, ah, ah." No real communication as yet. But wait! King smells the food. "King what are you thinking?" King replies, "Food, food, food! I have to get that food. Give it to me. Mine, mine, mine, yummy, yummy, yummy." Apparently all King can think about is, "I have to get that food." Leslie brings the target out, and naturally King smells the target. Leslie clicks the clicker, and she gives King some of his favorite grain. King replies, "Wow this is so good, no one has ever given me grain this way. Give me some more! Wow!" Leslie shows King the target. He looks at it again, and Leslie brings it to his nose. Click! Leslie gives King more grain. "King how are you feeling?" "Oh this grain is so good. I have to have more, more, more." King attempts to mug Leslie for the food, ignoring the target. King says, "I will just get the food myself. I know where it is coming from. I can get it. Where is it? I smell it. Where did it go? I know it is there."

Leslie ignores Kings advances. She zips up the pouch so King can not take what he wants. King continues to smell the pouch with a look of frustration on his face. How was he going to get the food? The target appears again, King looks at it, and Leslie makes sure that his nose touches it. Click, and Leslie proceeds to feed King. King says, "Its about time I was fed. I have been working for a while trying to get it." Leslie does not hesitate to show King the target again. King looks at it, and Leslie brings the target to his nose. Touch and click. Leslie feeds King. "King how are you feeling at this moment in the game?" "Well I am a little frustrated trying to figure out how to get the food, but I think it has something to do with that thing she is holding in her hand. For some reason a sound goes off just before I am fed what I want. I think I will look for that thing in her hand next time."

Leslie presents the target to King, and he touches his nose to the target. Click, and Leslie feeds King. "King, how did you feel about that round." "When I touch that thing in her hand, there is a special sound that I have never heard before today, then I get fed. So now I have to touch that thing in her hand. Where is it? Where? I touch it, there's a click, and I get fed." Looks like King is now really going for the target, getting the click, and getting what he wants. I would say they are both winning the game.

CLICKER TRAINING: COLT STARTING THE NATURAL HORSE

Leslie proceeds to move the target up high. King follows it up high, and touches the target. Click. Leslie feeds King. "King how are you feeling, do you feel like you're in the game?" "Yes, it was easy to figure out. The way to get the food is to follow the thing in her hand where it goes. Every time I touch it, this sound goes off, and I get what I want. It's simple. Where's that thing in her hand?" Soon, Leslie starts walking, and King proceeds to follow the target at a walk. King touches the target, click, feed. King is really going now. Leslie can tell he is thinking "Target." Leslie comments, "I am not sure yet if he is thinking click, food, or just target." I am sure she is aware that communication is beginning.

This game is coming to a close for the day. It's a very short game, only about 5 minutes. Time for King to go out to pasture. "How do you feel King?" King replies, "Target, food, target, food, click, food, target, click food." Correct answer King. Leslie proceeds to lead King to the pasture with him following the target. Leslie clicks, and feeds one last time, and proceeds through the gate. It is clear to Leslie that the session is over, but King has something else to say. "King, what is going through your mind?" King replies, "What? Where did she go? Where did that thing in her hand go? I want food! Come on! I am not done yet! Where did everybody go! I am willing to work for it. Come on!"

A few minutes pass, and King finally goes out to see his friends. King comments, "I am leaving now, but I will be back. If I see her again, I will be sure to show up. That was so much fun." Leslie how do you feel the game went? Did you start communicating? "Yes, I feel that King caught on very quickly. He really likes the target, and this is his favorite grain. We walked at liberty all the way to the pasture, and he continued to touch the target. The game was only 5 minutes, but he learned a lot, and we are both happy. I think we both achieved winning this game."

Session Two

Leslie takes one step outside King sees her, whinnies, and starts to run towards her. King looks very determined to stay in the game. "King, how are you today?" King replies, "Where is that thing in her hand? I am ready." King appears to be ready before Leslie. Looks like King has got the upper hand on this game. Leslie gathers herself, preparing herself mentally. King is looking at the target trying to get to it. Leslie opens the gate, and King follows the target. Touch, click, and feed. King is really on a roll. He can't get enough of that target. There is so much food in his mouth, and he is still going. Leslie clearly knows now that King understands the task-target, click, feed. King is willing to follow the target anywhere it goes.

"King how do you feel about the game today?" "It's easy, all I have to do is follow that thing in her hand, and the sound goes off, and I get my treat. Could this be any easier? I could do this forever." Leslie proceeds to walk towards the bridge that was set up for King to stand on. This will help with his trailer loading. Leslie walks toward the bridge. King looks at the bridge, click, feed. King has a puzzled look on his face, like he must have touched the target, and forgot he did, because she made that sound, and he was fed. King is looking for the target. Leslie puts the target over the bridge. King smells the bridge first, click, and feed. "King what could possibly be going through your mind right now?" "I know that if I could just get my nose on that thing in her hand I could get fed." "But King, you just got fed by smelling the bridge." King replies, "What!"

King seems to be zoned for target only, and has completely forgotten he was just fed a few seconds ago. Can King make it through the session? King looks down at the bridge, and smells the bridge again. Click, and feed. "King what happened? It seems you are getting what you want, but from a different source." King replies, "What? Where is my target? What did I do to get the food, I know I did something? Well, I will look for that target. Where did it go? I don't see it." King proceeds to smell the bridge again. Click, and feed. King just stops, and thinks. "King, are you there?" Is this the turning point in the game? Can he do it? King proceeds to touch his nose to the bridge. Click, feed. "King what was going through your mind? What happened?" "I just figured out that my target was gone, and that sound is telling me what I need to do. I can't believe this. Wow! I get it! I smelled the bridge, and there was the click, and I got what I wanted. The target must be in the bridge."

CLICKER TRAINING: COLT STARTING THE NATURAL HORSE

"Leslie, how do you think that it is going so far?" "He is very enthusiastic about the target, but we need to move on to other things to keep his interest. When he looks at the bridge I click, so he can make the connection between his actions and the click. He is getting there." King continues to smell the bridge. Click. Feed. He clearly understands that smelling the bridge is what is making the click for him, then he gets food. Leslie comments on how much King is increasing the behavior, and slowing down on the food. Leslie's agenda for the day is to work about 5 minutes, and have a good session. She is in hope of getting King to step on the bridge, but in this game there is no time frame, and they both need to succeed. It is crucial for both to feel they are successful.

Leslie withholds the click when King proceeds to smell the bridge. King continues to smell the bridge, waiting for the click. He accidentally bumps it with his leg. Click, and feed. "What happened King?" "I am not sure, but what I do has something to do with the click." King continues to smell the bridge. Leslie withholds the click. King is thinking. What is he thinking? Leslie waits patiently for King's next move. King lifts his leg in a little bit of frustration, and stomps the bridge. Click. Feed. King's face lights up. He goes right back to the bridge, puts one foot on top of the bridge, and taps it. Lets see if Leslie can get her timing down to get King's foot on the bridge. Leslie clicks when his foot is down the bridge, not before, or after. The click was made, and King was fed.

"King, how is it going now?" "If I put my foot on the bridge, I get some food. I am afraid of the bridge. It seems scary, and I don't want to do it myself. I need some time to think about it. Ok, here it goes. If I could just touch it with my foot once click! All right! I did something right. Food! I can do that again. Put one foot on bridge. Click, I got it right again! Wow! More food." "Leslie, how do you think it is going?" "King seems to be overcoming his fear, and now he is taking a big step toward getting on the bridge. King has to do this himself by thinking about it. I can't do that for him." King proceeds to tap the bridge with his foot. Click. Feed. "King, how is it going for you in the game?" "I am figuring out that what I do has merit. Leslie leads the way, and if I just think about it, I get a click. I like the clicks, because I can feel that everybody gets happy, not to mention I get my favorite food. I love that grain. This is a fun game. Wait! What, if I put my foot on the bridge, and lean on it?" Click. "All right! What if I pick up my other foot, and tap the bridge." Click. "All right! Wow, some more food." What if I put both front feet on the bridge?" Click, "All right!" Feed. "Hey wait a minute! I am not too sure that I want my feet on this bridge." King backs up, and shakes his head. "Leslie, now how is the game going?" "I think King has had enough for today. He just realized that he was on a bridge, and I think he is in a little bit of a shock. He looks a little tired. I think he needs to be put up for awhile to think about it." "King, how are you feeling about the game?" "I like the game, I know what to do, but I need to think about that bridge. It feels scary under my feet. I am not sure it is safe." Time to put King up for the day.

Session Three

It is a beautiful day here at the Clicker Games. Leslie has her game face on, and getting prepared to go get King. Leslie walks down to the pasture, and there is King patiently waiting to start this game. "King, how are you feeling today?" "I am ready to face the bridge. Lets get going." Leslie walks with King at liberty to the bridge without the target. King knows where to go, and heads for the bridge. Without hesitation, he stomps the bridge with one of his feet. Click. Feed. King thinks for a moment, and puts both front feet on the bridge. Click. Feed. "How are you feeling about the bridge today King?" "This is easy. I get it. Get on the bridge, no big deal." King proceeds to walk all four feet on the bridge. Click, feed, click, feed, click, feed. Leslie proceeds to give King a jackpot to hold his position. "Leslie, what do you think about King just putting all four feet on the bridge?" "It is wonderful that he just overcame his fear of the bridge. The goal was to have all four of his feet on the bridge. So I now can continue for a few clicks to let him know he did really well." "King, what do you think about the bridge now?" King replies, "Wow, that sure is good food." King is clearly embracing the moment. Leslie walks to have King follow her off the bridge. Leslie clicks King for stepping off the bridge. Leslie walks back to the bridge King follows. Leslie puts herself in a position for King to get back on the bridge. King puts 2 front feet on the bridge again. No click yet. King proceeds to put all four feet on the bridge again. Click. Feed. This session is over for the day. They have both won the game. "King, now how do you feel about the bridge?" "Well, I just walk on it, and wait, and I will get the click. That is easy." Now it is time for something else to do.

King not wanting to finish the game.

CHAPTER 3
CUES

I have a number of cues for working with a horse, and there are cues within cues. The cue for a young horse doing the same thing as a finished horse will not be the same. My finished horse will have a light cue, rather than the young horse that needs more guidance and a lot of cues.

If I look at my horse and walk towards him with a harsh look on my face, I would hope that he would move out of my way. If he just stood there, I would start making some noise to see if he moves. If that still didn't work, I might start tapping or pressing him on the chest. When he moved, I would stop the tapping. This is *Negative Reinforcement*. The next time I would walk towards him with a harsh look on my face, using my body language to make my intentions known, as if to say "Get out of my way, I am coming through," he should move. I don't want to have to jump up and down, or tap my horse every time for my horse to move out of my way. He should learn that a harsh look means move. It still depends on what we are working on. You have to keep the cues light. Horses are very sensitive, and it shouldn't take much to get a horse to move unless the horse was taught in a way that is harsh. Then they learn to only move with something harsh. We always have to keep working on our signals to keep them light. Horses can build up a resistance to pressure. The last thing that we want to do is have a cue that is firm every time. Lightness has to be practiced. It is an art that is formed, and we continually have to work on it. If I ask my horse to move forward, I will just lift my body up, not kick him to go. It becomes something mental when working with a horse. They feel everything. If you start with the mind, and think about what you would like to do, your horse will follow your lead.

An example would be with my horse Natchez. He takes a real nice extended trot, but I can only get that extension through power of my seat and body. If I just ride like a bump on a log, his trot will feel that way. I can ask him to trot the exact same way, but pulsating my legs and body to get the right strut. This changes his gait to something more intense. It is more of a strong dance. It is hard to explain how this is done. You have to feel it, then act on it. Natchez feels my intentions, and he follows it.

Your horse notices everything, even your position, what side your are on, how far you are away from the horse, and your body posture. It is as if your horse took a memory photograph of you when the cue was given, and that is exactly what your horse remembers. This is why when you ask for a maneuver with a cue, and sometimes your horse seems to not understand, the cue was given in a different way. Our memory is not as good as a horse, so things get mixed up. We think we did it that same way, and your horse would say, "You were standing one foot away from me, in the middle of my right side with a concentrated look on your face." If I were three feet away, and off to the side a little, they might see it differently. The key to this is to have a main cue, and practice it while you are standing in different positions. Good practice is the key. I incorporate Clicker Training with my own cues. I will show you step by step cues on how I get a horse to perform.

PHASING OUT CLICKER TRAINING WITH CHAINING

You do not have to Clicker Train your horse forever. You have to learn how to phase out Clicker Training. I incorporate it for retraining, and things they have not learned. Once they have learned it, phase it out, and move on to something more difficult. The phasing out part is when you add *Chaining,* putting behaviors together to make one task. Once the behaviors have been lumped together, you don't have to click for the first behavior any more. It has been learned, and the task becomes larger. For example, once my horse has learned how to be caught in the pasture, and it was taught in the positive, you will have no problems catching your horse out to pasture any more, so you don't have to click for that. Your horse should be very easy to catch, as it becomes a routine. When we walk to the barn, I don't have to click for that either, they know how to lead, and it was learned in the positive. I would then brush my horse. I don't have to click for that either. This was also learned in the positive and is now a regular routine. Saddling was also learned in the positive, and now a routine. Lunging was learned in the positive, and is now a routine. Mounting was learned in the positive, and is now a routine. At this point we might be working on our turns in their training. I would click for the horse giving a good turn with a cue, then this will become a routine and we will move on.

Horses learn very fast. You might be surprised how quickly you will have to phase the click out. Clicker Training is a wonderful aid in getting the point across for what you would like your horse to do. Once they have learned a task, it is time to add cues, or signals to it. For a more finished horse, I would click for the extra effort they give me, or maybe getting really specific on something that they might not be really good at. If you like, you can phase it out all together, but you will find out you might need it for fast results on something difficult. I have no problems working my horse, then going on a nice long trail ride. The trail ride is a reward for a more seasoned horse. I really don't feed my more experienced horses anymore than other people that don't Clicker Train. Most people give their horses special treats too. The horse just doesn't know what the treats are for, other than it tastes good. We will talk about phasing out the clicker more as we go.

SHOW ME WHAT YOU KNOW

With Clicker Training you have to get the horse to do the task first by chance, then add a cue to it later. This can be difficult. I like to set my horse up to do the task, which might be using some pressure, then wait for my horse to offer me the same behavior for the click. You can add the cue for a task, and then allow them to think about it, then they should repeat the task by their own free will. I call it *Show me what you know*. When you ask a horse to move without the assistance of Clicker Training, it is just moving away from pressure. The horse doesn't think they are going sideways, or back etc. Unless you get lucky, and the connection was made, or you repeat it over and over in the hopes that your horse is thinking of the task, not just getting away. It does happen, but not quite as often as if you had a little help. They are only moving away because of fear, or discomfort. Their mind gets blocked to where their feet are, and what the task is at hand. They don't think sideways, they think, "I must move." When you use 'show me what you know,' your horse has to decide what you want, sideways, or back, etc. They think and do the task on their own for the click. We don't cause it to happen, we WAIT for it to happen.

ANOTHER EXPLANATION

If I ask my horse to move their left front foot over their right front foot, there are many different ways to ask. I will ask by pressing my hand lightly where my foot would go if I would be riding. As soon as they cross over I will click and feed. I might ask this several times. Then I do nothing. If my horse reaches to beg for some food, we will know exactly where the mind is. It is begging for food, and that is not what I was looking for. I will show him with my cue 5 more times, then wait again. Believe it or not, they will slow down and think. The left front foot will cross over the right front foot without me telling the horse.

I remember I was teaching a young horse to pick up her front foot. When I asked for her foot she would wring her tail every time she lifted her foot for me. She was very consistent about it. She thought I was clicking for picking up her foot and wringing her tail. Your horse will tell you where they are if you just let them do the task on their own. She offered me wringing of her tail. Horses have ideas about what you want. We just seem to be oblivious to them communicating with us. So if they get into a habit of offering us behaviors, and we are both on the same page, your relationship will be much more solid. They understand the cue for the behavior, and I know they offered it to me. They will wait for your cue. Before my clicker days I worked many horses that just didn't get it, and somehow we didn't seem to be working together. The relationship seemed to not really be there so they didn't give much effort. Horses just want to know what you want.

ANTICIPATION VERSES OFFERING BEHAVIORS

Anticipation is when a horse will do the task before you ask. The behavior has been established with a cue, and we don't want the horse to produce the task until they've been asked. We have to think about why they are doing the task before we ask. In traditional training we use *negative reinforcement* as our main training method which is an unpleasant or painful stimulus that a horse can avoid by changing their behavior. The horse could be issuing the task before the cue is given because of the consequence it brings, which is discomfort or pain depending on who is giving it. It could be because they are anticipating what you want next because they have already learned it. It can be avoidance or beating you to the punch. Another reason why horses use anticipation is because they are bored with the task. If you practice the same task over and over again, the horse will assume this is what you want.

Anticipation can be a good thing to have. At least you know that your horse understands the task. The problem is we don't usually give the horse credit for figuring out what we want, and it is difficult to tell them that we only want it on cue. Starting another task, and going back later can help. If you are performing a pattern on a test or in a show, anticipation can be a problem. Horses are more intelligent than we give them credit for. They could do the pattern without us even giving any cues. When it is this way, they seem to get bored, and come up with other things to do instead. When I worked a horse with just *negative reinforcement* as my main training, I always felt out of sync. They usually wanted to be working on something else, and I could not give them credit when credit was due.

OFFERING BEHAVIORS

When we use *positive reinforcement*, the horse offers behaviors to us, even if they don't know what the cue is yet. We are noticing their behaviors, and marking them with a "yes" signal using a clicker. My horses will search for the answer by thinking of what they can do to get the click, which in turn gives them a reward. It might look like anticipation, but it cannot be because there is no cue to the action yet. There is no time schedule for the horse to perform. If the horse understands the task they will repeat it over and over again trying to get me to click the box. I will click the box, and reward multiple times to imprint the task as something that I want. Then I will add a cue to it as the horse is doing the task. As soon as the horse recognizes the cue for that task, I will only click when the horse does the task when the cue is given.

If my horse offers me the behavior without me giving the cue, this doesn't get the box clicked. The behavior is ignored. I will not click unless I ask with the cue, and they perform the action. Once they understand that offering this behavior out of the blue doesn't get the box to click, they will not offer it, because it doesn't work unless asked. They learn that waiting for the cue works best. I do not continue to repeat the cue. I don't have to practice the task any more with Clicker Training. It is recorded, and I give my horse credit for understanding it. It is time to phase out the click for that task and move on to another task and chain it together to make one task.

This type of work will allow you to be in sync with your horse throughout the entire session, and there is no confusion for the trainer, or the horse. Modern positive reinforcement training will allow both parties to understand every part of the session together in a positive way. So a Clicker Trained horse doesn't anticipate, they will wait for the cue, because that is how they are trained.

GETTING THE SAME RESULTS WITH DIFFERENT METHODS DOESN'T MEAN THAT IT'S SAME THING

This is a bit hard to explain. In the English language we can say the same words, but they mean different things. For example, if I say, "What are you doing," in a calm voice with a smile, we all know I am just asking a simple question. If I yell, "What are you doing?" That could mean several different things. "You're an idiot for doing that! I know what your doing, but why are you doing that!" "Stop that!" You will immediately know you're in trouble.

I was working on my colt Kiowa. He is the world's worst for not getting it. He likes to daydream. He is very good with negative reinforcement cues and pressure, but for him to offer it, especially something new, he blocks me out. I was asking him to trot in a circle at liberty in the round pen. This was new to him. (*Liberty* is when the horse is loose.) He understood the cues, and this worked just fine for him. I could really tell that he was not learning in a positive way by his body language, and his lack of enthusiasm. If I am using positive reinforcement the behavior has to increase, but he has to do it because of the reward, not because of a consequence. I have to get him to go forward without using anything negative. He was doing the task perfectly, but he would not do it on his own yet. I waited, and did nothing, waiting to see what he would do. He just stood there, and did nothing. We had practiced quite a few times, and this was the test. Was he going to go forward around me in a trot, or just stand there? He just stood there. He clearly didn't get the task.

I showed him several more times using some pressure to move him around. He soon started going forward on his own, but it wasn't because he wanted a reward. He was anticipating the task because I was backing it up with negative reinforcement to get him to move. He was going forward because he was afraid of the consequence. This was not what I was looking for, even though it looked the same. He needed to move forward because there was a reward in it for him, not that he was anticipating pressure (negative reinforcement). I was looking for his behavior to increase without him having any fear, or discomfort. His mind has to be in an "I want to do it" mode, for the reward of the click. That is the key. Until he offers this to me the task is not complete. As soon as he does, I know he understands it clearly, and his mind is with me in the positive. Then I can start asking for more.

This will stay with him longer and shorten my training time down. I am constantly looking for the positive. This is my goal as a Clicker Trainer. There will be many times that you will have to use negative reinforcement because you can't get along without it, but I am looking, watching for the positive in his mind. It took two more sessions to get Kiowa to offer it to me. How do I know that it was in the positive? I asked him to trot around me using some pressure. When he trotted in a full circle, I clicked, and fed him, then I did nothing. He backed up, looked around for awhile, stood there. I waited and waited. He looked like he was thinking. He turned and trotted in a circle without me doing anything. This is how I knew he finally understood it. He repeated it immediately several times, then we went to the other side. You have to know your horse's facial expressions when they perform a task. What kind of expression are you looking for? A scared look, a happy thinking look, or a pained look?

We also can't focus all the time. One time I was driving from Phoenix to Oklahoma, and I finally made it to Texas. I parked in the front of a store. When I came out I could not see my car. I had to go back into the store, and walk back out, and there was my car parked in the front. I was so tired from 12 hours of driving, I just couldn't think. Another one is, "Where's my glasses?" that are sitting on top of my head. Horses have a much better memory than we do. This does not usually happen to them. They can remember things from the time they are born. If you cannot get the mind to think about the task, it will never be stored as a memory. There is a department store that I go to on a regular basis, and they have number signs on their rows. I usually have to say in my mind that we are in row 5. If I do that, I can always find my car. Kiowa has to say in his mind, "If I go in this direction, I will get a click." Instead of, "She's going to pressure me so I better go." He only thinks about the threat.

IF YOUR YOUNG HORSE OR YOUNG FOAL IS NOT HALTER BROKE

I wanted to start out with a horse or a young foal that was not halter broke, or has had no human contact, because there are so many of them out there. If your horse is halter broke, but hard to catch, this can help get back to basics. I start all my horses in this way.

You have to remember your horse or young foal is only going to do what you teach them. There are two types of colts, friendly ones, and non-friendly ones. Some are friendly, just not started. Some are scared of humans, have never been touched, and will have no problem defending themselves. They both will take the same amount of time to start, because the ones that are friendly are most likely spoiled. The ones that are not, take more care. If the colt is spooking, they are scared and they don't understand. I am not into any type of physical force like roping them, or pulling on their head, or round penning until they are tired. Clicker Training is non-physical work. We work with the mind, and it is easier on both you and your horse.

CLICKER TRAINING: COLT STARTING THE NATURAL HORSE

Before my Clicker Training days I started a filly named Bobby Sox. It took me three weeks just to stand next to her. I tried feeding her, bribing her, habituation, round penning, comfort, discomfort, but nothing worked. I refused to put her in a chute. I wanted to train her, not lock her up and force it on her. With some patience, and a few weeks, I finally was able to get the halter on her, but she was so explosive you never knew what she was going to do. One day I was petting her at liberty, and she seemed fine. Someone walked by and she turned around, ran into the front door of the stall, and knocked herself down. I have started many young colts, and this filly was by far the worst. I finally put her out to pasture hoping that maturity would cure her. At the time she was only about six months old.

Two years later her full sister was 5 months old and just like her. Her name was Bobby Dee, and I felt that when she came in for weaning she was worse than Bobby Sox. She would run into the wall when someone would walk by. She was so afraid she would run out of the barn, and bang herself trying to get out. This was clearly a problem. She was recently weaned, and was angry about it. She was so terrified she injured herself many times. I knew I had to get to work on her before she injured herself even more. We still have to feed, and clean the barn. Just doing those things put her into a wild panic. She had plenty of room to get out of the way, but she still ran out so fast, she would hit something. She jumped into her feeder and broke it when someone walked by. I would not have even attempted working with her if I didn't have Clicker Training for assistance.

I waited about four days before I started working with her. She needed time to get used to eating grain and hay. I withheld food from her in the morning, and she had to eat with me watching her from outside her pen. She ate with no problem. During the day I would walk up and talk to her with food in my hand. She refused to look at me for the first few attempts. I clicked every time she looked at me. She soon took the hay out of my hand. I did not go into her stall, and I did not scare her. If we had a good session we did the same task the next session. I slowly built on her confidence with me. She soon would watch for me throughout the day. As soon as she understood the click meant food she slowed down and stopped running into the walls. This was the beginning of the communication that she craved. She improved tremendously every day. She started to target, and I finally walked into her stall. I even clicked for opening the door. She followed me all over the pen targeting. The fifth time I worked with her she stepped up on the trail-bridge. I was amazed that she understood the click so much that she was talking to me, and I was talking to her. She was extremely intelligent. She just didn't understand humans until I started Clicker Training her. The halter was on within a few days, and I didn't even scare her.

FACILITY

The stall has to be adequate for any horse, and for you. I prefer to have a shelter 12-feet by 12-feet and a run no less than 12-foot wide, by 24-foot long. I like portable panels that have a low gauge, thick steel pipe. Thin piped panels bend, and could harm your horse. Horses paw, and will rub their sides along the fence, so the fence has to be very forgiving. Plus, if your horse gets pinned under the panel you can just take them apart. I don't like a hot wire fence in a small area. It is great for large areas. And of course, take all barbed wire off your property. There is no place for barbed wire on a horse farm. You have to make sure that if the horse hits the pen, or puts a leg through it, they can't pull it down or bend it. For a young horse 5' high is adequate, but 6' is preferred for all other sizes.

Don't go into their stall. Set the stall up so you can water and feed from outside the stall. Spend a couple of days letting your horse get used to their surroundings. It can be a good idea to have another horse adjacent to them for comfort.

Most horses need to be vaccinated at some point, and their feet need to be taken care of, but not at the cost of your horse's mental well being. If they have never been touched, there is no way you are going to give them a shot or trim their feet.

CHAPTER 4
GETTING TO KNOW YOUR HORSE OR COLT

It is important that these tasks are done in the order that is presented in the book.

You will need clicker, and pouch of food.

By now they should be calm in their stall, and with you appearing around the barn. Some get into a habit of running away, so start withholding food from them and have them eat in your presence. If they leave and snub you, don't worry, they will come back. You might want to hold back the free grass hay for now. What will happen is they will eat the grass hay, and ignore you with the food. Let them get a little hungry. I will feed them by hand at first, either with hay or grain, and leave the rest so they can finish. I always make sure they do eat for their health.

I like to feed some alfalfa hay. It seems to be less aggressive to them when fed by hand. They will eat if they are a little hungry. Click for every time they look at you, then offer them some hay. If they are eating grain, you can use a small feed bowl, or hand feed them (see Hand Feeding Chapter 2). When you start using the clicker, you will notice they will become calmer. They will start to understand that the click means food. On average it may only take just a few clicks. They are much more intelligent than we give them credit for.

I like to keep safe, which means staying on the opposite side of the fence. I click every time they look at me, then I present the food, whether it is in a bowl or by hand. Take the food away every time they take a bite. If they stick to the food, and do not come up for air, I wait for them. Continue to do this for a few sessions. Keep thinking good thoughts about them. This will help you with your body language. Keep smiling. Sometimes talking to them helps. If there is food left, click for one last time, give them the whole bowl of food or hay and walk away. I like to feed them their grain rations for my sessions. You will be amazed how fast this works. It is actually the click that makes the difference, not the food. The communication with the human is what they are craving. They already know how to eat. We are taking something they already understand, and using it as a tool. It becomes a good thing to walk up to you, and look at you. They will start to get much more friendly.

Have your sessions run about 5 minutes long, but no more than 10. You will be able to tell when they are getting tired of it. They start to get less interested. When this happens end, the session.

I like to start with the target as soon as possible. This gives the food some meaning, and will help the horse start to think. (See Items You Will Need Chapter 2) I like to start outside the stall. The colt or horse will be scared of the target at first, so once they look at it, click and feed. They know that the click means, "YES that is what I want."

When this task is finished you should be able to:

Have your horse touch the target, and follow it through the fence.

Then click, and feed.

YES, THEY WILL KICK YOU

Horses communicate through body language. They bite, strike, and kick when they are scared or frustrated. A young horse's defense is to kick. They will kick you if they are trying to communicate with you. Horses kick to get higher in the herd and gain dominance. Young foals don't know where the best place is to be. Kicking is not on my list of desired behaviors, and I don't want to get kicked. You are still outside the stall, even though they are targeting, and doing some work. I have to teach them how to work around me so we both get along. If their hindquarters are away from you, they can't kick you.

I was working Bobby Dee, the very strong willed 5-month old filly. She would target while I was outside the fence just fine. I hadn't been inside the stall yet, so I went into her stall. My first task was to teach her to disengage her hindquarters, which means they cross one back foot over the other away from me, so I can be safe. I knew enough to stay away from her hindquarters. I wanted to teach her, not scare her. She was scared enough. She was trying to dominate me by walking away, which in turn put her rear towards me. She walked about 10 feet away from me. I was facing her. She saw my shadow, and she started kicking at the air. My presence in her stall made her so nervous she needed to defend herself. The space was not large enough to keep me completely safe from her. The next thing I knew, I saw a foot flying. I yelled out, and she took off. She was no-where near me, but she had no problems kicking out and defending her self. It didn't matter where I was. My yell was enough to get her to move her feet away from me. I put her in a larger area, and she ran around like a rocket, scared to death. When she stopped, she made sure she had her hindquarters to me to make sure she would stay safe.

Skylar was putting her hindquarters into me, so I asked her to move out of my way.

I carry a stick, which is a type of lunge whip about 5 feet long to make sure I stay safe also. I call this stick an *extension stick* because it is an extension of my arm. So what about this duel of wills? She was protecting herself, and so was I. How do I teach her that it would be better to move her hindquarters over without chasing her around, and showing her that I can be more dominant? I could get her feet to move with a yell, so she knew I was dominant. I needed to stay safe, and show her the way. Kicking didn't work for her. It only scared her more, and this made her run in mindless circles. Now she runs away instead of kicking if she feels she needs to. But, if she were cornered, she would kick for her defense. If I were cornered, I would take my stick, and come out swinging. This is not about fighting with each other. I want to teach her how to keep herself in a place where we both feel safe, and we both can relax. We have to find a happy medium. My stick is an extension of my arm to keep me safe. If she started to kick at me and came closer, I would swing my stick. When she came close enough to hit the stick, that is how she would get struck. If you can't get your horse to move with swinging the stick in the air or some contact with it, by all means RUN! Let the horse win. It makes no sense to get kicked. If you have to get out of the way, you need to rethink the whole process, and work on moving your horse's feet out of your way. Most horses are taught to fight back by the human.

Moving their hindquarters around will be the most beneficial thing you will ever do, but it won't have any meaning unless they understand what the click means. Disengaging of the hindquarters needs to be more important to a horse than kicking. (This is not a war. This is a partnership.) If I can just move her feet a little, that is enough to show dominance. I don't have to chase her around, and make her run like a maniac.

DISENGAGEMENT OF HINDQUARTERS AT LIBERTY

Liberty is when your horse has no halter on and they are free.

I like to have the horse in an area about 24-feet by 24-feet. If it is larger that will work just fine. If your space is any smaller you might get into trouble.

You will need your clicker, target, pouch of food, and an extension stick.

Your horse should be comfortable enough to stay with you just by having the target. Your horse wants the food, so clicking and feeding often will be a good key for success.

Let's get specific, and work on your horses left side. This means we are looking for the left hind foot to cross over the right hind foot. It really doesn't matter what side you start on, as long as you do both. You only have about 5 to 10 minutes of attention span. You might get more if they are having a good day, but plan on 5 minutes.

Stand in front of your horse.

Put the target in your right hand and present your target to your horse, and have them follow the target to your right. Click and feed.

If they just move their neck at first, that's just fine. Click and feed. They may start moving their front feet only. That's OK, we are just getting started.

Have them follow the target around until they move their hind feet away from you. I don't care if they cross. Any movement is worth a click. They may just walk in a small circle. They will be happy to do this if you click and feed often. As soon as they want to touch the target again, start moving the target around to their left side. Remember to move with your colt.

Rider is following the target.

Click when they move their hind foot over away from you. Soon they will just start moving their hindquarter over. Remember, your goal is the left hind foot crossing over the right hind. It might take some time to get to this. Soon you will notice that your horse will start to offer you this behavior before you get a chance to use your target. Wait and see if they can "Show you what they know." They should move their hindquarters over, or take a step over. Click as soon as they do. If they do not, repeat the same sequence until they do. Wait again, and repeat the same process about 5 times.

Now you can control one side of the hindquarters. Get this solid before moving to the other side. The reason that we want them to 'show us what they know' is that we find out exactly what your horse was thinking of at the time you clicked. Also if you use this method on one side and not the other, you will realize that the side that you used 'show me what you know' will be solid and easy. The side that you did not will feel weak and slow.

Rider is showing me what he knows by moving his hind foot away from me without me asking.

ADDING A CUE TO IT

Now it is time to add a cue to it. Your horse should be offering you this behavior. This is a good thing. While they are offering it to you, get your timing with your horse's movement.

Stand in front of your horse, step side ways about 2 feet to your right. I like to walk around in a circle, and point my finger towards the hindquarters. My focus and my body position should be enough to get them to recognize the cue. I do this just before I know they are going to offer me the behavior. All you are doing is adding more communication. Soon your horse will recognize your cue, and should be very willing to do it.

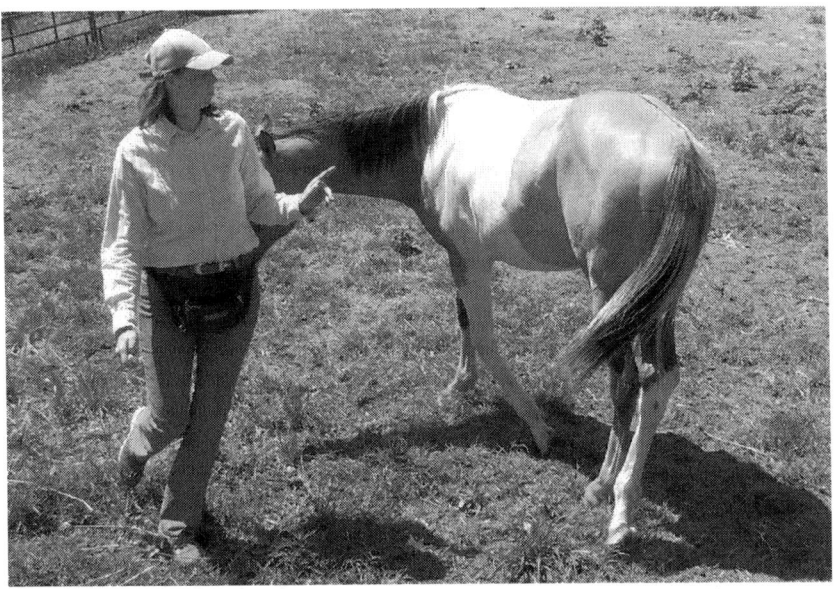

Focus and movement is a good way to cue your horse for disengagement.

If that doesn't work, you can make some noise by clucking, or stomp the ground towards their hindquarter to see if they will move. If they do not, go back to the target and try again. You will eventually phase out the clicker. If they do not do what is asked of them, they are thinking of something else, and need some help. It is your horse's responsibility to pay attention to you and your cues, and it is your responsibility to pay attention to your cues.

Do the same to the other side. The switch might take more time. Go back to your target for help in switching sides. Your horse will only want to do the side that they know, so it will take more patience. You are looking for 'show me what you know.' They need to offer the switch over as a behavior they thought of.

If you feel that they are a difficult horse, you can move to putting the halter on after you get one side of disengagement. You can work on the other side later on.

When this task is finished, you should be able to:

Point to their rear from the proper position. They should move it away from you.

Then Click and feed.

This task is very important for safety. I was working a young colt. He understood disengagement at liberty from both sides equally. I wanted him to walk in a circle, and follow the target. I put the target so he could follow it, and when he followed it he would continually move his hindquarters over away from me, and continue in a circle, even though I was not clicking for it. I liked this offering since it was a very small pen, and it kept me away from his hindquarters.

MISTAKES CAN HAPPEN

When you start working with 'show me what you know,' some horses like to show off more than others, your horse should understand the task itself, not your cues. You want a free offering of the task. An example with disengagement of the hindquarters is that you might feel your horse is putting their hindquarters to you. Sometimes you may mistake this as a horse getting ready to kick, but in reality your horse is showing you that they are just disengaging from the other side. Even if that means putting their rear into you, they are doing what you asked, just from the wrong side. Your horse should not be punished for this. It is not a hostile movement. It is a thinking movement.

FIXED, VARIABLE REINFORCEMENT SCHEDULE, AND CHAINING

Fixed Reinforcement Schedule is when every time the horse does the same thing, they are clicked and fed. A fixed ratio of 1 to 1 means that every correct performance of a behavior will be rewarded, however, when a horse is repeating a behavior 100% of the time, it is time to expand on the behavior to the next level of requests.

Variable Reinforcement Schedule means that reinforcement is distributed based on the average number of correct behaviors. A variable ration of

1: 3 means that, on average, one out of every three behaviors will be rewarded. It might be the first. It might be the third.

Chaining means making a chain of events that a horse can perform. Example would be trot slow, head down, and ears up. All of these things **together** would get reinforced. A general rule on chaining is that one task should lead into another task. Reinforcing the last behavior in a chain acts to reinforce the entire chain.

So far we have used a fixed reinforcement schedule for everything that has been done. We can expand that out to more and more things that your horse will do. Chaining is a large part of my program. I will use variable reinforcement on a more finished horse. They never know what I will be clicking for. If I like my horse standing still, I will click and feed. This keeps them alert and interested. In general, I will be using a fixed reinforcement schedule with chaining, and phasing out the click as we go, so we can move on to more interesting tasks.

CHAPTER 5
TOUCHING YOUR HORSE

TOUCHING YOUR HORSE FOR THE FIRST TIME

You will need your target, clicker, pouch of food, and extension stick close by.

By now you can start extending out the time with your horse to 10 minutes or even longer. Your horse will let you know how long it works for them. I don't go over 15 to 20 minutes unless they are still focused.

Now your horse is used to you, and you are able to go into the stall, and your horse understands that moving their hindquarters away from you is good. This may be all your horse is doing when you go into the stall, and that is a good thing. Now you will need to start touching your horse.

I like to call this the *approach/retreat method*. You will see how much your horse will accept you touching them without them moving away or spooking.

If your horse is still getting used to you, it might make you feel better working with your horse outside the stall. This is your decision. It is important when you are with your horse to always look at your position to the horse. There are all kinds of reasons your horse may spook, and it's very important to give them room to get away if they feel they need to. I work in a pen no smaller than 24- feet by 24-feet. The best place to stand is in the middle of the pen. If you do not give your horse room to run away, they may accidentally run over you.

Ask your horse to touch the target, click and feed.

Repeat targeting, but this time slowly move your other hand up in the air. Click and feed, if they stand still. When you bring your hand up, click and feed. If not, back up, and lift it 1/2 as much.

Bring your hand a little closer to their face or neck, depending where your horse is more comfortable. If they are afraid of their head being touched, the neck or the shoulder might be a better place to start.

Repeat targeting and move your hand up a little closer to your horse. Click and feed.

You might get to touch them on the first try, depending on the horse. Always go very slow. Move your hand a few inches in the direction of your horse. It is sometimes the movement they are worried about. It is hard for them to see. If they spook, back up and try again. The key is to keep them from spooking. This task needs to be very calm and easy. Move by the inch. Don't wait until your horse tells you that they won't accept it. Click when they do. If they move away, there is no click. Back up, and try again. Don't over click for what you have already touched. You get to touch a small part of their neck, click and feed. Then move another inch, click and feed. Progress to half of the neck, or the whole neck. Once it is recorded as a positive move, do not click for that part again, unless you are having problems. Then you need to start over. Your horse will tell you what they will accept, by letting you pet them. You have to keep working at it as long as it takes, until the horse can accept being touched. It might take many sessions.

As soon as you can touch a certain section, such as the whole neck, give them a chance to get used to being touched by stroking several times. (Remember not to pat your horse. Stroke your horse.)

Practice:

Stroke the area that you have clicked and fed for one full stroke, then click and feed.

Stroke the same area for 2 strokes, then click and feed.

CLICKER TRAINING: COLT STARTING THE NATURAL HORSE

Stroke again for 3 strokes, then click and feed.

Repeat until you get to 5 strokes, then move inch by inch to another part.

Phasing out the target is a good thing because some horses focus on the target too much, and you will be sneaking the stroking. I want the horse to think "touch me," not "touch target." Removing the target will help with this. Horses have a tendency to think of one thing at a time.

If your horse gets a little upset when you remove the target, go back to your target for their comfort and focus. I like to work really hard on the neck, head, and chest. You will need this to put on the halter. They must feel very comfortable with your presence, and you touching them.

When this task is finished, your chain of tasks should be:

You should be able to touch your horse on their head, down their neck to their chest and around to their shoulder on one side.
Then click and feed.

Do the other side! Most horses don't like you to go to the other side. The other side may be more difficult.

You might have to go outside the stall to pet the other side of your horse. Use your target and position the horse to touch the target with them looking at you with their other eye.

Do not pet them yet. Let them get used to you being on the opposite side first. This can take a few sessions. The important thing is that they stand calmly. It is your responsibility to make sure they enjoy the session.

When your horse seems comfortable, and they are consistently targeting, you can start to pet them.

Repeat the same steps. Get as far as you can outside the fence before you go back in. It never hurts to be too careful. Being in their stall with them can intimidate a horse a little more, and make them more fearful.

When this task is finished, your chain of tasks should be:

Touch your horse from both sides on their head, down their neck, and to their shoulders.
Then click and feed.

Try to touch all over their head, and don't forget any spot. It does make a difference. Then you can click and feed for chaining it all together. This gives you a good chance to get comfortable with each other. Remember about chaining. You have to move on when they understand the task, so we are expanding their learning. This is essential for Clicker Training to work.

Every once in a while you can catch your horse scratching on the fence. If your horse has not been touched much you can take advantage of this. One of my colts was scratching his tail on the fence, and I was not going to let this opportunity pass me by. I became the fence, and scratched his tail, even though I knew he wouldn't let me touch him at any other time. He was just in the right mood. This helped him know that I was not so bad. Since I don't like to click and feed too much for touching my horse, I don't worry about it when we are playing this game. It gives you and your horse a great opportunity to get to know each other better. The horse seems to feel safe because he knows the fence is there, and he can leave at any time. There are many different ways to get to know your horse without trapping them into it, and keeping yourself safe in the process. Many times I will just work in the barn, and wait for my horse to come around for another scratching session.

FREEDOM GAMES

I like to get my horses used to bridges, tarps, and flags, before they even see a halter. Since you have a target, there is not much need for a halter. This is work that is up to you and your horse. Your horse has the

CLICKER TRAINING: COLT STARTING THE NATURAL HORSE

decision to stay or leave. If I just put a halter on and walk off, it won't accomplish much other than dragging him around while he is not sure of it all. It's my job to make sure they understand.

When I started with Clicker Training, I had about 6 young horses to start that were not halter broke. I was having fun experimenting with this new discovery. We were walking on bridges, running around the pasture, walking on tarps, walking under things, and even going in the trailer. If I walked over a log, so did they. If I jumped a stream, so did they. It was so much fun, and all the horses were having fun, too. They all responded well to it. Some had more problems with the tarps than others but some never even spooked at all. Introducing the halter was so easy, and comfortable. They wouldn't leave my side. We built a strong bond.

Having fun in the pasture.

The next group of horses came along and there were 4 yearling colts that had never been touched. We went through our targeting with great success, and we were becoming friends. So I skipped the freedom games. I introduced the halter to them with ease. I had no problems teaching them to lead, but little incidents would happen. They would spook at small things around them. A cat would walk by, or my jacket would make a noise. They would spook, hit the end of the halter, and it was a big mess. They all did the same thing. They seemed to have a lack of confidence. We would have good days, but some days, it was a mess. No matter what I did, I could not get their confidence with the halter. When I took the halter off, everything changed. They calmed down, and started having fun. I brought a slicker out, and they all wanted to play the 'Walk on the slicker' game.

I was working with a colt named Dundee. I was very intent about gaining his confidence, and it took more time and work. I had the halter on him a few times, but he didn't want to lead yet. When he first came to me, he was scared of everything. He used to run and try to go over the fence when a human showed up.

I was working the colt next door with the slicker, and we were having fun. Dundee was looking at the slicker with curiosity. When I am finished with a horse, I usually place food on the object for them to further explore. I asked Dundee if he wanted to share the slicker with Royal, the black colt I had been working with. Dundee looked at me with curiosity. I pulled the slicker under the fence with half of it on Royals side, and the other half on Dundee's side. I placed some food on it, and left. The area that Dundee was in was way too small for me to give him a session, so Royal had to do this session for me. Dundee wanted to know what Royal had that he did not. Dundee walked right up to it, and ate the food off the slicker. He sure was not going to let Royal have it all. If it was good enough for Royal, it was good enough for him. I waited 15 minutes, then I moved Dundee to a safer area, and gave him a session of 'walking onto a slicker.' He walked right on top of it, he felt so comfortable. He was relaxed and calm, and so was I. We had so much fun playing the freedom games. I worked with the yearlings for over 2 hours switching back and forth from horse to horse. The Freedom Games gave them the confidence that was missing. If you can't do it with the halter, do it without.

The next day I was still working with the other colts with the slicker. Black Hawk, a 9-month old colt, was very flighty, and reacted in a huge way. He was the most sensitive of the 4 colts. When I asked him to walk to the slicker, he did because he understood the task. He would look up in the air and walk over it. If it moved, he would jump in the air and run off. It was hard to get out of his way, so I put some food on the slicker. I wanted to see if he could work it out himself. He did what I thought he would do. He walked to the other end of the pen and stood. He was not going to get anywhere near the slicker on his own. He was a very willing colt and understood the tasks, but didn't want to think about what he was walking on.

In this group of colts Black Hawk was the leader. He ate first, Royal second, Dundee third, and little Lucky fourth. I knew that Royal taught Dundee how to stand on the tarp the day before, so I wanted to try the same thing with Black Hawk. I usually don't let the colts out all together with only one food bowl, but I thought this would help Black Hawk. The food was still sitting on the slicker. The second I let Dundee out he headed for the slicker. Next Royal, then Lucky. They understood the slicker, and were confident enough to know it was OK. Plus they were both much calmer colts. Black Hawk, of course, knew they went for the food, and was not going to let them eat before him. He walked up, and spooked at the slicker right away. It took him a few seconds to think about it, snorting the whole time. You could tell he was thinking it was worth defending. He soon chased Dundee and Royal off. He stood on the slicker, and ate his grain. They all wanted to get to the slicker, but Black Hawk claimed it as his own, and there was nothing they could do to change that. He stood on it, and guarded it for 30 minutes after the food was gone. This made the slicker important enough to stand on. It had more significance to him now. You can have other horses help you in your training if they are available. It is a part of 'Setting up for Success.'

FREEDOM GAMES WITH OLDER HORSES

There is another reason why I always use the Freedom Games with all my horses, even the older ones. I have an Arabian gelding, named Natchez, who has been one of the biggest challenges I have come across. He is 18 years old now, and he still has trouble with the trailer. He will go in when I ask him, but he breathes hard, and starts to sweat. I have owned him for 12 years, and the first 5 years of his life he was considered UN-trainable. I bought him when he was 5 years old. He had never had his feet trimmed, not because they didn't want to, he wouldn't let them. I couldn't catch him, or even brush him. He had been through many trainers, and was still not broke to ride. Natchez and I were able to get along very well together. I was able to start him and we did fine, but he would have what I call moments. Just for him to walk into an arena without blowing up was progress.

When I started Clicker Training, I could get a young horse that was not even halter broke on the small bridge in a few seconds. I thought it would be easy for Natchez. I was so wrong. He was used to me telling him what to do. He didn't think he had any choices, so his efforts with Clicker Training were almost nothing. Natchez really has a good time with people, and doing the opposite of what we ask is how he has his fun. He was not about to let that go. He was going to wait me out. If I put the halter and lead on and used negative reinforcement to get him on the bridge he had no problems, he got right on, because he had to. If it was his choice, it was too hard for him. I did nothing but 'step on the bridge' task everyday. It was his choice, but this was different for him, and his choice was to ignore it, no matter what treats I had. About the 4th day Natchez was making some progress. We were able to get both front feet on the bridge. The back feet were another challenge. He just refused to step his back feet on the bridge. Natchez loves attention. He was testing me, trying to wait me out. After unsuccessfully trying to get Natchez to step on the bridge, I went to the other end of the pen, and stood in the corner facing the panel. I refused to even look at Natchez. This really sparked his interest. I fully knew he knew what I wanted. He is always looking for attention, any type of attention. So I just ignored him completely. I stood in the corner with my back to him for about 5 minutes. I started to hear a tapping noise. I turned around, and Natchez was on the bridge, tapping with his foot, looking at the bridge. I walked over to him, clicked and fed. We worked for awhile still trying to get his back feet on the bridge. He was really trying this time. He had a completely different look on his face. We were still unsuccessful, but Natchez and I had a different relationship. Natchez can't stand it if I take away his attention. It took 8 days to accomplish our goal.

CLICKER TRAINING: COLT STARTING THE NATURAL HORSE

What I discovered was that it was a fear issue. The drop off of the bridge scared him. He knew what I wanted, but he had to do it himself. He just could not bring himself to get over his phobia. When he finally stepped up and looked down, he seemed dizzied, and almost fell over. I asked him to target to the ground, and once he found out that the 4-inch drop off was not a plunge to death, he was fine. He is a good enough horse to do what I ask, but he needed those 8 days to get over a phobia that he had.

He was telling me of his phobia by shaking, and pacing back and forth when trailered. No matter how much I worked with him he still did it. Natchez needed to get on the bridge on his own, so he had time to soak it in, and get over his fear. Some people are afraid of snakes, spiders, or heights. Natchez was just afraid of falling. This was great therapy for him. Since the bridge he trailers calm and cool. And the drop off is not the endless pit anymore it's only the ground. With this task I figured out when I asked him to step up into the trailer he did it, but would not look down, so he avoided it. He is a different horse now, and happy our relationship has changed for the better.

For the Freedom Games I usually start out with them walking on a board or a bridge. This is a great exercise for your horses that are seasoned. I do the freedom games with all horses no matter how old they are. The Freedom Games will allow them to be more confident. I use the exact same methods for an older horse, as the young.

WALKING ON A BRIDGE TASK

Jackpot clicking is when you continue to click for the horse's position. If the horse is performing a task correctly, and it is a stationary position, I will click, feed, click, feed, click, feed. This will reinforce the task. An example would be standing still on a bridge or arching their neck, and holding it in position. It is the big "YES." I usually don't click and feed more than 10 times in a row, and I do not use this very often.

I like to start with the bridge as my first lesson with the Freedom Games. This will help you with trailering, getting used to strange objects, etc. You can use any bridge you like or a flat piece of wood, but it has to be strong enough for a large horse to stand on. The bridge that I use is made out of a pallet that is reinforced with 2 x 4's, and some plywood on top.

Place your bridge or your board in a large space, such as a pasture (it is better if there is no grass), arena, or large pen.

You will need target, stick, pouch, and food. No halter or lead is used unless you feel you have to, and your horse is halter broke.

Take your target and lead your horse to the bridge.

When they look at the bridge, click and feed. If they don't seem to understand that the bridge is the new focus, you can place the target on the bridge, then take it away when they are interested in the bridge.

This should take a very short amount of time. If they are afraid of it, continue to click for their efforts to get close to the bridge.

When they smell it with their nose, click and feed.

When they touch it with their nose, click and feed.

Continue this for a few clicks.

When you feel your horse understands that you want them to smell the bridge, you can move on. Wait until your horse bumps the bridge with their leg, or tries to paw it, then click and feed. If they try to come to you, walk around the bridge, not allowing them to get to you. If they follow, keep walking around the bridge away from them, so they cannot catch you. As soon as they look at or smell the bridge again, click and feed. Some take longer than others to understand that chasing you does not accomplish anything, and moving around the bridge will become its own keep going signal. This means they are not quite ready to get a click, so keep trying.

This is a crucial part. They will at some point paw the bridge, trying to get you to click. Some will lift their foot, but place it back on

CLICKER TRAINING: COLT STARTING THE NATURAL HORSE

the ground. Click when they pick up the foot, not when they put it down on the ground. When they paw the bridge, click when their foot hits the bridge, not when their foot is in the air.

We are not teaching pawing, even though some horses think that we are. Soon they will place one foot on the bridge. If they are pawing the bridge continually, click when their foot hits the bridge, no more than three clicks.

Wait until your horse puts their weight on their foot when placing it down on the bridge, then click and feed. Continue to click repeatedly, over and over about 4 clicks, to let them know this is what you wanted. You are reinforcing it with a 'jackpot.'

Withhold the click again, and wait for more effort. They should start lifting their other foot. When they lift their other foot, click and feed. Some horses understand right away, and walk right on, and others are more timid. Go slow. Click and feed for small efforts. It doesn't matter how fast they get up on the bridge, but how you reward them for it. Timing is everything.

When both front feet are on the bridge, click a 'jackpot,' then stop and wait.

Now you have both front feet on the bridge. We need the back feet on the bridge. If both front feet are on the bridge, withhold the click until they move one back foot. It doesn't matter if the back foot gets to the bridge, you are clicking for forward movement of the hind foot. Click for any movement toward the bridge. Some horses might get upset, back off, and walk around the bridge again. Put yourself in a position to have the horse get back on the bridge. Some will just go right back where they left off. If they do not, you can click for what they will give you. Your horse is not getting away with anything. They are still having problems, and clicking for this all over again can be a good thing. You wait them out so they can learn more. That can be the key. Wait and see how much they struggle, and when you feel that a click is in order, give them one. If they can't give you much more, end the session. They will be much better later on. I find that if a horse understands the task, they will offer it to you.

Once they have 3 legs on the bridge, give them another "Jackpot."

Wait to see if they will lift the last foot. When they offer forward movement of the last foot, click and feed.

As soon as all four feet are on the bridge, click immediately as they take the last step, and use your 'jackpot.'

Place some food on the bridge, and end the session. The next time you would like your horse to stand on the bridge, it will go much faster. I will continue the same method for about 3 sessions. When I am sure they understand, it is time to move on.

MORE SLICKERS AND FLAGS

We know that your horse can step up on a bridge. It is now time to get to know the noisy and scary looking things that pop up, that most horses don't care for. Living in Oklahoma the wind blows most of the time, and sometimes things do go flying in the air. One time I found some party balloons that blew over in the wind. We have no neighbors, so we don't know how far they came, but they were caught on the fence adjoining the babies pasture. I was lucky enough to discover it before the babies did, so I could time how long it took for the babies to walk up to it on their own. I knew they had never seen anything like a balloon before. When the first baby spotted it, he spooked and spun around really fast, so all the others spooked, not knowing what they were spooking at. There were about 5 young foals with a couple of older horses in this pasture. The older horses didn't seem to care about the balloons, but the foals were curious. They walked up to the balloons in a group. There is safety in numbers. They were all very cautious, bobbing their heads up and down trying to get a better look. They would take a few steps, bob their head, and continue. When one was brave enough to smell it, they all tried to smell it. When they figured out it was nothing serious, they all put their heads down and ate grass right next to it. It was enough to look at, but not enough to have a heart attack over.

CLICKER TRAINING: COLT STARTING THE NATURAL HORSE

All this only took 5 minutes from beginning to end. It is amazing how much a horse learns on their own. They only spooked at it once when they first saw it, because it was not there before. It was their choice to walk up to it or leave. The young foals knew if they were really scared they could escape, and this gave them more confidence. The older horses were not concerned and that added to the babies confidence. The human adds so much fear in a horse by restraining them. If the human knows in their mind that this is scary, then that will transfer to the horse.

Looking at strange objects can be fun for all. One year we had so much snow that I could not use the wagon for hay, and I had to use a tarp to lay the hay on and pull it with the A.T.V. The young ones never spooked or even seemed scared. Now when they see a tarp, it gets trampled. It was a part of their routine. I will tie bags to the fences and put bright beach balls in the pasture that they can chase. The horses have so much fun checking out all the neat stuff. This is very mentally stimulating to a horse, and I get to have a cup of coffee, sit down on the bench, and laugh too. Why do we make it so hard on our horses? Could it be the time factor, tradition, or we just don't know any better.

PLASTIC BAG TASK

Place some bags on the fence, but make sure it is in a large enough pasture so they can get away and not feel that they are going to be restricted by a fence.

See how long it takes your horse to look at it, walk up to it and smell it, and what their reaction is after they walk up to it.

Watch to see how they react in their own setting before you present it in your setting. This will tell you what type of horse you are dealing with. If they spook, you know what to expect in the future.

SOFT FLAGS

Now that your horse has been exposed to different types of things, they should be a little more relaxed. I like to expose them to a soft type of item that doesn't make any noise at first.

You will need clicker, pouch, rag, and extension stick to attach the rag to.

I will scrunch the rag up in my hand, and show it to my horse. Scrunching the rag up will make it seem smaller and less intimidating. When they look at it, click and feed.

Slowly open the rag up to show it to your horse. Click and feed when they target the rag.

Throw the rag on the ground, and have your horse walk up to it. When they target it, click and feed. Make sure you are in the middle of the pen, and the rag needs to be in a place where you can get out of the way just in case your horse spooks at it.

Pick up the rag, and drop it on the ground again. Click if they look at it, then feed.

Wait to see if they walk up to it, and smell it. When they smell the rag, click and feed. Pick the rag up again, and toss it on the ground a few feet away. Wait to see if your horse follows it. If they smell it, click and feed.

Wait for your horse to walk back over to the rag and smell it. Keep waiting to see what they do. If they paw it, click when their foot hits the rag, then feed. This shows curiosity, and learning what it is. When we go to the supermarket we might smell the orange or poke at an apple to feel if it is fresh. The same thing with a horse, looking, smelling, and pawing is learning. You never want to take curiosity out of a horse.

For now you just want to expose your horse to little things, not overpower them with slickers or tarps. To expose a slicker or a tarp at this stage would be too much. I only would lay them on a fence so the young horse can explore.

TARPS AND SLICKERS

CLICKER TRAINING: COLT STARTING THE NATURAL HORSE

A safe way to expose your horse to tarps and slickers is to hang them on the stall. If they are spooking just because of the tarp hanging, they are not ready for it yet, and you should do this when they are in a larger pen, or the pasture. If you don't have a larger pen or pasture, hang it from a distance away until your horse calms down. They will let you know what makes them comfortable.

Stand outside of the pen, hang your slickers, tarps or plastic bags on the fence one at a time. Be ready with pouch and food. I prefer to click and feed through a fence. As soon as they look at it, click and feed. If you have hung flags on the fence in a pasture, it should be easier on your horse.

Wait for your horse to touch your tarp, slicker or plastic with their nose, or to walk towards it. They might want to follow you towards the object. Whatever it takes to help your horse, I would do it. When the halter goes on for the first time, and your horse has been exposed to other things, they are less likely to spook. Work on this as long as it takes, until your horse becomes calmer.

I like to expose them to many different things that don't make too much noise, such as gloves, towels, brushes, etc. If you have a horse that you have worked with, and you are following this step by step, remember to try not to touch your young horse with the new item until you have gone through the correct process. You are just exposing your horse to different things right now, you are not touching them with it.

CHAPTER 6
THE HALTER

Now that your horse can do things that most can't do with a halter on, putting the halter on should be easy. The jumps and spooks will be much less, and you won't harm your horse's head and neck.

PUTTING HAND OVER NECK

You will need your clicker, and pouch of food.

To properly put the halter on, you will have to put your hand over their neck. I like to simulate this before I introduce the halter. Getting the halter on is all about your hand movements.

To do this I will slowly put my hand over their neck, and click, then feed when they stand still. Go slow. It is hard for them to see your hand on their other side. Work in inches, and keep progressing. Click and feed for every movement that your horse will stand still for.

The first step might be just to lay your hand on top of their neck, then click and feed. Slowly start to rub the other side of your horse's neck. Click and feed when your hand is on the other side of their neck. It can be a surprise to the horse that you can all of sudden be on the other side. Another big part of it will be working your hand under their neck. You will also have to put your hand under their neck to put the halter on. Make sure you can touch them under their neck and on the chest. Go slow. Click and feed every inch or so. If they jump or act scared, back up.

Putting hand over neck.

When this task is finished, your chain of tasks should be:

>Put your hand over your horse's neck.
>Pet the opposite side of the neck for a few seconds.
>Then click and feed.

Do the other side. You can use the target if you need to at any time, but don't forget to phase it out. Even though the halter is put on from the left side, your horse needs to be comfortable being handled on both sides.

SIMULATE PUTTING THE HALTER ON

You will need your target, rope halter, clicker, and pouch of food.

The type of halter I use is a soft marine braid rope halter. It is light, very quiet, and comfortable.

You do not need a lead.

Put the halter on the top of your target, and have your horse target the halter. Click and feed. Do this a few times.

Take the target away, and have your horse touch the halter. When they do, click and feed. Your halter is now the new target. If they have problems targeting something new, you can get your horse used to the new target by bringing the halter to their nose, until they figure it out.

By this time your horse should be very comfortable with their neck, head, and chest being touched. They should stand calm while you stand next to them. If not, keep working on the petting, and clicking. When you are putting the halter on, you have to do it safely. Always be prepared for anything.

They should be targeting the halter.

I like to touch my horse with the halter on their face, and slowly move to the neck and the chest, clicking and feeding all the way. Use the same method as for touching, but instead have the halter in your hand.

Do both sides.

I don't like to try to put the halter on right away. I simulate putting on the halter. I put my arm over their neck, separate the halter, and lightly pull it over their nose. Click and feed for every task, then chain the whole process together into one. It becomes a routine, and your horse should start to drop their head down after a few tries, while you bring the halter over the top of their head. This will help them learn to drop their head when they see the halter.

Have your halter in your left hand, and have it easy to grab with your right hand to open it.

Stand on the left side of your horse at their shoulder.

Put your hand over your horse's neck, and pet your horse. Click and feed.

Put your hand over your horse's neck, and pet your horse lightly. Open the halter with your left and right hand under your horse's neck. Click and feed.

Put your hand over your horse's neck, and pet your horse lightly. Open the halter with your left and right hand under your horse's neck. Touch your horse's nose with the halter. Click and feed.

Put your hand over your horse's neck and pet your horse lightly. Open the halter with your left and right hand under your horse's neck touch your horses nose with the halter. Slowly pull the halter over the top of your horse's nose. As soon as the halter gets to the top of the nose, click and feed.

Put your hand over your horse's neck, pet your horse lightly. Open the halter with your left and right hand under your horse neck. Touch your horses nose with the halter. Slowly pull the halter over the top of your horse's nose, and continue as far as your horse will allow, then click and feed. The goal is to pull the halter over your horse's head, then click and feed.

Repeat several times.

When this task is finished, your chain of tasks should be:

Put your arm over their neck.
Open halter.
Pull the halter over the face, then over the top of their head.
Then click and feed.

Repeat several times.

PUTTING HALTER ON

You will need the halter, clicker, and pouch of food.

Put your hand over your horse's neck. Open the halter, ask your horse to target the halter, and slip your horses nose in it. Click when the halter is over their nose, take it off, then feed.

Repeat this 5 times.

Soon your horse will figure out that what you want is their nose in the halter, and they should be offering it to you. Practice this several times before attaching the halter. I don't like to tie the halter right away, especially if they are not standing still. Tying a rope halter can take some time, and I don't want to have to sneak up on my horse to tie it. If you do, they will start jumping back, and it will get more difficult. I also do this because you don't want your fingers being pulled on if your horse spooks. I just pretend I am tying the knot.

Pull the halter over your horse's nose. Bring it up over their head. Put one end through the loop, but do not attach it, click and feed.

Put your hand over the neck and separate the halter.

Gently place the halter around your horse's nose.

Pull the halter up over the nose.

Loop the halter, but don't tie it.

CLICKER TRAINING: COLT STARTING THE NATURAL HORSE

Take it off, and repeat several times. If they move, the halter will just fall off. This is a good experience for your horse. They might only stand still for one second or so. As soon as they get used to you putting the halter on, and taking it off, hold the halter on with your fingers and count in seconds how long they will stand still.

Hold the halter for one second, then click and feed. If you cannot hold the halter while you click and feed, you will have to take the halter off, then feed.

Put the halter back on, hold the strap, and wait for 2 seconds. Click and feed.

Repeat the same sequence all the way up to 10 seconds. Figure out how long it will take you to tie your halter. That is how long you will have to simulate putting it on. When you are sure they will stand still long enough, go ahead and tie the halter.

When this task is finished, your chain of tasks should be:

Put your hand over their neck.
Open the halter.
Put the nose in the halter.
Slip the halter over their head.
Attach the halter with your horse standing still.
Then click and feed.
Repeat this several times.

As soon as the halter is on, let your horse get used to it being on their head before you do anything. Their heads are very sensitive. Let them walk around with it on. Do not leave them unattended. Rope halters do not break, and they can get their feet hung in them, or they can get it hooked on something. Carry a pocketknife with you just in case. You can move them around, and work on their disengagement. I suggest doing some targeting for a few minutes, and then take the halter off.

Click and feed for them standing still until you have enough time to take it off.

Repeat for a couple of sessions.

PRESSURE WITH HALTER

You will need the halter, clicker, and pouch of food.

Now that you have the halter on, they need to get used to pressure on the halter. If you just attach the lead, the weight of the snap might be too much for your horse, and they might spook. Because you are able to put a halter on does not mean you have control. We use the halter to lead the horse where we want to go, but if they do not understand, there is no point. Dragging a horse around is cruel and useless. Way too many people try to force their horses around, and if the horse wants to leave, they pull on their handler. Remember, a horse's face is very sensitive, and we don't want to make this a scary, or harmful experience. We want to work in the positive.

Without the lead on, I like to start out with putting pressure on the loop of the halter where the lead snap will be attached.

Hold your hand on the loop as light as possible, and count one second. Click and feed.

Repeat for 2 seconds. Click and feed, for up to 10 seconds. Your horse has to stand still for attaching the lead, so hold the hook very lightly in your hand, and click and feed for them standing still. If they pull away, it may be because you didn't pet them under the chin enough. Go back to that, and get this right. Make sure your fingers do not get caught in the loop. You never know when your horse could spook. Go slow.

I like for the horse to feel what pressure is, and tell them "that's right." I will pull lightly on the halter to the right or the left.

CLICKER TRAINING: COLT STARTING THE NATURAL HORSE

Put slight pressure on the loop. Click and feed for them standing still with the pressure. If you are too harsh, they will automatically back up. Let go, and start over again with a light feel. They will get used to it.

If they will stand still for touching the loop, I like to have them go with the pressure. To do this, direct their head to the right, with your hand on the loop. Click and feed as soon as they move with the pressure. I am not looking for their feet to move yet, just their head and neck. That is a good place to start. But if they do give you their feet, take it. Click and feed.

Do this to the right, and to the left.

When this task is finished, your chain of tasks should be:

Put your hand on the loop of the halter.
Lightly pull head to the right.
Then click and feed
Put your hand on the loop of the halter.
Lightly pull head to the left.
Then click and feed.

THE LEAD

You will need the halter, 12-foot lead, clicker, pouch, and food.

Remember there is no force when working a young horse. Don't think you have control of them now that you can put the lead on. If you get too pushy, you just might get into fight and it is not fair to the horse.

I like to use a lead that has a lightweight snap, not a big bull snap. That is too much weight on their face at first.

I will introduce the lead in the same way I introduced the halter. Rub it on their neck and head. When I feel that the horse feels safe in the presence of the lead, I will snap it to the halter loop. Your horse should stand still, since you worked on them standing still before the lead was introduced. They might move their head in a way that might bother them with the additional weight. The last thing you want is your horse to get spooked before you have a chance to let them get used to the lead and the weight. I like to have my target with me. I have them target, then click and feed. I do this so we don't get into trouble. Take your target, and have your horse follow the target just to get used to the new feel. When they touch the target, click and feed. Do this on both sides. End the session before you do too much.

When this task is finished, your chain of tasks should be:

Your horse should follow the target with the halter and lead on. Then click and feed.

DISENGAGEMENT WITH HALTER AND LEAD

You will need halter, lead, target, clicker, and pouch of food.

Your horse needs to learn what pressure is with the halter and lead. Repeat the slight pull to the right and to the left with the lead, instead of your hand on the halter. Click and feed for them following the pressure with the lead. If they go backwards, it is too much pressure. Stop and start over.

The first thing that I like to do is disengage the hindquarters. Now that you have the lead and halter on you can get this even better. Don't use the lead and halter yet. Your horse knows how to do this at liberty. Ask them to disengage from both sides and just hold the lead. Use your target for help. Work on your cues. Practice this a few times.

Now, since your horse understands a little about the pressure on the halter from the left and to the right, you now can use slight pressure on the halter, and disengage the hindquarters from each side. This is good practice for pressure on the halter.

When this task is finished, your chain of tasks should be:

Pull their head around towards you.

Point to their hindquarters.
They should move their hindquarter away from you.
Then click and feed.
Do this on both sides of your horse.

CHANGING HALTERS TO A WEB HALTER

I find that the rope halter is great for getting the horse used to a halter. It is soft, and lighter than a web halter. The problem with the rope halter is that it can be more severe on the head at first. If they spook, and they have never felt pressure on their head, it can be quite painful. If you hang on to the lead without them knowing what real pressure is, they could rear and even flip over. It adds fear, and with that you can get into real trouble. After the lead is attached for the first time, I will switch them to a web halter. The web halter is larger and makes some noise. But if you use the same methods, it should take no time for your horse to adjust to the change.

Make sure you are in a stall or a small area.

Put the web halter on and snap the lead to it.

Now that the web halter is on, you can drop the lead on the ground, and let the horse drag it around for a bit. I will change to a 6-foot lead that is stiff, and won't wrap around the horse's legs. They figure out really fast that stepping on it pulls on their head, and keeping their feet off of it releases the pressure. This way they can control the pressure. Some will just stand still and not move, and that is just fine. They are getting to know the lead and the halter on their own. The pressure could be much greater if you are holding the lead.

After every session I will change my halter to a web halter, drop the lead on the ground, and let them drag it around for no more than 10 minutes. If the halter and the lead are left on for too long, it could make their head sore. I recommend putting padding on a web halter to make it even easier on their head. Do not leave them unattended.

MORE ABOUT COMING FORWARD WITH PRESSURE

I like to practice walking forward by using my target to have the horse walk with me.

You will need halter, 12-foot lead, target, clicker, and pouch of food.

Before you put the halter on, I put the target in a position where my horse can follow it. Click and feed every time your horse touches the target. Walk off, and have your horse follow you. Click and feed for walking a few steps, then extend your steps until you can walk for about 15 steps, or as many as you wish. This will not take much time. If it does, you need to take the time, or make this your session for the day.

Put your rope halter and lead on. Drape your lead over your arm. Put the target in a position where your horse can follow it. Click and feed every time your horse touches the target. Do this a couple of times without using any pressure just to let your horse know what you want.

Show your horse the target again, and, as soon as they walk forward, give a slight pull forward with the lead. When they touch the target, click and feed. You are adding a cue to the walking forward task. When you pull on the halter with light pressure, your horse should walk forward.

Repeat this several times. I like to wait for them to show me what they know by waiting, and not adding any cues to it to see if they will walk forward. Click as soon as they do it on their own. Do this for a couple of times, then add the cue back to it.

Phase out your target, and, only using a slight pull, start walking forward. Your horse will know that walking forward is a cue also, so use your motion for help. Practice a few times. If you pull too hard your horse will automatically pull backwards. Just walk with your horse, keep the same pressure, and start over. It is very important that you do not pull on the halter. It should be light pressure. If you horse gets a little confused, try to disengage their hindquarters.

CLICKER TRAINING: COLT STARTING THE NATURAL HORSE

When this task is finished, your chain of tasks should be:

Walk forward, and your horse should follow.
You should be able to walk a full circle around the pen.
Your horse should come forward with pressure, or just follow you.
Then click and feed.

BACKING WITH HALTER

You will need halter, lead, target, clicker, and pouch of food.

Take your target, have them target a few times, click and feed.

Move the target under their chin towards their chest. When they start to follow it and touch it, click, then feed. Practice this a few times.

Keep bringing their head towards their chest. If they move their feet back, click when they take a step back, then feed. Repeat. If they are having problems, you can lay the lead on your arm, and press lightly on their chest with your hand to help them back up, while the other hand holds the target. This will help them using a negative to simulate what you want, then rewarding them. When you press on their chest, you will press very lightly. If that does not work, press a little harder. It should not take much. Do not cause any pain. Wait for the response.

If you are still having trouble, put your target away, and stand in front of your horse with the lead in one hand. Change your body to an aggressive pose, and make some movement towards your horse. They will back up at some point. Click the second they take a step back, then feed. If your horse blows up, the process you used was way too harsh.

Sometimes the best way is without your target. This process is the one I use on most of the horses. Put your hand below the snap of the lead. Apply some light pressure to cause your horse to go backwards. It does not take much for a colt to lean or make a change. As soon as they do, click, then feed. Make sure you only have enough pressure to cause your horse to make a change. There should be no pain or force, just light asking with the halter to back. If you feel the colt is stuck, just hold the light pressure until they move back. If they go forward, don't put any more pressure on your horse, just hold the same pressure, if you can, if not, start over and lighten up on your pressure. They are just searching to get the discomfort off, and, of course, that was the wrong decision. Moving forward will not get the release, but backing will. If they get upset, or move too much, your pressure was too much. Start over with lighter pressure.

Repeat which process works for you best, until they back up with ease.

When you feel the method that works for your colt is understood, you need for them to 'Show you what they know.' Wait and do nothing, and see what your colt will do. If they back on their own, click and feed. That is what you are looking for. If they don't, show them again with your method that works for them. I like to show them about 5 times in a row, and then wait and do nothing to see what they will do. At this point it really doesn't matter what method you use as long it is used in a gentle manner. We want the horse to back, and the task is what we are concentrating on. I want the horse to think that backing up on his own is desirable to the human and horse relationship, and will be rewarded.

By now your horse should be backing over and, over again on, their own. If they back up into the fence, they will walk forward very easily with just a light pull of the halter. Keep your sessions short. It can take only a few sessions to get this right, but once you do, it is there.

When this task is finished, your chain of tasks should be:

Your horse should back at least 3 steps on their own.
Then click and feed.

ADDING A CUE TO BACKING

Now they are backing, and have repetition. We need to click when they back with a cue.

CLICKER TRAINING: COLT STARTING THE NATURAL HORSE

Stand and do nothing and see if your horse backs on their own. When your horse is offering you backing on their own, put your hand below the snap of the halter. Put some light pressure for your horse to go backwards. When they take a step back with your pressure, click, release pressure at the same time, then feed.

Practice:

Ask your horse to back 1 step. Click the moment the step was taken, then feed.

Ask your horse to back 2 steps. Click the moment the second step was taken, then feed.

Ask your horse to back 3 steps. Click the moment the third step was taken, then feed.

Continue this process until you get 10 steps or more if you wish. Remember you are clicking for the chain of steps. When you get the 10th step, your horse has to back 9 steps before the click and feed. That is chaining the whole process.

When this task is finished, your chain of tasks should be:

Ask your horse to back 10 steps.
Then click and feed.

COMBINING BACKING AND COMING FORWARD

We know that the cue for walking forward is slight pressure on the lead in front of the horse, and backing is putting some pressure on the halter for backwards.

Ask your horse to back, with the cue taught, click and feed for about 3 steps. Your horse does not have to 'show you what they know.' This has already been done.

Ask your horse forward with some pressure, and step in front of your horse when they come forward 3 steps. Click and feed. If they get stuck walking forward, you can arch to the right or the left, then straighten up. This can help get them unstuck. If you need your target, use it. At this time, you are clicking and feeding for the back up and walking forward.

Practice:

When you practice this for a few sessions, it is time to combine both of them into a chain.

Ask your horse to back 3 steps.

Ask your horse to come forward 3 steps. Click and feed.

Ask your horse to back 4 steps.

Ask your horse to come forward 4 steps. Click and feed.

Practice until you get up to 10 steps in each direction. You can now phase out the clicker for every step. You can use the clicker if they get stuck, or for when the effort is really there. There are many different combinations you can do. When you are sure they understand, combine them.

When this task is finished your chain of tasks should be:

Have your horse back 10 steps.
Ask your horse to come forward 10 steps.
Then click and feed.

ANOTHER EXERCISE

You will need halter, lead, clicker, and pouch of food.

Stand in front of your horse. Keep your feet still. Ask them to back with the halter until you cannot reach your horse any more. Do not click. They already know how to do this.

CLICKER TRAINING: COLT STARTING THE NATURAL HORSE

Take the end of the rope in your hand, have the rest of the rope lay on the ground. Stand up big and tall and give your horse a strong focus.

Start to wiggle the rope a little with your wrist. You can see the movement of the snap wiggle on the halter. If your horse backs up, you are just adding another cue to it.

If the wiggle of the rope does not work, make some motion with your body. As soon as they take a step back, click and feed. Repeat with the same cue of focus, and a wiggle of the rope. When they take a step back, click and feed. Click and feed for every step. When they move away from you, do not let them come to you to get the food. You need to walk to them to give the food. When the click is made they are supposed to freeze, and wait for the food to come to them. It is like a pause. Everything stops so you can reward them. Walk back to the exact same position, and continue. This won't last long. You will be phasing out the click very soon.

When your horse gets to the end of the rope, ask your horse to come back to you. Take the rope in your hand. Put a slight pressure on the rope with some rhythm. Your horse may want to back some more, or may walk forward. Click and feed when they come forward when the pressure is given. If they take one step, click, walk up to your horse and feed. Stand back, and ask again to walk forward. Take very small steps in the beginning.

When they have walked forward toward you while you are facing them, repeat the backing process. Try to get your cue lighter and lighter. Strong focus is really light. Right now you are clicking for them backing all the way to the end of the rope. Walk up to your horse, and feed. Get back into your position, and ask your horse to come to you with light pressure. Do this several times.

When this task is finished, your chain of tasks should be:

Ask your horse to back to the end of the rope.
Ask your horse to come in back to you.

Then click and feed.

I will mix this up a bit. Sometimes I will click and feed for backing only, then ask them to come in. I will not click for them coming in. Ask them to back again. Click and feed. Ask them to come forward. Click and feed.

MORE FREEDOM GAMES TARGETING OBJECTS

You will need target, clicker, and pouch of food.

Now your young horse understands how to act a little better with you around them. It is time to go outside the pen. Just because your horse is working well in the pen doesn't mean they will act the same way out of the pen. They will be scared and nervous about new surroundings. I like to go to a small pasture, or arena, at liberty, and have them target as they walk with me.

If you do not have a place such as this, keep the halter on, but go slow.

Take your target, and have your horse touch the target, click and feed. Open the gate, and ask them to come out. If you have a halter, don't use the halter. Have the halter there so your horse won't get loose. This exercise is not for using the halter. I like my young horses to feel free to make choices at this point in their training.

Your horse may seem to be scared, and might slow down and not want to come out unless this is their normal turn out area. If they take off, that is just fine. Wait for them to come back. They should. If they start off to eat some grass, let them. This is what they want to do not what we want them to do. If you cannot get their attention, wait a few hours. It is best if you have a place where there is no grass to eat. Most horses will be more into the target.

Ask your horse to follow your target to other places in the pasture.

Place the target on top of a strange object and have your horse touch the target. Click and feed. Have them focus on that object. If they look at it again, then click and feed. Continue doing this until they touch the object with their nose, click and feed. You want your horse to be curious, and look at scary things. You can reinforce them walking up to different things, and record it as positive in their mind. Once they figure out that the particular object is safe, and you have clicked and fed for them touching it with their nose, you can find another object. It can help to put your target behind your back for phasing out the target. You want them to focus on the other object as a target. You can lay your target on the object, then take it away. Horses are very curious, and this is a fun task for them. This task should take 10 to 15 minutes.

Do this with many objects in the pasture, from buckets to barrels, cars, logs, and even trailers. All we are looking for is for them to look at it, and touch their nose to it. You are building their confidence. Soon your horse will want to walk right up and look at everything for the click. This exercise makes the scary not so scary. If you make your horse do this with a halter and a lead, this can add more fright to your horse. It makes it very hard for them to think on their own. When your horse is at liberty, your horse understands how the clicker works, and you can tell them yes, and it is so much more enjoyable. I have seen many horses walk up to things like bags, tarps, and tractors in the pasture, on their own. In the pasture when there is fear of a new object, a horse can and will figure it out, even with out our help. They have to learn that they can do this in our presence as well.

When this task is finished, your chain of tasks should be:

Walk up to a strange object.
When your horse touches the object with their nose.
Then click and feed.

CHAPTER 7
EXPANDING ON TOUCHING YOUR HORSE

Now it's time to work on touching your horse a little more. We know that we can touch our horse on their neck, head, under the chin, chest and shoulder. I like to repeat the process of clicking and feeding for other parts of the horse. We have not touched their back, underside or back legs as of yet. Since your horse knows you a little better this is a good time to start.

STROKING YOUR HORSE WITH AN EXTENSION STICK

The Front

You will need clicker, pouch with food, extension stick (lunge whip), halter and lead. The stick is an extension of your arm and, if you make a mistake, the stick keeps you out of harms way.

Put your rope halter on. We will be starting on the horses left side.

Take a long lunge whip or stick and stroke your horse on their neck. Click and feed for what they will let you touch. We click when the touch is given. Remember we don't want the horse to move, so click before they do. Progress inch by inch with your stick, if your horse is afraid of the stick, you can have them target it a few times. Click and feed.

Drape the lead over your arm. Stroke your horse's neck to their shoulder with your stick, click and feed.

Start again at the left shoulder and stroke down inch by inch, clicking and feeding all the way down the outside of their front legs to their hoof.

Take 1 stroke from their neck all the way down to their hoof, then click and feed.

Take 2 strokes in a row from their neck all the way down to their hoof, then click and feed.

Repeat up to 5 strokes in a row, then click and feed.

When you can do this, switch to the inside of the leg. On the inside of the left leg, start at the underside of the neck. Stroke to the chest, click and feed. If they do not let you stroke from the neck to the chest, back up and click inch by inch until you get to the chest. Since you have not touched the inside of their legs, you need to click inch by inch for them standing still while you stroke down to their hoof. Remember, work very short sessions. It can take a few sessions to get this. Go slow.

Take 1 stroke from their chest, go to the inside of the leg all the way down to their hoof, then click and feed.

Take 2 strokes in a row from their chest to the inside of the leg all the way down to their hoof, then click and feed.

Repeat up to 5 strokes in a row, then click and feed.

When this task is finished, your chain of tasks should be:

You will be able to stroke the outside of the front left leg with your stick from their neck to their shoulder to the hoof, then move your stick to their chest and stroke the inside of the left leg down to their hoof.

Then click and feed.
Repeat this chain up to 5 times.
Do the other side.

Back and Side

I like to move to their back and then go to the underside of their belly with my stick before I start using my hands. When you stroke your

CLICKER TRAINING: COLT STARTING THE NATURAL HORSE

horse with your hands, you will be standing very close to your horse, and you are vulnerable while stroking their legs. We want to get as much in as we can with the stick first.

Stroke the top of their neck until the stick gets to their back. Click inch by inch. Some might let you get away with more than an inch. Take it if they give it to you. Your horse will tell you what they like or dislike. Repeat a few times.

Practice:

Stroke from their neck to half of their back 1 time. Click and feed.

Stroke from their neck to half of their back 2 times in a row. Click and feed.

Continue up to 5 strokes in a row, then click and feed.

Stroke from their neck to their back, continue to the top of the hip, 1 full length, then click and feed.

Stroke from their neck to their back, continue to the top of their hip 2 full lengths in a row, then click and feed.

Repeat up to 5 strokes in a row. Then click and feed.

Repeat process on other side.

Stroke your horse's shoulder, and continue half way to their belly on their side. This might be sensitive, so click inch by inch for better results.

Stroke from their shoulder and continue half way to their belly on their side for 1 stroke, then click and feed.

Stroke from their shoulder and continue half way to their belly on their side for 2 strokes in a row, then click and feed.

Repeat up to 5 strokes in a row, then click and feed.

Stroke your horse's shoulder and continue to their belly on their side all the way to their flank. This might be sensitive, so click inch by inch for better results.

Stroke from their shoulder and continue to their belly on their side all the way to their flank for 1 stroke, then click and feed.

Stroke from their shoulder and continue to their belly on their side all the way to their flank for 2 strokes in a row, then click and feed.

Repeat up to 5 strokes in a row, then click and feed.

Repeat process on the other side.

When this task is finished, your chain of tasks should be:

Stroke from their withers to their hip.
Move your stick and start again from shoulder to their flank at least 5 times in a row.
Then click and feed.

The Underside

For the underside, you want to start at the shoulder and go to the elbow, to the girth, and under their belly. It does not matter what side you start on. Start from the elbow and go under the belly inch by inch, clicking and feeding, until you get halfway underneath their belly. When you can stroke from the elbow to the middle of their belly in one stroke, then click and feed.

Stroke from the elbow to the middle of the underside of their belly. Click and feed.

Stroke from the elbow to the middle of the underside of their belly 2 times in a row. Click and feed.

Continue this process until you get to 5 strokes before you click and feed.

Repeat the same on the other side.

When this task is finished, your chain of tasks should be:

Stroke from the elbow to the middle of their belly at least 5 times. Then click and feed.
Do the same on the other side.

STROKING WITH OUR HANDS

I like to work as much as I can on the front before I attempt to go to the back parts of the horse. Your horse needs as much time as possible before we attempt to do the back legs and hip.

You will need halter, lead, clicker, and pouch.

I repeat the same process as with the stick, but instead I will use my hand. Stand next to your horse's front legs facing toward their hindquarters, and run your hands from the shoulder to your horse's foot on the outside. While doing this you will be bending down. Do not tilt your head towards your horse's rear. They still can kick you. Keep your head upright while you bend your knees to touch their legs. Always be cautious of where you are standing, and don't forget to let your horse have room to move away if they need to. Your hand will feel different to your horse, and you might have to repeat inch by inch, clicking all the way.

Repeat the same process as if you had a stick in your hand. Your horse will tell you what they are okay with and what they are not. Do not touch where they have not been clicked for yet. We don't want any unexpected spooks or shivers, and we certainly don't want to invade the horse.

Repeat the same process on both sides.

When this task is finished, your chain of tasks should be:

Touch your horse where you have taught, with your hand.

Go from one side to the other.
Then click and feed.

Touching the Back Section of your Horse with your Stick

This can take twice the amount of time.

You will need halter, lead, clicker, pouch and stick.

Stand at your horse's shoulder. Take the stick and stroke from their withers to the middle of the back. Remember where you left off last time. Stroke inch by inch, clicking and feeding, from the middle of the back until you reach the top of their tail. You should be able to stroke half way, then click and feed. Continue the stroke to the tail. The next stroke should be a complete stroke from your horse's withers to the top of their tail, then click and feed.

Stroke 1 full stroke from the wither to the top of their tail. Click and feed.

Stroke 2 full strokes in a row from the wither to the top of their tail, then click and feed.

Continue this process until you get to 5 strokes in a row before you click and feed.

When this task is finished, your chain of tasks should be:

Stroke from the wither to the top of their tail 5 times in a row.
Then click and feed.

Stroking the Hip and Back Legs with your Stick

Stand at your horse's shoulder. Stroke from their withers to the top of their tail. Click and feed. Start again from the top of their tail and stroke down inch by inch, clicking and feeding until you can stroke down their hip to the hoof.

CLICKER TRAINING: COLT STARTING THE NATURAL HORSE

Stroke from the top of the hip to the hock. Click and feed. From the hock, go to the inside of the leg, stroke inch by inch, clicking and feeding until you get to the foot.

Stroke 1 full stroke from the top of the tail, down the hip to the hoof, then click and feed.

Stroke 2 full strokes in a row from the top of the tail, to the foot, then click and feed.

Continue this process until you get to 5 strokes in a row before you click and feed.

Stroke 1 full stroke from the top of the tail, down the hip to the hock, to the inside of the leg, to the hoof, then click and feed.

Stroke 2 full strokes in a row from the top of the tail, down the hip to the hock, to the inside of the leg, to the hoof, then click and feed.

Continue this process until you get to 5 strokes in a row before you click and feed.

Repeat the exact same process on the other side.

When this task is finished, your chain of tasks should be:

Stroke with your stick from the top of your horse's withers to the top of the tail, down the hip and continue down to the foot.
Then click and feed.
Stroke with your stick from the top of your horse's withers to the top of the tail, down the hip and continue down to the hock, then move to the inside of the leg to the foot.
Then click and feed.

I don't like to just start touching the horse's back legs with my hands yet. Some horses feel very uncomfortable with this. I like to work on some other things first. This will get your horse more used to you, and be safer for you when it is time to work on touching your horse's back legs. It's one of those things where you just have to get to know your horse a little bit better first. We haven't touched the underside, private parts, or ears. I prefer to wait until my horse gets more comfortable with me before I touch those parts. It is a little too personal.

PHASING OUT TOUCHING YOUR HORSE WITH YOUR HAND

When you can touch your horse on the shoulder and you have clicked and fed for it, phase it out by counting the strokes. Pet your horse's head, neck, and front leg, click when you get to their foot. Repeat with more strokes until you have so many strokes that you won't be feeding for stroking any more. The stroking will be reward enough. Try to see which parts your horse likes to be scratched on their front sections. This will also give your horse time to get more used to you. The scratch should be reward enough. I like to introduce a brush to them at this point.

INTRODUCING THE BRUSH AND BRUSHING YOUR HORSE

You will need halter, lead, clicker, pouch and soft brush.

It does not matter what side you start on. Introduce the brush as if it were a target. Slowly start brushing your horse. You can click and feed when you feel that it is appropriate. Your horse will let you know if they have a problem with it. Once your horse has learned that brushing feels good, don't click and feed for brushing in those parts of the body any more. I don't want my horse to expect me to feed him for petting or grooming. Spend some time getting your horse used to different brushes. Do their front section only.

TOUCHING THE BACK SECTION OF YOUR HORSE WITH YOUR HAND

If you feel your horse is calm enough and ready for you to start on the back section, begin touching them on their back, hip and back legs.

CLICKER TRAINING: COLT STARTING THE NATURAL HORSE

Repeat the process the same as if your arm was your stick. Stand at your horse's shoulder, touch with your hand as far as you can reach, click and feed inch by inch.

When you feel comfortable enough, take one step toward their midsection, stroking the part that you have touched. Click and feed. You will have to walk to your horse's front to feed. When you get back into position, touch your horse's shoulder stroking all the way back to where you last were, and continue. Stand as close to the horse as you can. Remember to pay attention to where your head is. Standing close to your horse will prevent a kick if one should happen.

Continue the process with one more step toward their hind leg. Your leg should be standing next to your horse's back leg. They cannot kick you when you stand close to their leg. The most they will do is knock you back with their hip. This is important for your safety. Only touch where you have touched with your stick. We don't want any surprises.

Just stand next to your horse's hip and don't touch your horse, click and feed for them letting you stand next to their hip for at least 5 clicks.

My Arabian gelding Natchez is very well trained and understood all about the feet and touching. I tied him up and went to get some things in the barn. I was boarding at the time and the owner of the place let her dogs out. While I was in the barn, the dogs (which were cattle dogs) decided to bite Natchez's back legs for fun. Natchez kicked at them and they stopped right away. It only took a few seconds for him to solve the problem. I heard some noise but was unaware at the time of what happened. I went to clean Natchez's back feet and I, of course, stood as close to him as I could. The next thing I knew, I was 5 feet away from him on the ground. He kicked out and knocked me to the ground. If I were standing a foot away I would have been seriously hurt. His hip hit me in the cheek and pushed me away. I figured out what had happened as soon as I saw the dogs. Never forget the horse's power. You never know what is going to happen, so always keep yourself safe.

Stroke the back of their hip. Click and feed for every inch. I like to spend some time stroking. You will need to double the amount of time that you spent on the front part of your horse.

Stand facing toward the back of your horse and continue to stroke the hip very lightly and softly. You will have to move to feed. Remember everything stops for the horse when you click, so walking up to your horse to feed is not a problem. Always stroke all the way back to get back in position so you won't startle your horse. If your horse starts to move away from you, go back to their midsection and work from there. Always back up if there is a problem.

Continue to face the back of your horse, standing as close to your horse's leg as possible. Start stroking the leg and click for what they will allow. You shouldn't have to click inch by inch because you have already done that with your stick. You can be the judge of your progress. If you have problems, go back to your stick. Keep in mind not to drop your head down too far. Keep it upright while you go down their leg with your hand.

Repeat on the other side.

This task will take a few sessions and this should be the only thing that you work on. Soon your horse will walk up to you at liberty and get into position. They are in the habit of showing you what they know. When they feel comfortable with you being at their hindquarter, it is time to move on.

When this task is finished, your chain of tasks should be:

Stroke with your hand from the top of your horse's withers to the top of the tail, down the hip and continue down to the hoof.
Then click and feed.
Stroke with your hand from the top of your horse's withers to the top of the tail, down the hip, continue down to the hock, then move to the inside of the leg to the hoof.
Then click and feed.

Continue this task with the brush when you feel your horse is ready, remember, we have yet to touch the inside of their ears and private parts. We will get to that when your relationship gets a little closer.

CHAPTER 8
CRUCIAL TASKS

SHOW ME WHAT YOU KNOW CHECKLIST

If your horse is already halter broke you can start here, but you will need to read all the previous chapters especially 'show me what you know' in Chapter 3.

Now that your horse is getting used to you, it is time for some real skills of managing your horse. We will be working on 5 different tasks.

Disengagement of hindquarters, from the left side.
Disengagement of hindquarters, from the right side.
Backing.
Moving the forequarters over from the left side.
Moving the forequarters over from the right side.

DISENGAGEMENT OF HINDQUARTERS FROM THE LEFT SIDE

You will need the halter, lead, stick, clicker and pouch of food.

There are many different cues you will be using with your horse to move their hindquarters over. I am not too concerned about the cues right now, just the task itself. We will add cues later. Good disengagement can help you with side passing and lead changes, not to mention that the control of your horse is through their hindquarters. I will show you different cues to get your horse to move their hindquarters, but for now I want the task imprinted.

For this task you want your horse to disengage their hindquarter from their left side, which means the left back foot crossing the right back foot away from you. If you have been following this manual, we did this at liberty with a horse that was not halter broke.

Have your horse in a halter and lead.

Stand in front of your horse facing him.

Walk around to your right to their hindquarters in a horseshoe, tapping the ground with your stick. Make sure you are out of kicking range of your horse. You want to stay at least a stick and arm length away to the side. The stick does the close up work for you. Your horse should move away from you. If they do not move, you can tap their hip with your stick.

Click the instant they take a step over, and at the same time stop tapping the ground, then feed. You have to stop the cue for comfort, and click at the same time for learning in the positive. The comfort, stopping the tapping on the ground, is usually the only reward a horse gets. When we add Clicker Training, they get the release reward, plus they get rewarded with a tasty treat for moving their hindquarters over, and the click communicates 'yes, that is what I want.'

Repeat the same process 5 times in a row.

Now wait and do nothing. Check to see what your horse does. They might beg for food, walk up to you and beg, just stand there, or they might disengage their hindquarters and repeat all on their own what you have been practicing on. This is using 'show me what you know.' Your horse should cross over their hind legs just as you showed them for a treat. When they do this, click and feed. You might have to stand facing your horse's hindquarters to hint at what you want. Horses are very perceptive of your position.

If your horse does not respond, it is not in their mind yet, and it's not their idea, so repeat your cue 5 more times in a row.

Again, wait for them to offer it to you.

CLICKER TRAINING: COLT STARTING THE NATURAL HORSE

If they offer it to you, click then feed. One step is good. They need to understand that this is a movement that we desire, and it will get them a treat. When they start offering this behavior to you, click when they cross their back feet over away from you. Wait again for them to show you, then repeat up to 10 times.

Now that you have one side of disengagement working well, and your horse really likes to offer this to you, you can ask with your cue for 2 steps, click, release, and feed. Repeat this several times.

Wait for your horse to offer you 2 steps of disengagement.

Repeat several times. What this does is imprint to the horse that moving away from you is what you wanted, it was thought about by the horse, so the task will stay with your horse for a life time. If you use pressure all the time your horse might not be 'thinking.' This is so powerful that I very rarely have to go back to 'show me what you know.' They will always remember this. Once this task is finished, I can check the box on my 'show me what you know' checklist, which is listed at the end of this section. There are only 6 directions a horse can go, up, down, forward, back, and side to side. Right now we are working from side to side on their hindquarters, which should always be the first thing we work on for safety. If you control the hindquarters, you control the horse.

Time to do the other side. This can be tough, but what we are teaching the horse is to pay attention to us. Ask your horse to disengage from the other side by standing in front of your horse, walk around to their hindquarters on their right side in a horseshoe, tapping the ground with your stick. Wait for your horse to disengage their hindquarters, click, stop tapping, and feed, Repeat all the same steps. It will be easy for your horse to move away from pressure, but it will take longer for them to think of the task in the opposite direction.

Repeat with tapping of the stick 5 more times and wait. It will take longer because your horse will be stuck on what you showed them before. They might even disengage their hindquarters towards you, and repeat what you worked on last. You have to talk to your horse by showing them with a cue, click, release, and feed several times. You will notice your horse is offering from the other side as they did before. You are having a real conversation with your horse now. It may be a bit of an argument. Your horse really believes that they are getting clicked and fed for the other side, because in their mind it worked and they are fixating on that. This is called an *Extinction burst*. No matter how many times you click for the new task they still think you are clicking for the old task. They have to slow down and think. Once they do they will get it. We also go through extinction bursts. If you turned on the light switch and the light bulb suddenly went out you would flip the switch many times trying to get the light to go on even though you know that the light bulb went out. You might do this for several days before you get out of your routine or until you change the light bulb. If the light always turns on every time I flip the switch I am being reinforced every time with the light going on. My mind is a non-believer that the light is out because I have been reinforced so many times by getting light when the switch is flipped on. It would take several tries to make me a believer.

This is why, when you use cues all the time without this exercise, your horse does not get a chance to really 'think.' We are working with the 'thinking' horse.

Soon your horse will get the message. Click and feed for them offering you this behavior. Repeat up to 10 times.

Ask for 2 steps of disengagement and have them 'show you what they know.'

BACKING

The next most important task for your horse to learn is backing. Horses sometimes seem to get a little pushy with us, and having a horse that understands that backing is better than begging will help you with your training. You might have already done these earlier. If your horse was not halter broke, repeating it at this time is a must. If your horse has already shown you what they know on backing, only use your cues.

CLICKER TRAINING: COLT STARTING THE NATURAL HORSE

Have your horse in a halter and lead with clicker and pouch. Stand in front of your horse.

It doesn't matter what cue you use for this. You can tap the ground to get your horse to back, you can use pressure on the halter, release and click when they back up, or you can wiggle the rope until they take a step back.

I will use the rope wiggle for an example.

Stand in front of your horse. Wiggle the rope until your horse takes one step back. Click the instant they take a step back and at the same time quit wiggling the rope, then feed.

Repeat with the cue of wiggling the rope, click, stop wiggling the rope, and feed.

Repeat 5 times in a row.

Wait and do nothing, check to see what your horse does. They might beg for food, walk up to you, just stand there or they might disengage their hindquarters for you instead of backing. What you are looking for is backing, nothing else. If they seem to be confused, show them with the cue 2 more times, then wait and do nothing. We are still teaching 'thinking.' They will soon start backing on their own.

Click and feed for them offering it to you without you adding a cue to it. All you want to see is if the horse is making the connection to the task in a positive way.

Watch your horse and have them repeat 'show me what you know' about 10 times.

MOVING THE FOREQUARTERS OVER FROM THE LEFT SIDE

Moving the forequarters over will assist you with your lunging.

You will need the halter, lead, stick, clicker and pouch of food.

There are a few different ways to teach your horse to move over on their forequarters.

Having them follow the target until they cross over.
Tapping the horse until they move away.
Pressing with your hand until they move away from the pressure.

We can start with the target since your horse has no clue of what you want. The first thing that we need to do is to just get your horse to cross one front foot over the other foot.

If you have a long target, this is a good time to use it. If your target is short you can use it, but you will have to walk with it to get your horse to cross over.

You will be asking your horse to move their front end over to their right. Place the target in your left hand.

Stand in front of your horse.

Ask your horse to touch the target, then click and feed.

Move the target to the left about a foot, click as soon as your horse touches the target, and feed.

Move the target to the left again, and continue to move the target even further to the left about 2 feet. When they touch the target, click and feed.

Repeat again until your horse moves their feet over. Click as soon as the foot moves over, then feed. They don't have to touch the target this time.

Repeat the same 2 more times. At this point you might have to walk with the target to get them to cross their foot over. When they do click and feed.

Repeat this several times.

MOVING OVER WITH YOUR STICK

Take the target and your lead in your left hand and ask your horse to follow it, and at the same time take your stick in your right hand and start tapping your horses neck or shoulder on their left side. You will have to be holding your clicker and the stick in your right hand. You will be holding your lead and target in your left hand. This might take some coordination, but I am sure you can do this. Having an assistant will work also. Tapping on your horse's neck is the cue to tell the horse to move over away from you.

Phase out your target so you will only have your lead on your left hand. Make sure there is distance from you and your horse. Take your stick and tap your horse's neck or shoulder until your horse steps over away from you one step click and stop tapping at the same time, then feed. If your horse doesn't move over, keep your tap very light for a couple of taps, then you can tap a little harder until they take a step over. Some horses might walk forward. You can wiggle the rope a little to discourage walking forward. Continue tapping. The tapping doesn't have to be hard, just enough to cause irritation. If your horse is giving you a reaction, the tapping doesn't have to be increased. Your horse is just searching for what you want. Continue to tap until your horse takes a step over away from you. Whatever you do, don't stop tapping your horse until they step away from you. When you stop tapping is when your horse learns what you want. You are looking for them to cross the left front foot over their right front foot. Remember, when you click, stop tapping, then feed.

Repeat the same process until your horse understands to step over one step. Repeat the same process 5 times with cue and click.

Wait to see what your horse does by doing nothing. See what they will offer you. Your horse should be getting better at having you show them what to do, and then following your lead by repeating it on their own. It might take some time, and if you have to repeat the cue 5 more times, that is what you have to do. I have worked on this for many sessions, even repeating with a cue and putting them up for the day. Wait to see what they can show you again. If they move away from you without having to give them a cue click, and feed. Have them offer this about 10 times in a row. I have had to work for several sessions on one side before they were ready to go to the other side.

You will need to repeat the exact same sequence, but on the other side.

This is the beginning of expanding this to all other things that your horse will learn. Now that this has been done, we will add many other cues to it, but we don't have to use, 'show me what you know." Your horse will offer it to you more easily. You should get better disengagement and moving over quicker. They understand what you want, and it will make it easier for them to react to your cue.

Now you can check everything in the, 'Show me what you know checklist.'

It is very important that all of these are checked off before you move on.

____ Disengagement of hindquarters from the left side
____ Disengagement of hindquarters from the right side
____ Backing
____ Moving, the forequarters over from the left side
____ Moving, the forequarters over from the right side

PRACTICING DISENGAGEMENT WITH YOUR CUES

I like to practice with my cues to have my horse understand better. It can be more like a dance. You have to practice to get lighter on your feet.

CLICKER TRAINING: COLT STARTING THE NATURAL HORSE

Ask your horse to disengage their hindquarters by focusing on them. If they don't move over, start tapping the ground. If they still don't move over start tapping your horse lightly until they move over. You should have a very willing horse that will move over with very little effort from you. Click and feed when they move over.

Practice:

Ask your horse to disengage their hindquarters for 1 step, click and feed.

Ask your horse to disengage their hindquarters for 2 steps, click and feed.

Ask your horse to disengage their hindquarters for 3 steps, click and feed.

Repeat this until your horse can do a full circle.

If you have to ask with your cue again and again to get all the steps, that is fine.

When this task is finished, your chain of tasks should be:

Ask your horse to disengage their hindquarters for a full circle.
Then click and feed.
Repeat the exact session, but on the other side.

We have already checked our list off for this task, and now we can start phasing out the click by chaining steps together. We have to remember that Clicker Training is for unlearned behaviors, retraining, or if your horse gives you a big effort and you would like to reward them. You don't have to click for disengagement any more. You can even ask for 2 full circles without clicking anymore. It's not necessary to over-click for a horse that understands the process.

BACKING WITH A CUE

When you ask for backing, you will be wiggling the rope and

releasing the moment your horse takes one step back. You will also be clicking when they take the step back.

Stand in front of your horse. Have your horse at least 2 feet away from you.

Take the end of the lead. Wiggle the rope very lightly and see if your horse will back up from soft pressure. If they do not, wiggle it a little harder. If they still do not back up, wiggle it a little harder until there is enough discomfort for your horse to back up. You need to go slow and give them a chance to back up. You should not have any problems with this task. They should back up very lightly if 'show me what you know' was done correctly, and you have checked it off your list.

Stop wiggling the rope the second your horse takes one step back. Click and feed.

Practice:

Ask your horse to back up for 2 steps. Click and feed.

Ask your horse to back up for 3 steps. Click and feed.

Ask your horse to back up for 4 steps. Click and feed.

Repeat this until your horse can back up at least 10 steps.

When this task is finished, your chain of tasks should be:

Ask your horse to back up for a full 10 steps.
Then click and feed.

Now that backing has been practiced with a cue, you don't really have to click for backing anymore with this cue. If you use a another cue, you can click and feed for them understanding another cue, but you will only click and feed when that cue is given. 'Show me what you know' for backing has already been checked off. Then you will only click if your horse backed up really fast and it was impressive. You get to judge what they get clicked for now. Great effort can be clicked for, but it isn't necessary.

COMBINING BACKING AND COMING FORWARD

We know that the cue for walking forward is slight pressure on the lead pulling forward, and backing is putting some pressure on the halter pushing backward.

Ask your horse to back with the cue taught. Click and feed for about 3 steps.

Ask your horse forward with some pressure by pulling on the lead as light as you can or until they make a move forward. Have them walk 3 steps then click and feed. If they get stuck, you can arch to the right or the left. This should help them get unstuck, then straighten up. If you need your target, use it.

When you practice this for a few sessions, it is time to combine both of them into a chain.

Practice:

Ask your horse to back 3 steps.

Ask your horse to come forward 3 steps. Click and feed.

Ask your horse to back 4 steps.

Ask your horse to come forward 4 steps. Click and feed.

Practice until you get up to 10 steps in each direction. You can now phase out the clicker for every step or combination of steps. You now can use the clicker when they get stuck, or when the effort is really there. There are many different combinations you can do.

When this task is finished, your chain of tasks should be:

LESLIE PAVLICH

Have your horse back 10 steps.
Ask your horse to come forward 10 steps.
Then click and feed.

CHAPTER 9
MAINTANCE

Now that your horse is a little more manageable, it is time to work on maintenance. The horse's feet need to be worked on, they need to be given shots, and even their teeth looked at.

TONGUE CLICK SECONDARY CLICK

The tongue click is from the middle of the mouth. It is not from the side of the mouth, as a smooch that we typically use to get a horse to move forward. It doesn't matter what you use, but this will be your secondary click, the back up when you can't get to your clicker. I have also heard some people using the word, 'excellent.' For some reason the horse hears the "X," which makes the word more distinctive. I don't usually use my secondary click when I have access to a clicker. I still have some horses mistake my secondary click for a smooch, and it can get a little confusing.

VACCINATIONS

Now that you can touch your horse almost all over, it is a good time to start working on getting them vaccinated.

This is a great task for horses that have never been vaccinated, and horses that are afraid to be vaccinated. Giving a horse a shot is more about how the human acts. If the shot giver is nervous about giving a shot, your horse will know it and sense it. The needles are so sharp most horses don't feel it if it is done properly. It is the fear within us.

I was not good with needles and that bothered me, so I took an orange and practiced stabbing it over and over again with a needle. With practice, I figured out it was no big deal, and that did the trick for me. I just pretended my horse was an orange.

My Arabian, Natchez, was the worst horse I've ever had with vaccinations. He could see a needle a mile away, and throw a huge fit. He had felt pain when given shots, because I would give a shot when he was tense. When he moved, it hurt, so he associated the shot with pain. I became nervous when giving shots and things only got worse. One day I started giving him his vaccinations in the pasture. It was all over before he knew what had happened, then he got a treat. That was the last day he was afraid of a shot. He was associating the place, time, sight, and most of all, the fear of my intentions. Vets never have been able to give him a shot, because he sensed the vets intentions. If you have a real problem giving a vaccination to your seasoned horses, think about who is giving it. This task can help.

You will need halter, lead, clicker, pouch of food, and a syringe without a needle.

I like to pinch my horse in the spot where I give the shot. That is usually in the neck.

Tap in a small spot 3 times with your finger, click when the last tap is given, then feed. Do this a few times.

Tap then pinch, click while you are pinching, then feed. The pinch should not cause pain of any kind. What we are doing is focusing on a certain part of your horse's body, so your horse will be more comfortable. Focusing on a small part of a horse's body with anxiety can cause them to get a bit nervous. Continue doing this for a few sessions.

Do both sides of your horse.

Get a syringe without a needle. Your horse will have to stand still for a period of time. Pretend you are giving your horse a shot by tapping the skin with your fingers and adding the syringe to that location. Hold syringe in that location for 1 second, then click and feed. You might have to use your secondary tongue click.

Tap the skin 2 times, add the syringe to that location, hold the syringe for 2 seconds. Click and feed.

Tap the skin 2 times, add the syringe to that location, hold the syringe for 3 seconds. Click and feed.

Tap the skin 2 times, add the syringe to that location, hold the syringe for 4 seconds. Click and feed.

Continue this process until you can hold it for 10 seconds.

Tap the skin 2 times, and add the syringe to that location, hold the syringe and pull it back slowly, just as if you were going to give a real shot. Push the plunger of the syringe in and click while you are pushing it in.

Repeat the same several times. Only click if your horse stands still.

Do the same on both sides of your horse's neck.

When this task is finished, your chain of tasks should be:

Tap the skin 2 times, and add the syringe to that location, hold syringe and pull the plunger back slowly. Push the plunger of the syringe in and click while you are pushing it in.
Then click and feed.

They should be good for a shot. I don't tell people how to give a shot. That is your decision, but most often it will be your veterinarian. Have a friend walk up to your horse and act like a vet and see how they do. You might have to practice.

CHAPTER 10
FEET

To handle a horse's foot can sometimes be a physical effort, and when you have many young horses that need their feet worked with, it takes even more physical effort. It doesn't make much sense to over exhaust yourself.

Since you have been working with touching your horse, you can start to ask for their foot. I don't like to just grab a foot and hope for the best. For some reason I have more people complain about the feet. For example, they won't hold the foot and they pull away. It is lack of confidence in the human and the method.

I was asked to come and look at a mare named Cha Cha that was having trouble with her feet being worked on. I was informed that the farrier was unable to trim her feet because she had white line disease and trimming her feet was painful, and sedation made the matter worse. The mare's reaction to her feet being worked on was for her to blow up, pull back, rear and strike. Nuria the owned was at her wit's end on how to deal with her mare. Cha Cha was handled quite a bit with her feet before her white line disease. She was trained for feet work, but something was missing in their communication.

I went to see Cha Cha and she seemed really sweet. She seemed to like her owner and people. I was also informed that no one other than Nuria has ever been able to walk up to her and pick her feet up without a fight. I just didn't walk up to her and pick her feet up. I introduced her to a target (which was a plastic bottle). Cha Cha was very sharp in understanding the target to the click. We target trained for about 15 minutes before I asked for her foot. I explained to Nuria that if she is willing to pick her feet up, she understands about having her feet done, and it was just fear. If she doesn't willingly pick her feet up, she doesn't understand her feet being picked up, and it is a combination of her not understanding and fear. I was hoping she understood. I would rather it just be one problem instead of both. If she understands it, you can get farther faster.

I bent down and petted her leg and clicked while I was petting her. She understood. I asked for her foot by tapping her chestnut lightly. It only took 2 taps. She gave me her foot for 1 second. I clicked and fed her. She had a thinking expression on her face as, "I know what this is." I continued to ask for her foot, but this time she gave me her foot before I asked her. I held it for 3 seconds, clicked and fed. She was very relaxed, but I felt that if I held her foot any longer she would have felt claustrophobic and panicked. She needed to know that what she did had merit, and that I would reward her for her efforts also. I held one front foot for 10 seconds and then held the other front foot for 10 seconds. It was time to end the session. I had no problems with her. Nuria wanted to work with her and achieve the same results as I did. She even picked up her back feet with no problems.

Nuria was amazed how fast Clicker Training worked. She never even considered using this method, until she had no choice. She now knows how fast positive reinforcement training works, and that it is the key to real success. Nuria had three weeks to continue working with her mare before the farrier was scheduled to come back. When the farrier came, she was able to trim all four feet, without sedation, for the first time since Cha Cha's white line disease diagnosis.

GETTING STARTED WITH THE FRONT FEET

You will need halter, lead, clicker, and pouch of food.

Make sure your horse is standing square. It is hard for a horse to pick up their foot if they are leaning on it. Stand next to your horse's shoulder facing the back end of your horse. I like to tap the chestnut as the cue for them to pick up their foot. Take your hand from their shoulder and slide your hand down to the chestnut. Tap on the chestnut continually. You can also pinch the chestnut if tapping is not successful. Most of the

CLICKER TRAINING: COLT STARTING THE NATURAL HORSE

time they will pick up their foot. If that doesn't work, go down the leg just below the pastern on the back of the foot, where it gives in a little just before you get to the hoof. Place your hand there and add some light pressure. They should pick up. This seems to always work.

Remember, you don't want to cause any pain or panic to your horse to get them to pick up their foot. If you are really having problems, you can ask them to walk forward and when they pick up their foot, click and feed. You might have to get creative. I usually continue tapping until they move their foot. As soon as they pick up their foot, click and feed. Your timing has to be very good. You want to click when the foot is in the air. If your timing is off, they will think you want it down rather than up.

In the beginning of this process your horse may pick up their foot and put it down really fast. Don't worry. This is normal. Repeat by tapping the chestnut. When they lift their foot, click when it is in the air. They are so fast that you might have to click just before they lift it to get the timing correct. At this point your horse might want to start pawing to show you that they figured out what you wanted. They will think that lifting the foot up and bringing it down really hard and fast is what you want. If your horse starts to paw continuously, ignore the pawing and wait until they are done, then start over. Put them up if it gets really bad.

To fix the pawing horse, tap the chestnut and hold the foot for 1 second, click, place the foot down nice and calm, then feed. Do not hold the foot if the horse wants to paw or pull away. Let them. It is all a part of the process of their learning. They can paw their way to China and it still won't get the click. It is up to your horse what they do. They have to figure out what gets the click. The only way to do that is to work with what they think, they understand.

Repeat and hold (when I say hold that only means to support) the foot for 1 more second. Click and feed. Hold the hoof part of the horse not the bone. If they try to pull away let them. It didn't make the box go off. Keep trying, they just need some time to think. As soon as you can hold the foot for 1 second, next time hold it for 2 seconds. If they start to lean on you, let the foot go. You are looking for them to hold their own foot up. You are just helping them along at this point. You can also count out loud. Horses do know how to count. There are many times that I have counted, and my horses have known exactly how long they have to wait. They even know when I count in my head.

Practice:

Tap the chestnut. When they pick their foot up, hold for 2 seconds, click and feed.

Tap the chestnut. When they pick their foot up, hold for 3 seconds, click and feed.

Tap the chestnut. When they pick their foot up, hold for 4 seconds, click and feed.

Continue this process until you can hold it for 10 seconds. It should be a light hold, just to support them.

You will start to notice your horse figuring out that you want them to hold their foot up. They will start slowing down and helping you hold their foot.

When this task is finished, your chain of tasks should be:

Stand at your horse's shoulder, slide your hand down to the chestnut, and tap the chestnut (don't be surprised that your horse picks his foot up before you ask), hold the foot for 10 seconds.

Then click and feed.

Now do the other side. You will still be working with short sessions of 5 to 10 minutes. Working with feet does take some time.

It took some time to get my colt, King, to be good with his feet. Since I trim my horse's feet, the horse has to hold their foot a certain way or I cannot trim the foot. I brought King in from the pasture after a few weeks of layover, and I started to trim his feet. Straddling the feet can be a strain on my back. King picked his foot up, and held it on his own so I could trim the foot. At the time, I didn't train King to hold his own foot up. He offered it to me. He is so funny. If he thinks that the foot is not high enough he continues to hold it higher and higher. I saw an ad for a footstool, so you won't have to hold the foot while you trim their feet. King eliminated me having to go out and buy a footstool to trim his feet. I am not so particular about having a horse rest their foot in my hand for trimming, as long as they do not lean on me. The most important thing for me is that they hold it still so I can trim the foot without any mishaps. Since I work with so many young horses, a footstool looks like a great idea for most horses.

CLEANING OUT THE FRONT FEET

You can now start to clean their feet out. You know your horse will stand still for about 10 seconds. Ask your horse to pick up their foot. Clean the foot out with one stroke, tongue click while you are cleaning out the foot, place foot down very politely, then feed.

Ask to pick up the foot, clean the foot out with 2 strokes, tongue click, then feed.

Repeat this process until you can clean out the whole foot, which should be about 10 strokes.

When this task is finished, your chain of tasks should be:

Pick up the foot, clean the whole foot out, then click, place foot down, and feed.

Repeat the same process on the other front foot

STRADDLING THE FRONT FEET

It can be a surprise to a horse that you have to hold their feet between your legs, so this needs to be practiced. I had a mare that was horrible about feet, and we needed to get her feet done. Her foot was very sharp and would cut my leg if she pulled away while I was straddling her foot. She had been in training for awhile, and now her feet were in great need of work. I had to straddle her leg to properly trim her front feet, but she would only hold it for about 5 seconds. If it was not OK with her, she would pull away very fast. I put her in the most comfortable spot I could find. The tongue click came in handy for this.

I straddled her foot and nipped one small section of foot, and put her foot down. I clicked while I was nipping. She had no idea what I was doing, but she liked it. She figured out this was fun. As soon as I fed, she would hold her foot up again waiting for me to straddle it. I have never worked so hard and it was all her idea. I put her in the right mood for the work. I withheld the click up to two nips, then clicked. She had a good time. To this day, she is the best foot horse I have. It is so much fun to her. Now I can nip the whole foot and click. She loves to get her feet done.

We took the time it takes to get it right. It can take a long time and some horses are better at it than others. I trim all my own horse's feet and have always had problems. It used to take me a week to trim one horse because they would lean on me or pull away. Now that they have been overhauled with Clicker Training, I can trim up to 5 horses in a day.

Ask your horse to pick up their foot. They should be used to holding it up for 10 seconds. Slowly straddle the foot for 1 second. Click and feed.

Tap the chestnut. When they pick their foot up, straddle it for 2 seconds, click and feed.

Tap the chestnut. When they pick their foot up, straddle it for 3 seconds, click and feed.

Tap the chestnut. When they pick their foot up, straddle it for 4 seconds, click and feed.

CLICKER TRAINING: COLT STARTING THE NATURAL HORSE

Continue this process until you can straddle it for 10 seconds.

Do the other side.

TRIMMING YOUR HORSES FRONT FOOT

If you want to work on your own horse's feet, that is fine. If you are getting ready for the farrier, you can simulate that same task. For nippers you can use a pair of pliers, for the nails you can tap their foot with a hammer. Everybody should have a rasp.

Pick up your horse's foot and straddle it with your legs. Take your nippers or your pliers for simulation. Nip or squeeze one time. Click at the same time as the nip or squeeze, place foot down softly then feed.

Straddle your horse's foot. Nip 2 times. While the second nip is given, click and then feed.

Straddle your horse's foot. Nip 3 times. While the third nip is given, click and then feed.

Straddle your horse's foot. Nip 4 times. While the fourth nip is given, click and then feed.

Continue this process for about 10 simulations, or until your horse's foot is done.

When this task is finished, your chain of tasks should be:

Straddle your horse's foot. Nip 10 times. While the tenth nip is given, click and feed.
Repeat on the other front foot.

We are looking for patience in your horse. This will help you physically when you clean out their feet, and when they get their feet trimmed or get shoes.

RASPING THE FRONT FEET

This is done in the same way.

You will need halter, lead, pouch of food, and rasp.

Pick up your horse's foot, hold it or straddle it. Take the rasp, and rasp once across the foot. While the rasp is moving across the foot, click with your tongue click, then put your horse's foot down softly, and feed.

Practice:

Straddle or hold the foot, rasp 2 times. While the second rasp is given, click and then feed.

Straddle or hold the foot, rasp 3 times. While the third rasp is given, click and then feed.

Straddle or hold the foot, rasp 4 times. While the fourth rasp is given, click and then feed.

Continue this process for about 10 simulations, or until your horse's foot is done.

Repeat the same on the other front foot.

When this task is finished, your chain of tasks should be:

Rasp the foot 10 times. While the tenth rasp is given, click and then feed.

SHOES FOR THE FRONT FEET

You will need halter, lead, pouch of food, and hammer.

Most likely you will have shoes put on at some point.

Take your hammer and pick up your horse's foot and straddle it.

Take your hammer, tap on your horse's foot lightly 1 time. At the same time, click with your tongue click, place foot down softly, and feed.

Practice:

Straddle or hold the foot, tap with the hammer 2 times. While the second tap is given, click and then feed.

Straddle or hold the foot, tap with the hammer 3 times. While the third tap is given, click and then feed.

Straddle or hold the foot, tap with the hammer 4 times. While the fourth tap is given, click and then feed.

Continue this process until you can tap about 10 taps.

Repeat the same on the other front foot.

When this task is finished, your chain of tasks should be:

Straddle or hold the foot, tap 10 taps. While the tenth tap is given, click and then feed.

You may notice that when you ask your horse to pick up one foot, they may want to pick up another foot. That is because they got fixated on the last foot you worked with. I've learned that if you continue to ask for the foot you want, they will figure it out. All the horses that I work with have done the same thing. It takes time to get the cue to the foot.

GETTING STARTED WITH THE BACK FEET

Working with the back feet is a bit different. You need to spend some time next to your horse's hip with the 'Touching Your Horse for the First Time' in Chapter 5 exercises before you start to work on their back feet. Your horse should be very comfortable with you standing at the hip.

You will need halter, lead, clicker, and pouch of food.

Watch your horse for a moment. What you are looking for is them resting one of their back feet. When they rest their back foot, click and feed. Your horse will have no clue what you are looking for at this point. Click and feed a jackpot click for 3 clicks if they continue to rest their foot.

Sometimes it is best to do this task after a good work out. They will have a tendency to rest their foot more often.

Repeat. Work on this for no more than 5 minutes at a time. You will notice that your horse will be resting their foot more for you.

Drape the lead over your arm and walk towards your horse's hip. Pet your horse all the way back to their hip. Wait until your horse rests their foot. If you are having problems with your horse resting their foot, you can tap their chestnut or tickle it until they pick their foot up. You do not want to click for them picking their foot up. You want to click for when they rest it. They will at some point rest their foot. You can also rock them back and forth by the hip to get them to rest their foot. This should be easy if they caught on to the task above. If not, just keep waiting, they will relax. When they rest their foot, click and feed a jackpot for 3 clicks.

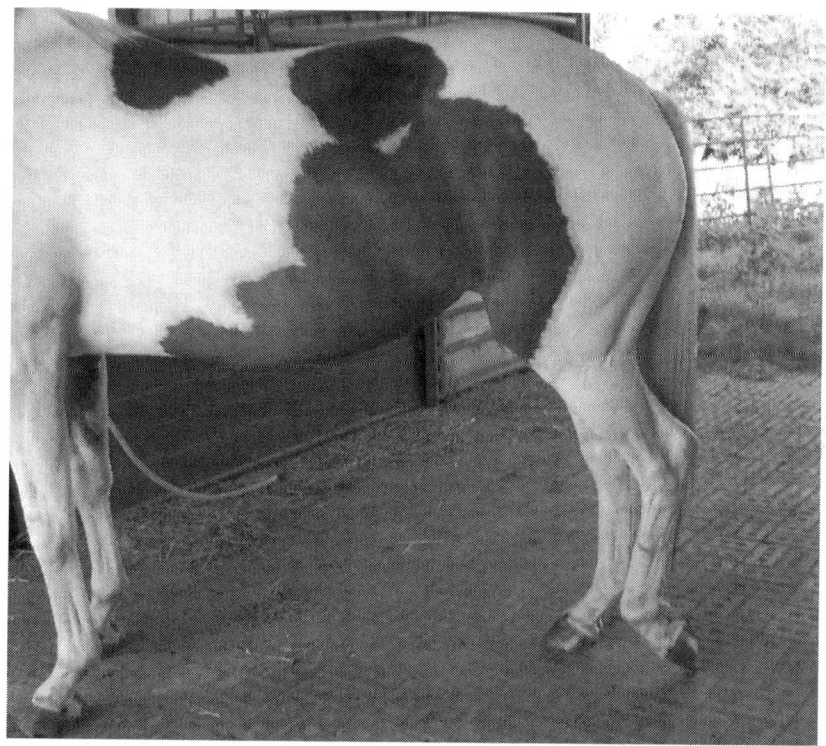

Resting the hind foot.

Practice:

While their foot is resting rub their foot, then click and feed.

Rub the foot and leg for 2 seconds, click and feed.

Rub the foot and leg for 3 seconds, click and feed.

Rub the foot and leg for 4 seconds, click and feed.

Get to where you can rub for about 10 seconds while your horse is resting their foot.

Now it is time to do the other side. You will notice that your horse will be resting the opposite foot. You can try a few things such as tickling the foot until they rest it or moving the hip back and forth.

Repeat the same process.

When this task is finished, your chain of tasks should be:

Walk to the back of your horse while touching them all the way back.

They should rest their back foot for you for about 10 seconds while you touch their leg. Then click and feed.

What this does is let the horse know that they can relax while you are standing next to their back foot. If you ask them to lift their foot first, they may lift it high and smash it down hard, and they may start to kick a little bit. It is very easy for a horse to pick up their back foot. This is way too much power for me. I want my horses to turn to gel when I work with their back feet, and starting with resting the foot will help. This is something that is relaxing.

ADDING A CUE TO RESTING THE FOOT

Stand next to your horse's back hip, slide your hand down their leg, tap on the chestnut or tickle it. If they shift their weight enough to rest the foot, click and feed. You are now adding a cue to the resting of the foot. I want my horse to rest their foot first, before they pick it up. This will slow them down.

Repeat this several times.

Do the other side

I like to teach my horses how to rest their foot so I can clean out their feet without holding it up. It is easier on my back. I even trim their foot that way, and only have to pick it up to trim the toe. You can also teach them to hold it on a stool. I tend to be too lazy to find the stool.

When this task is finished, your chain of tasks should be:

Ask your horse to rest their foot for up to 20 seconds. You can add more if you like.

CLICKER TRAINING: COLT STARTING THE NATURAL HORSE

Then click and feed.

PICKING UP THE HIND FOOT

After you have worked on resting the back foot cue on both sides, you can move on to having your horse pick their foot up.

You will need halter, lead, clicker, and pouch of food.

Ask your horse to rest their foot with your cue. Since the hind foot is resting, most of your horse's weight is on the other leg, so picking it up is easy.

Physically pick up the foot about 4 inches, click while it is in the air, then feed. Your horse will have a tendency to want to rest his foot more, so the lift will be less dramatic. When I first started Clicker Training I didn't teach the resting of the foot and the results on all horses were the same. They all gave me a big lift with a kick at the end.

Practice:

Pick up the foot and hold it for 2 seconds, click, lay foot down softly and feed.

Pick up the foot and hold it for 3 seconds, click, lay foot down softly and feed.

Repeat this until you can hold it for 10 seconds.

If it is hard to hold, you might be forcing your horse too much or holding their leg too high. Taking a deep breath and relaxing will help.

Do the same on other side.

When this task is finished, your chain of tasks should be:

Pick your horse's foot up. Hold it lightly for 10 seconds.

Then click and feed.

HAVING YOUR HORSE HELP YOU PICK UP THE FOOT

I was working with a mare named Sugar that was having a hard time relaxing. I needed to work on her back feet, but she was 7 years old and had never had her back feet worked on. I always try to get the horse to rest their foot, then click and feed. I just could not get Sugar to rest her foot. She would bring the foot up really high, but would not rest it. I worked on her for 4 days just trying to get her to rest her foot. I could have worked her first, then had her rest her foot, but I wanted to teach her how to relax without being tired. I pushed on her hip a little bit to get her weight off of her leg in the hope that she would rest it. She did not. She would pick up her foot, and I clicked for the foot coming down to a rest. It happened so fast that I was not sure she caught on. I waited and did nothing to see what she would do. She pawed, sniffed me, and wiggled her hips. I guess she didn't quite get it yet. The wiggle of the hips was cute, but that was not what I was looking for. I continued to ask her to rest her foot by laying my hand on her back hock. She picked it up higher than I liked. I was picking her foot up and clicking for it when it went down. I still could not get her to relax enough to rest her foot. She kept thinking that I wanted her to pick her foot up. I thought that maybe my timing was off for her, so I clicked 3 seconds before I thought she would pick her foot up, which meant 3 seconds before I even asked her to. The first time I did this, she dropped her foot down to 2 inches above the ground. The next time she rested it for only about a second, but a second was a great place to start. I soon was able to click just for her foot resting. Your timing can have a lot of affect on the outcome. Sugar's mind was racing and anticipating something that I did not want. To slow her down I had to work on the timing of the click.

When we physically pick up the foot, we show our horse how we would like them to pick their foot up. I don't want to keep picking the foot up. I want the horse to hold it up for me.

You will need halter, lead, clicker, and pouch of food.

CLICKER TRAINING: COLT STARTING THE NATURAL HORSE

Stand next to your horse's back hip, slide your hand down their leg, tap to have them rest their foot, click when they rest their foot for you, then feed.

Slide your hand down their leg, tap to have them rest their foot again and continue tapping until they pick their foot up about 4 inches. Anything will do for now. Do not hold the foot at this point.

Your horse should take the foot down in a rested position while you feed. If not, continue to ask in the same manner. 1 tap, rest foot, click, feed, second tap, pickup foot, click, feed.

Tap the chestnut until your horse picks it up for 1 second. Click when the foot is in the air, then feed.

Repeat this 5 times.

Practice:

Tap the chestnut until your horse picks their foot up and hold the foot by the pastern for 1 second. Click and feed.

Tap the chestnut until your horse picks their foot up and hold the foot by the pastern for 2 seconds. Click and feed.

Tap the chestnut until your horse picks their foot up and hold the foot for 3 seconds. Click and feed.

Repeat the hold in the air until you can hold it for 10 seconds.

Do the same on the other foot.

When this task is finished, your chain of tasks should be:

Tap the chestnut until your horse rests their foot. Then tap your horse's chestnut until they pick their foot up and hold your horse's foot for 10 seconds.

Then click and feed.

CLEANING OUT THE BACK FEET

You will need halter, lead, clicker, pouch of food, and hoof pick.

You can now start to clean their back feet out. You know you can hold your horse's foot for about 10 seconds. Ask your horse to rest their foot, then ask to pick up their foot. Clean their feet out with one stroke, tongue click while you are cleaning out the foot, place foot down, then feed.

Ask to rest the foot, then pick up the foot. Clean their feet out with 2 strokes, tongue click while you are cleaning out the foot, then feed.

Ask to pick up the foot, clean the foot out with 3 strokes, tongue click, then feed.
Repeat this process until you can clean out the whole foot.

Repeat the same on the other foot.

When this task is finished, your chain of tasks should be:

Pick up the foot. Clean the whole foot out, then click, place foot down, and feed.

STRADDLING THE BACK FOOT

To trim or rasp the back feet you will have to straddle the foot. The last thing that you want is for your horse to pull away while you are straddling the back feet. This is very hard on your knees and your horse has to feel very comfortable. I have seen so many people hold up their horse when they straddle their feet. Your horse will tend to lean on you and make you their foot. Leaning on you becomes a game to your horse.

You will need halter, lead, clicker, and pouch of food.

You should remember to ask for the resting of the foot, wait about

2 seconds, then continue to ask for the foot to be picked up. If you skip the resting of the foot and just pick it up, that is fine, but only if they are polite.

Ask for your horse's foot and have them rest the foot, then continue to ask again for your horse to pick it up. You do not have to click for the resting of the foot.

Straddle the foot for 1 second. Click when you feel that your horse is holding their foot up. Place the foot down very softly and feed. We are looking for the horse not to lean on you. If they lean let go. Do not hold it for any reason. Start over. You might need to back up a task or two. They should not lean, if you clicked correctly in the earlier tasks.

Ask for your horse's foot. Straddle it for 2 seconds, click, place foot down, then feed.

Ask for your horse's foot. Straddle it for 3 seconds, click, place foot down, then feed.

Ask for your horse's foot. Straddle it for 4 seconds, click, place foot down, then feed.

Repeat this process until you can straddle the foot for 10 seconds.

When this task is finished, your chain of tasks should be:

Ask for the foot. Straddle it for 10 seconds.
Then click and feed.

RASPING THE BACK FEET

Rasping the back foot is done in almost the same way as rasping the front foot.

You will need halter, lead, pouch of food, and rasp.

Ask your horse to pick up their back foot. Hold it or straddle it. Take the rasp, and rasp one stroke across the foot. While the rasp is moving across the foot, click with your tongue click, then put your horse's foot down softly and feed.

Practice:

Straddle or hold the foot, rasp 2 times, then click and feed.

Straddle or hold the foot, rasp 3 times, then click and feed.

Straddle or hold the foot, rasp 4 times, then click and feed.

Continue this process for about 10 simulations.

Repeat the same on the other hind foot.

When this task is finished, your chain of tasks should be:

Rasp the foot 10 times.
Then click and feed.

TRIMMING THE BACK FEET

You will have to straddle the foot for trimming. This will be very simple if you have been working on the above tasks. We will be repeating the same task as for the front feet.

You will need halter, lead, pouch of food, and nippers or pliers.

Pick up your horse's foot and straddle it. Try not to pull your horse's foot out too much to the side. If your horse starts to pull on you, it may be because you have put them into a position that is uncomfortable for them. It is up to you to find the best spot for your horse.

Take your nippers or your pliers for simulation. Nip or squeeze one time, click when the nip or squeeze takes place. Place the foot down softly, then feed.

CLICKER TRAINING: COLT STARTING THE NATURAL HORSE

Practice:

Straddle your horse's foot, nip 2 times, then click and feed.

Straddle your horse's foot, nip 3 times, then click and feed.

Straddle your horse's foot, nip 4 times, then click and feed.

Continue this process for about 10 simulations.

Do the same on the other hind foot.

When this task is finished, your chain of tasks should be:

Ask your horse to pick up their foot, straddle it. Nip 10 times. Then click and feed.

CHAPTER 11
ROUND PENNING

DOMINANT HORSES

There was one particular horse that I had a hard time figuring out. He was a young colt named Dundee. We could pet him in the pasture and he was the best baby we had that year, but things soon changed. One day when he was about 4 months old he decided that we couldn't pet him anymore. Why, I'm not sure. He soon ran away from us, and that was the last day we could play with him in the pasture. He was not scheduled for halter work for a few more months, so I left him alone. When we brought him up for weaning, we led his mother to the stall and he refused to follow her. He was the only colt that we had problems with that year. I put his mother in the front stall and locked her in, and had the second stall open but ready to shut when the little colt went in.

We went in the house and waited for Dundee to go into the stall on his own. He had to go in the stall to get close to his mother. We watched for an hour and he finally went in, so we went out and shut the gate. I knew he had been touched all over and I remember giving him body massages in the pasture and he loved it, until that one day, when he said, "No, I am leaving. No more." He was a problem from then on. I made some progress with him, but he was inconsistent. The things I thought would scare him didn't, and the things that I thought he would accept, he didn't. I used my same Clicker Training techniques as with the others, but every day seemed to be a new day for him. I was not getting real improvements. He was not motivated by food, so I had to make sure he was in the mood for it. I knew he was extremely intelligent and it was my job to figure him out. I always gave him the opportunity to succeed. When he had learned enough skills to put to the test, he ended up failing.

One day I put a tarp down for him to walk over. He was on it in 30 seconds, as calm as a horse could be. I was still having problems catching him. I could not figure him out. The big test was when I brought him in from pasture after a 3-week layoff. How was I going to get Dundee in the stall this time? I had to get him in a 2-acre pasture, a round pen, another pasture, then the stall. Dundee did follow the other horses to the round pen from the 2 acres and into the last pasture. Dundee refused to follow the target to the stall.

The main problem I had was the grass was really tender, and he just wanted to eat. When I walked up to him he walked away. I could get him to target a little, but soon he would leave. When he would leave I would follow him. I didn't care where he went or how fast, as long as his feet were moving. When he would try to eat I would kiss to him and he would pop his head up. I was getting a different look from him. He took off and I followed. The pasture was quite large so I had to do some walking. He had a mental round pen in his mind and he did stay at one end of the pasture, which helped me out.

He made 2 runs around his pasture and stopped. I immediately turned and walked away. He now figured out this was a good place to be. It was as far from the stall as he could get, but that was OK. As long as he could stand still, he was OK. I offered him the target and he walked up to me. I clicked and fed for walking up to me. I tried to get him to follow the target towards the stall. He took two steps and immediately ran off, so I followed. He looked a bit bothered and he ran right back to the same spot. Every time he would try to eat grass, I would kiss to him and his head would pop up. I was becoming very difficult for him. He wanted to stay and eat, but running around seemed to be the game for him.

Since I couldn't get him to follow the target, I retrieved the halter, in hopes that I could get the halter on him. He took one look at the halter and ran off. He ran around the corner and went in the stall. He had a look on his face as if to say, "This is too much monkey business. I think I shall go in the stall now, so you will leave me alone." I closed the door to his stall and left him alone.

CLICKER TRAINING: COLT STARTING THE NATURAL HORSE

After that day he seemed to come around and our relationship changed. Just because he isn't an aggressive horse doesn't mean that he isn't dominant. I'm still giving him the opportunity to succeed, but he prefers not to participate and I know full well that he understands. Comfort and discomfort can be a great help. The good thing is, he is really lazy, so it didn't take much for Dundee to participate. He is becoming a great horse. I have a saying, "There is a time and a place for everything," and for him it was time for comfort and discomfort training. Some horses never show me this type of behavior, and some do, depending on the horse.

ROUND PEN WORK

There are some of us out there that don't have much dominance in them and the horse knows it. No matter what they do, the horse still doesn't seem to respect them. Round penning is a great way to help the not so dominant person. If you ask a horse to get out of your way, they better get out of your way. You have to show your horse that you are the dominant one.

You have to show this to all of your horses, but I think that this shouldn't be taken to the extreme, when the point has already been taken by the horse. We try to dominate more than be a partner. Once we have established that we are the more dominant, we can show them how to be a good partner. I could seem more dominant just by the way I am with my experience. Some will have to work at it harder. There is no excuse for any horse to dominate their owner. If you feel that you are being dominated, get some instruction before you get hurt. The horse will tell you everything you need to know by their actions.

I went to a Colt starting clinic. There was a lady there who was a professional colt starter and she wanted to upgrade her skills. I will never forget her, because when she led her horse up to the gate, the horse tried to kick her from the side almost every stride. I'm not sure what their relationship was, but it looked extremely dangerous to me, and I was glad that she went for help. The clinician addressed the problem right away. When she was round penning the colt, the colt kept trying to kick at her. At one point, I thought the colt kicked her in the head, but he just missed. It took some time, but she finally had the horse move away from her without kicking at her. This helped their relationship and the rest of the clinic went very well for her. I was really surprised how well they did after that.

I have one mare in the pasture named Spider, who thinks she's the boss, even when I am in the pasture. I was getting another horse out of the pasture. Spider usually leaves me alone, but since she had been in training, she wanted to come in. When I went to bring in the other horse, she tried to run the other horse away from me. She didn't know that this would be a problem. I chased her off to let her know that she is never allowed to chase any other horse while I am in the pasture. It took some dominating, but she got the hint, and now all I have to do is look at her. I learned this from Baby, the most dominant horse in this pasture. She is respected because of her loving nature, but if you don't move when asked, you will get it. When Baby is around, no one picks on anyone. She likes a calm pasture. I feel the same as Baby. When Baby walks up everybody stands still and behaves no matter what horse they are standing next to. Baby has a huge amount of respect for people. Spider just needed to be filled in.

There are many times that I need to be around horses and direct them without the halter on, such as having them back up and get out of my way safely.

If I were going to take a horse like Spider to a round pen, she would already know that I was the more dominant and I could get her to move out of my way. Most horses are respectful enough. All I have to do is tap my foot and they're gone. I don't want to scare them more in the round pen. I want to teach them to leave me with a cue, or stay with a cue. You don't have to have a round pen to show dominance. You can do this in a stall or a pasture. If the horse leaves, you have shown dominance. This is how I taught Spider. I would swing the rope continually like a fan and walk towards her and, if she didn't move, she got hit by the rope that she clearly saw coming at her. She has plenty of time to get out of the way. All horses are different and some like to stay a little longer than others, with some, all I have to do is give them a dirty look, and they're gone.

The same horse that I could just look to leave could take a lot of effort from someone else to get to leave. Horses perceive people differently. The one thing that I want to make clear is, don't overdo the domination game. Learn to be more of a partner.

When we round pen, our horses are free (if you call being in a round pen where they have no where to go but around in a circle, free.) The pen itself is just one big halter. I'm not big on throwing ropes at horses to get them to run in mindless circles while they are already running. Let's try to remember the word **teach** again. I do want my horse to get out of my way, but I also want to teach them what direction to take, and how to stop. There is an order to round penning. After you horse has learned the basics they might, at times depending on the horse, believe that they can do what they want. When you round pen, this allows you to communicate in a different manner. To have a little more control without being crude. The horse figures out that they are free to leave, but in just a small circle. Soon the circle becomes boring so they come to us for relief. Again we don't want to click and feed our horse forever, but we have to have some type of control.

My Paint mare Cheyenne learned a great skill from round penning. I wanted to teach her how to follow me if I asked. If I asked her to follow me, she would even if she didn't want to. I proved myself to her that if I ask her to come with me she would know that I would not give up until she did what I wanted. This was accomplished first by starting in the round pen. A lead mare accomplishes this in the same way. Cherry, a half-Arabian mare, was the caretaker of 3 weanlings and 4 yearlings, Cherry likes the herd to be together so she can watch them. Cherry takes her job very seriously. She wants to care for these young horses and she takes pride in it. Duchess was an independent yearling that didn't care for Cherry. Cherry singled her out because Duchess wanted to eat alone. Cherry followed her around until Duchess went back to the herd, then Cherry was happy, Duchess soon would escape and do her own thing, so Cherry would have to go get her again and direct her back to the herd. This took about 2 weeks until Duchess gave up. King my stallion did the same with a new mare named Star that was introduced into the herd. Star was a loner and didn't like the mares. She would wander off by herself. The mares would try to get to know her, but she would leave. King allowed this for about a week. Kings job, as a stallion, is to keep the horses together. Instinct tells him that they are safer in a herd. I went out to check on the horses and I couldn't find King or Star. Soon I saw Star trotting towards me, then King not far behind. Star was soaked with sweat and so was King. Star stopped in the middle of the mares and King stopped and rested. They must have been running for a while. King was not mean to her. As long as she was moving, he was fine. She got to rest when she did what he wanted, which was for her to be in the herd. When she did, he rested. If she got too far, King would start it all over again, that was the last day I saw her far from the herd. I am simulating the same with Cheyenne, but you have to be as persistent as King and Cherry without being crude. It didn't take long for me to teach Cheyenne to follow me.

ROUND PENNING TASK

You need an area no smaller than 24-foot by 24-foot for a young horse, but much larger for a big horse, up to a 60- foot round pen.

Objective: Having your horse go around you in a circle.

You will need clicker, pouch of food, and an extension stick. You do not need a halter.

Your horse should be very friendly.

We will be working with 'show me what you know.' (See Chapter 3)

Put yourself in the middle of the round pen.

Make some noise by jumping up and down or tapping your stick behind you. When your horse leaves, click and bring your horse some food.

Repeat the same about five times. Soon your horse will learn to walk off on their own, chances are they will stick to one direction. You are just following their lead, recognizing what they are doing, and marking it with the clicker.

Wait and see what your horse does. They should 'show you what they know' by moving away from you in that direction. Remember, you cannot cause them to leave. They must do it on their own. You have already shown them what to do. Wait for them to 'think.' You have not yet taught them how to walk around you in a circle, so don't expect them to. Wait for them to show you how they walk away from you.

When they take 1 step away from you on their own, click when they leave, then feed.

Then wait. When they take 1 step away from you, encourage them out a little by causing some pressure. You can be the judge of what works best for your horse for the pressure. When they take a step or two more away from you, click after the step has been made, and feed. I like to bring the food to them, but if they like to come in for the food, that is OK for now. Wait for your horse to offer to leave again. If they refuse to leave jump up and down or use your stick to cause pressure so they will leave. They should take the extra steps that you clicked for before. Now encourage 1 more step. Click as soon as the last step was taken, then feed.

By now your horse should be moving away from you and walking at least three steps around.

Practice:

Wait for your horse to offer to leave again. They should take 3 steps, encourage the 4th step with some pressure. When the fourth step has been taken, click and feed.

Wait for your horse to offer to leave again. They should take 4 steps, then encourage the 5th step. When the 5th step is being taken, click and feed.

Wait for your horse to offer to leave again. They should take 5 steps, then encourage the 6th step. When the 6th step is being taken, click and feed.

Continue for a full circle. This will take more than 1 session. I would stick to 5 to 10 minutes at a time. Start right back where you left off for the next session.

When this task is finished, your chain of tasks should be:

Your horse should move around you in a full circle in the direction you have been working on. Click and feed while the last step is being taken.

We have to click and feed for every step that is made. It must be recorded in the positive. Once it is, we are finished with that part of the training and we can move on. If you think about it, you have successfully made one circle. That circle is done at liberty and you will not click for them going around in one circle anymore, but you will click for them going around you in one circle and 1 extra step. Sometimes your horse will offer you more than that one extra step, take the extra step and move on. I don't want my horses getting bored. They are just showing that they understand and we should move on. How many times should your horse go in a circle? I think that a good number would be no more than 4 at a time. You need to remember your horse is going in a circle with complete understanding and they are thinking of every step.

ADDING A CUE TO IT

What your cue will be for this task will be up to you. I like to point in the direction that they are going to go and refine it later on.

Point in the direction that your horse will be going as the horse leaves, put your hand down. You will have no problems getting them to move, because they will be showing you automatically without you doing anything. You are just adding a visual marker to that behavior. Remember they need to go in a full circle before you click and feed. Once they have accomplished a full circle, click for a full circle and 1 extra step.

Your horse will catch on to this really fast. You might be getting up to 4 circles much faster then you think. Your horse will offer you more once they understand the task.

Point again. Your horse should move off. They need to complete 1 full circle and 2 steps. Click after the 2nd step, then bring your horse food.

Point. Your horse should move off. They need to complete 1 full circle and 3 steps. Click after the 3rd step, then bring your horse food. If your horse gives you 5 or 6 steps take it, but expect 7 steps next time.

Continue this until you get to 4 circles, or until you feel your horse understands the task.

When this task is finished, your chain of tasks should be:

Point in the direction your horse offers to you. They should go around you in 4 circles. Then click and feed.

You will notice that your horse will stop coming to you for food. They will allow you to bring it to them. Some horses don't have time to eat. They are thinking about getting right back to work. I like this, and I want everything to stop when I click, including them coming in to me. I prefer to take the food to them.

DISENGAGEMENT OF HINDQUARTERS FOR STOPPING

While your horse is at a stand still, ask for disengagement from the same side that you have been working on, by looking at their hindquarter and drawing their eye. This is to check to see how well they disengage in the round pen. If you followed the tasks, this should be easy.

If your horse just takes off in hope of you rewarding them for a circle, that is fine. Wait for them to think. They will stop sooner or later to check in. If they do not respond, it is because you have never asked them to stop while they are away from you.

No matter what position you are in, you still look different. What will help is to look at their eye and walk backwards, drawing your horse's eye to you. Then add pressure to the hindquarters. Some horses might still ignore you. If they do, wait for them to stop on their own. They will get bored with running in a circle. When they offer to stop, add your cue of disengagement of hindquarters. Then click and feed. Practice this for about 5 times with a cue every time. This will tell your horse that you would like to add this to the circle.

Ask your horse to go around you in the direction you have been working on. This is now a cued task. If they take off, that's OK. Take what they give you. Ask your horse go around for one complete circle, cue them for disengagement, and for stopping. This cue can be you pointing towards the hip and drawing your horse's eye to you by taking a step back. If they do not stop, wait. They will. If they stop and do not disengage their hindquarter, do not click until they do the disengagement task.

You are chaining all of these tasks together as one task. Repeat the process a few times until they catch on. If your horse keeps ignoring you, ask for the stop once or twice. If you are still being ignored, do nothing until they offer it to you. Trotting around in a circle can get very boring after awhile, and they find out they are not going anywhere but in a mindless circle. Soon they will start paying attention. Some horses get confused and just need to move their feet.

Practice:

Ask your horse to circle. Have them complete 1 circle, then ask for a disengagement, then click and feed.

Ask your horse to circle. Have them complete 1½ circles, then ask for a disengagement, then click and feed.

Ask your horse to circle. Have them complete 2 circles, then ask for a disengagement, then click and feed.

Ask your horse to circle. Have them complete 2½ circles, then ask for a disengagement, then click and feed.

I like to mix it up a bit. This is when you start using the cues more.

GOING THE OTHER DIRECTION

Now that your horse is a bit brain washed to one side, switching sides can be tough.

Ask your horse to disengage from the side you have been working on. They should swing around enough to show you their other side.

When they show you their other side, click and feed. You can even walk to the other side and put yourself in position before you ask them to move off. Pet them a couple of times on that side, and click and feed. This will let them know you would like them to stay there.

Ask them to walk away in the new direction with the point of your finger, and back it up with some pressure. If you need to, tap the stick behind your back. If that still does not work, tap your stick a little closer to your horse. If that still does not work move it closer. That should do it.

Click and feed for one step away from you. Some horses might just walk off and then turn around to show you that they can go around in a circle on the side they first learned. There is nothing wrong with it other than this is not what we are working on. It's not a big deal. Wait your horse out, and they will soon come back to you to ask a question. Do not punish the horse for this, or make them do something else. This is a good lesson for your horse. I will ignore it and let them extinguish the behavior. When they stop and look at me, I will ask them to disengage again and start over. This type of behavior could go on for a while. Your horse is learning how to listen to what was clicked for last, so they can learn, and not get stuck on one thing.

Ask again for them to go around you in the new direction. They should turn in the new direction. If they do for even one step, click and feed. Ask again in the new direction, and try to get more steps when they go around you, even if it is only 2 steps. Click and feed. Continue to click and feed for more steps until you get a full circle.

If they move away from you, and they keep you on the new side, click when they move away, and feed.

Repeat the same in the new direction.

MIXING IT UP

Now that your horse can go around you at liberty in both directions, mix it up a bit.

I will ask for my horse to go to the right for 1½ circles, then ask for a disengagement. I point in the new direction and have my horse move off in the other direction for a few steps. Click and feed. I want to concentrate on the turn to the other direction. I will repeat this several times. You will notice if you stay with 1½ circles for a few times, your horse will automatically stop at 1½ circles. So I won't ask at 1½ circles every time. I might ask for a change at ½ of a circle, or 2 circles, and so on. If your horse turns before you ask, go with it. This means they are offering it to you.

Change to the other side, and repeat. You can get creative with this task by mixing it up. You are clicking for them listening to your cues.

ADDING THE HALTER AND LEAD

You will need halter, lead, at least 12-foot long, clicker, pouch, and an extension stick.

We need to add a halter and a lead and call it lunging. Adding the halter to the situation will add extra stimulus that may cause some confusion. They may think they can't run in a circle with a halter on. Some get confused, and others just continue on as if there is no halter or lead.

Pretend the halter and lead are not on. If you are going to the left, point to the left holding the lead in your right hand. You want to hold the lead in your right hand so as not to add too much too fast to your horse. We are still trying to pretend the halter and lead are not on. Your horse should go around you in a small circle. If they make a full circle, click and feed.

Repeat the same steps as for Round Penning Task, in Chapter 11, but still trying to pretend the halter is not on them.

Once you feel your horse is doing well with having the halter on, you can add some more cues to it.

Stand in front of your horse.

Stand still.

Take the lead into your left hand and lead your horse to the left. Most will just start going around you, but some might get confused. If they get confused, click for every effort they make for you. Even it is just turning their head in that direction. Always assume that your horse is confused. If your horse does not do what you ask, it may not be your horse. It may be how you are asking. It could be your position, or the way you are looking at your horse.

If you are having problems, click for them just moving their head toward the direction you would like them to go. Ask again, and if they move their front feet over in the direction, click and feed.

You might have to repeat all the steps for lunging at liberty. Some horses will take to it real easy and others need more direction. Give them the direction and help them, as they need it. As soon as they understand it, they will offer it to you.

Repeat this on the other side. You might have to repeat it all over again. Don't worry, it does not take as long as it sounds.

LUNGING WITH THE HALTER AND LEAD WITHOUT A ROUND PEN

If you have a horse that you need to teach to lunge, and you do not have a round pen, that is just fine. Some of us would like to retrain our older horses with Clicker Training, and we don't have access to the facilities that we wish we could have.

Your horse must have completed the Show Me What You Know Checklist, in Chapter 8 and the cues that go with it before we start working on this.

Your horse should already move away from you when you tap on their shoulder.

It is natural for a horse to go forward if there is pressure behind the withers. If a horse runs up to another and tries to bite them on their withers, the horse naturally goes forward. We want to simulate what is natural to a horse.

Your horse's instincts tell them that if they get bit behind the withers, it means go forward. But what is unnatural is, we are not another horse. To top it off, we are going to ask the horse to go forward by tapping behind their withers with our extension stick. That is also unnatural, so your horse may be confused.

We will be asking your horse to go around us to the left.

Stand in front of your horse.

Take the lead in your left hand.

Stand still.

Lead your horse to the left. If they just stand there take your extension stick in your right hand and lightly tap on their shoulder until your horse turns a few steps away from you to your left. If they just stand there, take your stick and tap your horse lightly just behind their withers. If they get confused they just might start going backwards, or come to you. If they come to you tap the shoulder for them to move their shoulder out of your way again. Continue tapping on their withers, trying to lead them in the correct direction at the same time. Continue to tap until your horse takes one step in the direction you wish them to go. Click as soon as a step is taken, stop tapping, then feed.

Repeat this same process 5 times.

Wait and do nothing to see if your horse can 'show you what they know.' When they can walk away from you and give you 1 step on their own, click and feed. You can encourage them to take that extra step by leading them or giving some pressure towards their withers for the extra step. When they take 2 steps, click and feed.

Practice:

Ask for them to take 3 steps. Click, stop asking, then feed. If they are showing you what they know, go with it and have them do it on their own, just encourage more steps. It only takes a few times of offering it to you. Then you can move on.

Ask for them to take 4 steps, then click and feed.

Ask for them to take 5 steps, then click and feed.

When this task is finished, your chain of tasks should be:

Ask your horse to walk around you in a full circle.
Then click and feed.
Do the same in the other direction.

WORKING AT LIBERTY WITH A ROPE IN THE ROUND PEN

I like to put a rope over the horse's neck and ask for liberty work. The rope I use is a soft marine braid rope, but you can use any type of rope. Before you perform this task, you should be able to put the halter on, be able to touch your horse with your hand or stick, and have your horse drag the lead around. They need to have gone through some round pen work. They need to know how to go around you. You should be working in a round pen or stall no smaller than 24-foot by 24-foot.

You will need round pen or a pen, rope at least 24-foot long, clicker and pouch of food.

You will be working at liberty with a rope around your horse's neck that is at least 24-foot long. Place the rope over your horse's neck. Slip it over their head. It can be a slipknot.

Ask your horse to move around at liberty. Get your horse to move to the right and to the left. This will let the horse get used to the rope around their neck.

Ask your horse to stop.

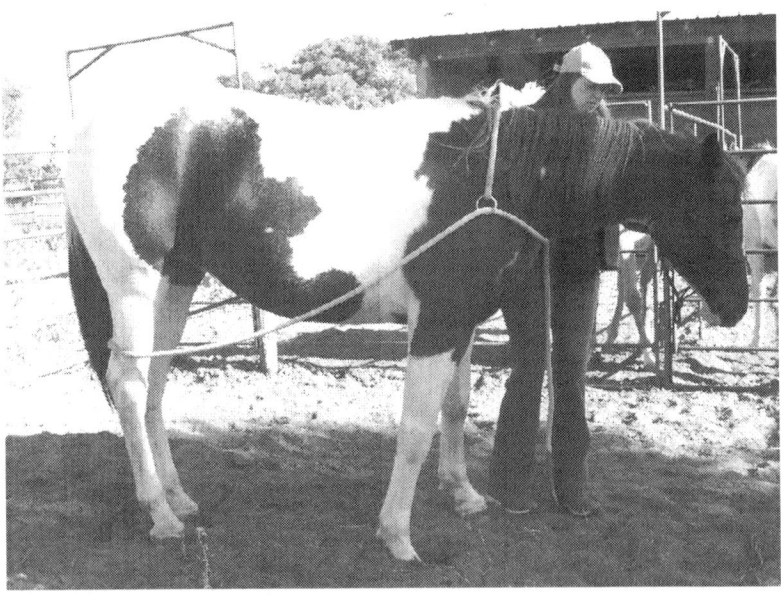

Cherry is showing the rope around her neck and hindquarters.

While the rope is still wrapped around your horses neck take the end of the rope and slip it over your horse's back and have it drop behind your horse's hindquarters to the legs, ask your horse to go around in a circle. The rope will be hitting your horse's rump and legs. This will help the horse to get used to the rope on their legs and behind him. If your horse is going to the left, the rope should be draped around the right side of their body. Your horse will be zoned for the liberty circle, so they should go around with no problems. Ask for a complete circle at the walk, then click and feed.

Repeat the same in the other direction.

CHAPTER 12
CONTINUATION OF FREEDOM GAMES

This is the sequence that I use with these tasks.

With the Freedom Games, we went through the introduction of slickers, flags and tarps. We didn't touch your horse with these items.

With plastic, the noise factor sometimes determines how your horse reacts. If you take a slicker for example, it will not sound as loud as a plastic bag. A tarp also doesn't sound as loud as a plastic bag, but the tarp is larger, which can be more intimidating to the horse. A flag that doesn't make any noise will be much easier to put on your horse at first.

I always make sure that I can touch my horse with flags, slickers, tarps, and plastic. The last thing that I want is a piece of plastic blowing by, and my horse spooks and runs off. I want to know what the reaction to plastic is before we start the process of riding. I don't like starting this process until your horse is more comfortable with you, and you have worked together for a while. That is why we don't do this task with the Freedom Games until you have a closer relationship.

TOUCHING YOUR HORSE WITH A CLOTH OR TOWEL

You will need a halter, lead, clicker, cloth flag or small towel, and pouch of food.

I use the same techniques for touching the horse with the flag as seen in Chapter 5 Soft Flags, and Chapter 7 Touching Your Horse. Your horse should have completed all the steps for touching in Chapters 5 and 7, and they also must have completed the steps for the More Slickers and Flags, in Chapter 5 before this is attempted. Your horse must be very confident with you touching them before we start this task. If they are afraid of their head being touched with the flag, the neck or the shoulder might be a better place to start.

Make sure your horse has a safe place to go if they need to. Your horse will tell you what works best and, if they seem scared, back up and try again.

We will be touching your horse all the way to their rump.

Scrunch the flag up really small in your hand.

Ask your horse to target the flag. Click when they touch the flag with their nose, then feed.

Repeat 2 more times.

Slowly move your hand up in the air with the flag in your hand scrunched up. Click and feed if they stand still when you bring your hand up. If not, back up and lift it half as much.

Bring your hand a little closer to their face or neck, depending on where your horse is more comfortable. Click and feed when you feel that you have come closer to touching them.

You might get to touch them on the first try. Always go very slow, moving your hand a few inches in the direction of your horse. It is often the movement they are worried about. Go very slow. If they spook, back up and try again. The key is to keep them from moving. This task needs to be very calm and easy. Don't wait until your horse tells you that they won't accept it. Click when they do. If they move away there is no click. Back up and try again. Don't over click for what you have already touched. So if If you get to touch a small part of their neck, click and feed, then move another inch, click and feed. Progress to half of the neck or the whole neck. Once it is recorded as a positive, move on. You have to keep working at it as long as it takes until the horse can accept being touched with the flag in your hand. It might take many sessions.

As soon as you can touch a certain section, give them a chance to get used to being touched with the flag in your hand by stroking several times.

Practice:

Stroke the area one full stroke, then click and feed.

Stroke the same area for 2 strokes in a row, then click and feed.

Stroke again for 3 strokes in a row, then click and feed.

Repeat until you get to 5 strokes, then move on inch by inch to another part.

Continue until you can touch your horse all the way back to their hip. This can go very fast depending on the horse and how your horse feels about you.

Now, let the flag open up a little so they will see more of the flag, then repeat all over again.

Repeat on the other side.

When this task is finished, your chain of tasks should be:

Brush your horse with the flag from their head to their rump with the flag open full on both sides. Then click and feed.

If your horse gets a little upset go back and have them target the flag for their comfort and focus.

Now that you have introduced the soft flag or towel, you can introduce something that is larger. You can move on to something like a blanket or pad and repeat the same exercises. The pad is hard to scrunch up to make it small, so you just have to go slow. Most horses accept this well. If they do not accept it, your chances of them accepting something that makes noise will be much less, so get the non-noisy things working well first, then move on to things that make some noise.

STANDING ON TOP OF BLANKETS, JACKETS, AND TARPS

When you have introduced blankets, jackets, and tarps to your horse, we can move on to standing on top of them. I like to do this before I touch them with noisy objects because it gets them used to the object and they can investigate it more at their own pace. This makes it easier to touch them with it.

I use the same techniques as the bridge, just different objects. Your horse must have completed the Walking on the Bridge Task, in Chapter 5.

You want your horse to step on something other than a bridge, such as a blanket, tarp, or jacket. Since these objects are much lighter, you have to make sure that they do not get hooked to their feet and have it follow them. This will scare them.

I usually start out with an old saddle blanket.

You will need halter, lead, saddle blanket, clicker, and pouch of food.

No halter or lead is needed, unless you feel you have to. If you do, pretend you do not have it on.

Place your blanket in a pen, arena, or large stall. If it is in a stall, make sure it is in the middle so there is plenty of room for your horse to move around it, just in case they spook.

Take your target and lead your horse to the blanket.

When they look at the blanket, click and feed. If they don't seem to understand that the blanket is the new focus, you can place the target on the blanket, then take it away when they focus on the blanket.

CLICKER TRAINING: COLT STARTING THE NATURAL HORSE

When they look at the blanket, click and feed. This will take a short amount of time. If they are afraid of it, continue to click for their efforts to get close to the blanket. If you have done your homework with the Walking on Bridge Tasks Chapter 5, this will go very fast.

When they smell it with their nose, click and feed.

When they touch it with their nose, click and feed.

Continue this for a few clicks.

Then wait until your horse paws the blanket with their foot, or if they accidentally step onto it, click and feed. What usually happens is your horse will try to get to you for the treat, because they smelled the blanket and they are sure you clicked for it. They will be trying to come to you for food, and they don't understand that you would like them to stand on top of the blanket, which at this point is impossible to some horses. If they try to come to you, walk around the blanket, not allowing them to get to you. In a way, you are running away from your horse. When they follow you, keep walking around the blanket away from them, so they cannot catch you. As soon as they look at or smell it, click and feed. Some take longer than others to understand that, chasing you does not accomplish anything, and moving around the blanket will become its own "Keep going signal". This means they are not quite there yet to get a click, so keep trying.

When they are chasing you around the blanket, they will accidentally stand on it or smell it again, so make sure you click and feed for the accidental step. It doesn't take long for them to figure out that chasing you around does not get the click, and all you will have to do is take one step away from them for them to figure out they need to go back to the blanket and start over.

This is a crucial part. They will at some point paw it, trying to get you to click. Some will lift their foot, but place it back on the ground. Click when they pick up the foot, not when they put it down on the ground. When they paw the blanket, click when their foot comes down on the blanket, not when their foot is in the air. We are not teaching pawing even though some horses think that we are. Soon they will place one foot on the blanket. If they are pawing the blanket continually, click when their foot hits the blanket, for no more than three clicks.

Wait until your horse leans on their foot when placing it down on the blanket. Click and feed. Continue to click repeatedly over and over about 4 clicks to let them know this is what you wanted. You are reinforcing it with a "Jackpot."

Withhold the click again and wait for some more effort. They should start lifting their other foot. When they do, click and feed. Some horses understand right away and walk right on and others are more timid. Go slow. Click and feed for small efforts. It doesn't matter how fast they walk on the blanket, but how you reward them for it.

When both front feet are on the blanket, click a "jack pot," then stop and wait.

Now you have both front feet on. We need to get them to walk over it. If both their front feet are on the blanket, withhold the click until they move one back foot forward. It does not matter if the back foot gets on the blanket. You are clicking for forward movement of the hind foot. Some horses might get upset and back off and walk around it again. Put your self in a position to have your horse attempt to get back on the blanket. Some will just go right back where they left off. If they do not, you can click for what they will give you. Your horse is not getting away with anything. They are still having problems, and clicking for this all over again can be a good thing. Wait and see how much they struggle and when you feel that a click is in order, give them one. If they can't give you much more, end the session. They will be much better later on. I find that if a horse understands the task, they will offer the task to you.

We just want them to walk over the blanket. The blanket is way too small for them to stand with all four feet on it. You can give a jackpot click, if you feel they need one, but they have to have at least 2 feet on the blanket to get one, either the front feet or the back feet.

CLICKER TRAINING: COLT STARTING THE NATURAL HORSE

Place some food on the blanket and end the session.

When this task is finished, your chain of tasks should be:

Have your horse walk over the blanket with all four feet. Then click and feed.

When that is accomplished, you can move on to a jacket.

WAVING AROUND A JACKET

You will need jacket, clicker, and pouch of food.

When using a jacket, make sure there is some type of noise factor to it. It can be a slicker, but I prefer that it is not as noisy as a tarp.

Have your horse at liberty in a stall or a large pen. Do not be in their pen with them. I like to just walk around with the jacket in the barn, waving it up and down, not looking at my horse. I want them to get used to it before they stand on it.

Walk around the barn waving the jacket and check to see what your horse's reaction will be. If they get scared and run around their pen, you will know this is too much for your horse. Move back farther from them. Keep waving the jacket until your horse calms down. Move closer, still waving the jacket. Don't stop waving it. The only thing that you change is the distance. We are getting your horse used to scary objects. When something is flying around, you are not always going to be there to click and feed. They need to get used to things on their own, and learn to calm down and accept things. Move closer and closer and let your horse gauge how close you get. I have been as far as 100 feet away to start off. Practice this for a few sessions. I will routinely carry a jacket, a plastic bag, or a tarp and wave it about when I am working in the barn. You may not be able to get close to your horse while waving the jacket. If you can get at least 10 feet away, then this task is done.

STANDING ON JACKET TASK

Take your horse to the same area where you worked on standing on the blanket.

Place your jacket on the ground.

Repeat the same as if it were the blanket. When they paw the jacket or slicker, they might scare themselves, because it will move and make noise, so be prepared for them to jump back.

The next time you would like your horse to stand on the jacket, it will go much faster. I will continue the same method for about 3 sessions. When I am sure they are comfortable, it is time to move on.

TARP

Don't forget to wave around your tarp first to get them used to it.

You will need halter, lead, tarp, clicker, and pouch of food.

I use the exact same techniques for the blanket, but now with a tarp. The only difference is that the tarp might move, so you have to be extra careful to stay out of your horse's way. I usually do this task without a halter, but if you are concerned about your horse, use a halter for assistance if they get scared.

Use a tarp no larger than 6 foot long. It will be easier to wave. Repeat walking around the barn waving the tarp. This might take a little bit longer, because a tarp makes more noise.

Place your tarp in a large pen, arena, or large stall. If it is in a stall, make sure it is in the middle so there is plenty of room for your horse to move around it, just in case they spook.

Lay the tarp on the ground and fold it about 1 foot wide. Leave the length of it long. It is something that your horse can step over, but not go around.

Put some dirt on it to weigh it down. It will look less threatening to your horse if it looks like part of the ground.

Take your target and lead your horse to the tarp.

When they look at the tarp, click and feed. If they don't seem to understand that the tarp is the new focus, you can place the target on the tarp, then take it away when they focus on the tarp.

If they are afraid of it, continue to click for their efforts to get close to the tarp. If you have done your homework with the walking on the bridge work and the blanket work, this should go very fast.

When they smell the tarp with their nose, click and feed.

When they touch the tarp with their nose, click and feed.

Continue this for a few clicks.

Some horses will paw the tarp and others will just walk right over it. Some will even stand on it. Most will walk or jump over it. Click as soon as they do any of these things. After they walk over it and you have clicked and fed, they will turn around and smell it again. Withhold the click until they smell the tarp again. If they pawed it, it will move, so be prepared for them to jump. Do not click if they paw it and then jump. Click if they paw it and they stay and investigate.

Angel, a paint filly likes to paw the tarp under her belly. She thinks that is fun. She will paw it until it flops under her belly, then she will back up and do it again.

If they do paw it, you will have to put it back into place and cover it up again. This task can take some time.

As soon as they walk over it or investigate it enough, you can open it up and have it 2 feet wide and repeat the same process. They will step over it, so they do not have to stand on top of it. Our goal is for them to stand on the tarp. This is hard for a horse because the tarp is large, loud and intimidating. Some horses really do have a problem with this and others take to it right away. If they are like Angel, this will be easy for them to walk on.

Open the tarp about 2 feet wide and put some dirt on all ends, and even in the middle. Spread the dirt around a little. Ask your horse to walk up to the tarp. Withhold the click until they walk over it or on it. One foot is good for now. When they put one foot on the tarp, click and feed.

Open the tarp about 3 or 4 feet wide. Again put some dirt on it to lay the ends down.

Ask your horse to walk on the tarp by standing on the other side of the tarp in front of your horse or beside them. Remember your horse just might try to jump the tarp, so stand far enough away.

If your horse starts chasing you around the tarp, they may accidentally stand on it or smell it again, so make sure you click and feed for the accidental step. It doesn't take long for them to figure out that chasing you around does not get the click. All you will have to do is take one step away from them so they figure out they need to go back to the tarp and start over.

Some horses will at some point try to paw it, trying to get you to click. When they paw the tarp, click when their foot comes down on the tarp, not when their foot is in the air.

We are not teaching pawing even though some horses think that we are. Soon they will place one foot on the tarp. If they are pawing the tarp continually, click when their foot hits the tarp no more than three clicks.

Wait until your horse leans on their foot, placing it down on the tarp. Click and feed. Continue to click repeatedly over and over, about 4 clicks to let them know this is what you wanted. You are reinforcing it with a small "Jackpot."

Withhold the click again and wait for some more effort. They soon will start lifting their other foot. When they lift their other foot, click and feed.

When both front feet are on the tarp, click a "Jack Pot" click.

Now you have both front feet on the tarp. We need the back feet on the tarp. For some horses it can be difficult. If both their front feet are on the tarp, withhold the click until they move one back foot. It doesn't matter if the back foot gets onto the tarp. You are clicking for forward movement of the hind foot. Click for any forward movement toward the tarp. Some horses might get upset and back off and walk around the tarp again. Put yourself in a position to have the horse attempt to get back on the tarp. Some will just go right back to where they left off. If they do not, you can click for what they will give you. They are still having problems and clicking for this all over again can be a good thing. Wait them out so they can learn more. Wait and see how much they struggle, and when you feel that a click is in order, give them one. If they can't give you much more, end the session. They will be much better later on.

Once they have 3 legs on the tarp give them another, "Jackpot" click.

Then wait to see if they will lift the last foot on to the tarp. When they offer forward movement of the last foot, click and feed.

As soon as all the four feet are on the tarp, click immediately. As they take the last step, use your "Jackpot," clicks. Continue to click for up to 10 clicks. If they just walk over it or run over it, you can click for the time they are on the tarp. If they run over the tarp, try to get them to slow down by starting over. If they keep on running over the tarp, don't keep on clicking. You will have to start over and click for them slowing down and even looking at the tarp.

When they stand on the tarp, end the session and put some food on the tarp so your horse can explore even more.

When this task is finished, your chain of tasks should be:

Ask your horse to stand on a tarp with all four feet.
Then click and feed.

TOUCHING YOUR HORSE WITH THE SADDLE PAD

It is always best to touch your horse with something less scary at first. So a pad will do just fine.

You will need blanket, halter, lead, clicker and pouch of food

Ask your horse to smell the saddle pad first, then click for them targeting it.

Repeat.

Rub your horse with the pad on their neck. Click when the pad touches your horse, then feed.

Move it to the shoulder, click and feed.

Repeat, but start at your horse's neck and move towards their withers, then click and feed. Click and feed step by step until you can complete the whole chain from the neck to their withers.

Repeat.

Move it to their back. Click and feed.

Continue to move it towards their rump, click and feed.

Repeat.

Drape it over your horses rump, click and feed.

Repeat.

CLICKER TRAINING: COLT STARTING THE NATURAL HORSE

Do this on both sides.

When this task is finished, your chain of tasks should be:

Take your saddle pad and rub it on your horse's neck to their withers to their rump, walk back to their shoulder and go around their front and continue rubbing your horse on the other side from their neck to the withers to their rump.

Then click and feed.

RUBBING THE SADDLE PAD ON THEIR LEGS

You will need blanket, halter, lead, clicker and pouch of food.

Ask your horse to smell the saddle pad first, then click for them targeting it.

Repeat.

Rub your horse with the pad on their neck. Click when the pad touches your horse then feed.

Move it to their front leg, click and feed.

Repeat, but move the pad down the entire front leg, then click and feed.

Repeat a few times.

Rub your horse with the pad on their neck, to their shoulder, to their withers to their back, and to their rump, and continue to go down towards their hip, then click and feed.

Rub your horse with the pad on their neck, to their shoulder, to their withers, to their back, and to their rump, and continue to go down towards their hip to their hock, then click and feed.

Rub your horse with the pad on their neck to their shoulder to their withers to their back and to their rump and continue to go down towards their hip to their hock and continue down their leg to the hoof, then click and feed.

Repeat several times.

Do the same on the other side.

When this task is finished, your chain of tasks should be:

Take your saddle pad and rub it on your horse's neck, to their shoulder, to their front leg, to their hoof, then go back up to their shoulder, and rub their back to their rump down to their hock and then to the hoof. Go back to their front and do the same on the other side.
Then click and feed.

Now that you understand the task, you can rub them on their sides down to their legs, then click and feed.

LAYING THE PAD ON YOUR HORSES BACK

Rub the pad on your horses shoulders, then lay the pad on the horses back. Click and feed.

Take it off and lay it again on your horses back, click when the pad is laying on your horses back.

Repeat, but have the pad stay on your horses back for 2 seconds. Click at 2 seconds, take the pad off, then feed.

Repeat, but have the pad stay on your horses back for 3 seconds. Click at 3 seconds, take the pad off, then feed.

Repeat, but have the pad stay on your horses back for 4 seconds. Click at 4 seconds take the pad off, then feed.

CLICKER TRAINING: COLT STARTING THE NATURAL HORSE

Repeat the same for 20 seconds, then click and feed.

Do the same on the other side.

When this task is finished, your chain of tasks should be:

Have the pad lay on your horses back for at least 20 seconds Then click and feed.

Now jump to 30 seconds 50 seconds to minutes then phase out the click for laying the pad on your horses back.

WALKING WITH THE PAD ON

Put your pad on your horses back. Ask them to go for a walk. Click and feed if they do well. Practice this for awhile. Try to phase out the click for walking around with the pad on. You can be the judge of when your horse accepts it.

HAVING THE PAD FALL OFF YOUR HORSE

Take the saddle pad off while they are walking and drop it on the ground. Click when it hits the ground.

Repeat a few times on both sides.

Let the pad fall off the horse and land on the ground, click and feed when it falls to the ground.

Repeat several times.

Soon your horse will turn around and smell the blanket, and that is what you want. If they turn around and look at the blanket or smell it, click and feed.

Do this on both sides.

TOUCHING YOUR HORSE WITH A JACKET, SLICKER AND TARP

Introducing a slicker.

We will be doing the same as with the blanket and soft flag. It will be harder to touch your horse with the jacket and tarp, so scrunch it up using the same method as the Soft Flags section in Chapter 5. You also want to lay it on your horses back, have them walk with it and have it fall to the ground. Sometimes you have to pull it off yourself, then have your horse look at it.

The reason that I do this is some horses get scared if something falls to the ground, and they may back up and kick at it. I had a young mare in for training. Every time the jacket would fall off, she would kick at it. If she was trotting forward and the jacket fell off she would stop, back up and kick it. If someone fell off her she just might stop, back up, and kick. When she would stop and stand still I would click and feed. It took some time, but she finally stopped kicking at the jacket.

Another horse that I was working with, named Junior, had a problem with scary things. If I asked him to go into a circle he was fine, until he saw something, and he would take off, scared to death. There was no stopping him, he would turn his hindquarters and bolt. I used the jacket on him to correct this problem. He was just fine with me touching him with the jacket when he was standing still, but when he moved, the jacket would make some noise and he would bolt. I worked with his disengagement, and then put the jacket on his back and asked him to trot around me. When the jacket fell off he bolted, but I managed to get him to disengage his hindquarters. Then I clicked and fed. I continued to repeat the same until Junior offered to stop, turn around and look at the jacket. As soon as he did, I clicked and fed him. This gave him a chance to get used to scary things, and the bolting stopped.

KILLER PLASTIC BAGS

Junior also had a problem with plastic. Apparently some plastic had blown over into his pen and he ran off, almost running his owner over. Junior's owner knew that there was a problem that needed to be addressed. So she sent Junior to me to work on his fear of plastic.

Junior seemed to not fear tarps, just plastic bags. If he was not properly introduced to plastic before he was ridden, I was not sure what he would do. I needed to know what his reaction would be to plastic before even attempting to start him under saddle. I didn't expect miracles. I just wanted to know if I could help this horse.

I took an old slicker and hung it all over the stall. Junior had plenty of room to get away if it was too much for him. We worked on Clicker Training with plastic and it was going well, but Junior still didn't like it. This poor horse lived plastic for 7 days straight! That is all we worked on. I still didn't get him to accept it fully, but he did stand still for it and that was all I could ask. There is no guarantee what his reaction to something blowing in the wind will be, but I feel better that he has been exposed to it, and that he knows he didn't die when he saw plastic.

TOUCHING YOUR HORSE WITH A PLASTIC BAG

I don't usually start off with the plastic bag right away. It is very noisy and most horses don't like it. Now that you have successfully worked your horse with a jacket and a tarp, the plastic bag should go much smoother.

Take your plastic bag and tie it to the end of a stick. Repeat the same, waving it around while your horse is in a pen or pasture, just to see if they can get used to it on their own.

While the plastic bag is tied to your stick, wrap it around your stick. It will look really small and the noise will be much less. Repeat the same exercise as for the flag. Go very slow. Unwrap the plastic bag a little and repeat until the plastic bag is fully open.

Repeat the exact same sequence as the soft flag in touching your horse. Scrunch the plastic bag up really small in your hand, slowly open it up, and rub your horse all the way to their hip.

Now that you have successfully worked with the pad, jacket, tarp, and plastic bag, you need to repeat all of it again, but this time you will need to touch them on their belly and on their legs.

TOUCHING THE BELLY AND LEGS WITH ALL THE OBJECTS

You will need to use the same sequence as rubbing the saddle pad on their legs in this chapter, but this time you will be using all kinds of different objects. For smaller objects don't forget their face. You can use the same task as Soft Flags in Chapter 5.

Take your blanket or pad and rub you horse with it on their shoulder. Move slowly to their legs, then click and feed.

Repeat the same from their shoulder to their chest and to their legs. Click and feed.

Repeat the same from their shoulder to their chest, to their legs, to the middle of their belly. Click and feed.

Repeat the same from their shoulder to their chest, to their legs, to the middle of their belly. Repeat from the belly up towards their flank. Click and feed.

Repeat the same from their shoulder to their chest, to their legs, to the middle of their belly. Repeat from the belly up towards their flank and continue down the back legs. Click and feed. Remember, on the back legs, if they are scared, back up and try again in a place more comfortable.

When this task is finished, your chain of tasks should be:

Rub the blanket from their shoulder to their chest, to their legs, to the middle of their belly, from the belly up toward their flank, and continue down the back legs.
Click and feed for each step.
Do the same on the other side.

JACKET

Repeat the same with the jacket, but remember that the jacket makes more noise, so it can take longer. Don't forget to scrunch up the jacket and slowly open it up.

When this task is finished, your chain of task should be:

Rub the jacket fully open from their shoulder to their legs, to their chest to the middle of their belly, from the belly up toward their flank, and continue down the back legs.
Then click and feed.

TOUCHING WITH A TARP

Repeat the same with the tarp but remember that the tarp makes even more noise and it is larger, so it can take longer. Don't forget to fold up the tarp, and then slowly open it up.

Do the same on both sides.

When this task is finished, your chain of tasks should be:

Rub the tarp fully open from their shoulder to their legs, to their chest, to the middle of their belly, from the belly up toward their flank, and continue down the back legs.
Then click and feed.

When I put a saddle on Boltus, a pony in for training, he lifted his head up and put his ears back. He was afraid of things on his back, even though they had been riding him for a few years. He never had the training that he needed with noisy objects. The owner complained of him running off with her. Boltus seemed to be rushing everywhere. He would stop, but he would still run off. The owner thought this was normal. What was happening was Boltus (which is an appropriate name for him) was running away all the time because he would hear noises while the rider was in the saddle, so would run off in fright. He was easy enough to stop, but he had it in his mind that he had to run away from the noise. When I brought the tarp out, he bolted to the other side of the pen. I worked with him for days, and he seemed to be a little bit better, but habits are hard to break. Running away from noisy things was ingrained in him. I did get to my goal of having him stand still while I brushed with a tarp on him, but he looked scared. Because he was not introduced to tarps in the correct way, Boltus created a habit of running away from the rider. He couldn't get rid of the rider, so he always looked a little panicked. He hadn't figured out that bucking could get the rider off, or he just didn't have the urge to.

One day while I was riding him, I just decided to let him run if he wanted to until he figured out that he was not running anywhere. He had to learn the hard way. He ran around the pasture for about 45 minutes. until he figured out that slowing down and standing still was easier. He soon slowed down, and I clicked and fed for him trotting and cantering slow on a loose rein. My only criteria was, he had to stay in the pasture we were working in. We don't want to have to fix this problem this way. This is why I am so strict about flags and tarps.

After Boltus was in training his owner Bryce (6 years old) can now canter on a loose rein.

HAVING BLANKET, SLICKERS AND TARPS FALL OFF WHILE TROTTING

You will need halter, lead, saddle blanket, clicker, and pouch of food.

It doesn't matter, what side you start on, but you will have to do both sides because you want your horse to see the blanket fall off on both sides.

With the pad or the blanket on your horses back, ask them to go for a walk. Take the pad off while they are walking and drop it on the ground. Click when it hits the ground, even if your horse jumps.

Put the blanket on your horses back, and ask your horse to trot in a circle. When the blanket falls off, click and feed. If this scares your horse, and you think that they are having a problem with the blanket falling off, just continue letting the blanket fall off for a few clicks. Then you can get specific to the action, withhold the click until your horse lets the blanket fall off without them jumping. Reinforce them for stopping and looking at it, or even if they ignore it.

Repeat.

Put the blanket back on and ask your horse to trot in a circle. When the blanket falls off, ask your horse to stop, turn, and look at the blanket. Click when they look at the blanket.

Repeat the same 3 more times.

Put the blanket back on your horses back and ask your horse to trot in a circle again. When the blanket falls off, wait for your horse to stop, turn around and target the blanket, then click and feed.

Repeat 3 more times.

Repeat the other direction.

Repeat the exact same task for the jacket and tarp, but the jacket and the tarp need to be fully open. Remember it will be much harder for them to accept the tarp, so go slow. This might take a few sessions.

Make sure you do both sides.

CHAPTER 13
TRAILERING

IMAGE'S LIFE THREATENING ORDEAL

I check my horses that are out on pasture on a daily basis. I noticed that one horse was missing, my paint horse, Image. I looked in the trees, and she was standing by herself. She seemed OK, just resting. I almost left, but I thought, "Well I should say hi to her, and see if she is OK." When I rode up on the A.T.V, I could see she was very relaxed, but I noticed that she had blood on her back legs. She was bleeding and swollen. I walked to the back of her, and to my amazement, she had a foal hanging from her. The baby was dead, and cold to the touch.

I rode home to call a vet. We live in a very remote area, and getting a vet out is very difficult. We called everywhere, and no vet. She was acres away from the house, in the pasture, and in the trees! We hooked the trailer up and managed to drive to her. We got about 10' away. She was now laying down. I felt to see where the foal's legs where, and they were both clearly stuck. She must have been pushing for hours. Image would die if she did not see a veterinarian.

I always have prescribed pain killer for horses at the house for emergencies. I gave her some, and soon she started calming down, and relaxing. About 10 minutes later she got up, but wanted to go down again. I put a halter on her, but didn't get the lead on. My husband walked her out of the trees with just the halter. I encouraged her to move from behind.

When we arrived at the trailer, I thought she was going to go down again. I let her go, and asked her to try loading. She looked at me, and followed me right in the trailer. I didn't have any food, or a clicker, but she knew what she had to do. I had taught her to load in a trailer earlier at liberty with Clicker Training. We shut the door, and took off for the veterinarian's clinic. When we arrived, she was still standing, and she walked out and right into the chute. It took 10 minutes to get the baby out. The foal was very large. The vet said that he wasn't sure that Image would be ok, but she didn't go into full shock, which is a good sign. He gave her a 50/50 chance to live over the next 12 hours.

When we arrived home, Image drank 5 gallons of water and started eating. She made it the twelve hours, and had a full recovery. She had only been on one trailer ride in her life before this incident, but we had used positive reinforcement for loading her. She knew when she saw the trailer she was supposed to load. It saved her life. Everyone is saying that the only reason she survived was because of her training. I also feel that the positive relationship that we have together helped keep her from going into shock. The vet was also very surprised that she lived. Have you ever begged for a horse's life before? I made a promise to Image that I would make her my horse, if she lived. I had planned on selling her. I guess she really wanted to be my horse. I am proud to own a horse as tough as her.

Image after her ordeal enjoying a nice ride.

CLICKER TRAINING: COLT STARTING THE NATURAL HORSE

PICKING THE RIGHT TRAILER

At some point you are going to have to trailer your horse, or you may have a horse that is afraid of trailering. The trailer should be a happy place. It should not be associated with something scary. Some horses take to trailers right away, some don't seem to care, and others just can't seem to get over it.

We have to make sure that the trailer is adequate for the horse. Some trailers can be more difficult for horses to load into than others. The trailer that comes to mind is a small, straight load 2 horse. Horses like to have a lot of space. The smaller the space the more difficult it can be on the horse. I think most people would agree, that horses would rather ride backwards instead of forwards. I have a stock trailer and I usually let the horse be loose in the trailer, so they can find the best way to ride. Most of the time, it is backwards. Whether you have a straight load, stock, or slanted trailer, it is your job to make sure your horse trailers well.

Before we start with trailering, your horse has to know how to lead, disengage their hindquarters, and back up.

Try these tasks before you try trailer loading.

HAVING YOUR HORSE FOLLOW YOU THROUGH A GATE

I want you to do these tasks because it is a good simulation of trailer loading.

You will need halter, lead, clicker, pouch of food, and extension stick.

Stand in front of your horse.

Ask your horse to walk through a gate by pulling on the halter with slight pressure. If they walk forward 1 step, click, release pressure, and feed.

Repeat the same until your horse follows you through the gate. Expect 2 steps, then click and feed, expect 3 steps, then click and feed.

To turn around, disengage their hindquarters, then click and feed when the disengagement is complete. Ask your horse to walk back through the gate. Pull on the lead with slight pressure, click and feed when they come forward. By this time you will be clicking for 2 or 3 steps, Your goal is to click only when they completely walk through the gate, no matter how many steps it takes.

Repeat the same, on the other side.

When this task is finished, your chain of tasks should be:

Have your horse follow you through a gate.
Disengage their hindquarters.
Walk back through.
Disengage the hindquarters
Then click and feed.

HAVING YOUR HORSE WALK WITH YOU

This is a good simulation of you and your horse walking into the trailer together.

Cue your horse to go around you in a circle.

When they are facing in the direction you would like to go. Start walking with your horse inline with their shoulder. At first your horse might stop. Your position beside them looks different, and it might feel a little strange.

CLICKER TRAINING: COLT STARTING THE NATURAL HORSE

Cheyenne was lunging around me in a circle, and I just started walking with her.

Ask your horse to go in another circle, and start walking with them again. If they stay in a walk, click and feed.

Ask them to go forward again and walk with them. If they walk with you, click and feed. If they feel they have to go into a circle around you, that is OK, but only click for them walking with you at their shoulder. This will let them get used to you walking with them.

Do this on both sides.

When this task is finished, your chain of tasks should be:

Walk with your horse. If your horse offers to walk with at the shoulder, click and feed.
Do this on both sides of your horse.

HAVING YOUR HORSE WALK THROUGH A GATE FIRST

This is a good simulation of you asking your horse to go into a trailer first. This is very helpful when there is no room for you to go into the trailer and this will keep you out of their way.

Find a gate, or a small opening that is safe for your horse to walk through.

Stand at the gate. You will not be walking through the gate with your horse. Keep your position in the same place.

Stand on the left side of your horse.

Extend your left arm towards the gate opening, leading your horse in the direction of the opening. If they do not want to go through the gate, and they just stand there, bring your focus behind your horse's withers. If they still do not walk forward, lift your extension stick up in the air, and motion towards their withers. If that does not work, start tapping just behind their withers. Your horse should understand what this is, and take a step forward. Keep tapping until one step is taken forward. If your horse backs up, just keep tapping lightly until your horse takes a step forward. Click and release pressure, then feed.

Ask for another step to move through the gate. Click, stop tapping, then feed.

CLICKER TRAINING: COLT STARTING THE NATURAL HORSE

Having your horse walk through a gate first.

Ask for another step until your horse walks completely through the gate. Then ask for disengagement so they can face you, then click, release pressure, then feed.

Move to the other side of the gate, and ask your horse to go back through the gate on their other side.

Repeat the same sequence.

When this task is finished, your chain of tasks should be:

Ask your horse to walk through the gate, disengage their hindquarters, then continue to ask your horse to go back through the gate, disengage their hindquarters.
Then click, then feed.
Do the same on the other side.

You will need to practice these tasks several times before you start to introduce trailer loading. They will also help you with your relationship with your horse.

INTRODUCTION TO THE TRAILER

You will need a clicker, target, pouch of food, and a trailer

You don't need a halter unless the trailer is in a place that you feel your horse can get loose. If you have the means, move the trailer into the arena, big stall or pasture so your horse can be loose.

This task should be what your horse wants to do, and what we present to the horse, not what we want. This is a learning experience, and your horse needs to learn on his or her own.

Open all the back doors of your trailer. As soon as they walk up to the trailer, click and feed. It might be a good idea to tie the doors back so the doors will not slam onto your horse. We will not be shutting the doors for a few more sessions. Leave the front openings closed. You don't want your horse jumping through the front doors. At this point, we are not going to ask the horse to go into the trailer, we are only going to introduce the trailer.

Place yourself in a position so that if your horse gets spooked, they won't run over you. I usually stand at the edge of the trailer.

Ask your horse to follow the target to the trailer, or you can just walk to the trailer, or lead them, depending how far along your horse is in their training.

As soon as they even look at the trailer, click and feed. This task is completely up to your horse. If your horse does not want to walk up to the trailer, click for what they will give you, even if it is a glance in that direction. You can use your target to try to get them closer.

If they smell the trailer, click and feed. I don't care if they smell the front of the trailer or the back.

Walk around the trailer and see if your horse will target the trailer in different places.

GOING INTO THE TRAILER

As soon as your horse seems to be comfortable with targeting the trailer, walk to the back of the trailer and see if your horse will smell the back of the trailer. When they do, click and feed. They should be very curious, and will want to smell the trailer even more. Phase out the target as soon as you can. If you worked on the bridgework earlier, your horse will want to stomp the trailer with their foot.

When they pick their foot up, or accidentally bump their leg on the back of the trailer, click and feed. When they tap the trailer, click and feed. If your horse doesn't attempt to step up, and you use your target to get them in they just might start to lean and forget that they have to pick up their feet to go into the trailer. This is why I will phase out the target, and click for forward movement of the feet.

If your horse puts one foot in the trailer, click and feed. It can be hard to feed your horse if you are standing outside the trailer when your horse is in the trailer. You can feed through the window or have an assistant feed, or you can ask your horse to come out of the trailer to get their food. You can also step up into the trailer to feed, if you feel you can be safe if they need to come out. Most horses figure out what you want, and will repeat it without the target. The important thing is to stay out of your horse's way, and if they want to leave, that is their choice. You have to let them, and try to set the process up better for success on the next session.

For this session, it is better if you stop while you are ahead. Only let them put two front feet in and call it a day.

When this task is finished, your chain of tasks should be:

Have your horse put two feet in the trailer.
Then click and feed.

You might want to repeat this task a few more sessions, before having your horse walk into the trailer with all four feet.

I was working with Black Hawk, a 2-year old colt that had never been off the farm. It is not unusual for a 2-year old at my farm to have never seen a trailer. Black Hawk was the kind of horse that would do things before he really thought about it, then scare himself. I had the lead on him when he first saw the trailer. I have a stock trailer that is extra wide and extra tall. I unlatched the front escape door just in case I needed to escape, but the door appeared closed. Black Hawk did what he usually does. He walked right into the trailer calm and cool. I walked in with him, clicking and feeding every step. I then dropped the lead on the floor, and escaped out the escape door. The worst thing that I could do would be to get in his way. I continued to click, and feed him from outside the trailer. When he would smell the trailer wall, I would click and feed. I had a hay bag in the trailer. I knew that this hay bag could cause a problem. He targeted the hay bag, scared himself, and ran out the trailer full blast. Then he turned around and snorted. He came back and we tried again. I took the hay bag down. This time he was much more cautious about loading, and he was thinking about it more. I should have only allowed him to just put 2 feet in the trailer and ended the session.

Now that your horse is calm and they have explored the trailer a little, I like to make some noise around the trailer before they go all the way in. Trailers are noisy and your horse needs to get used to it.

Ask your horse to walk up to the trailer, have them target the trailer, click and feed. Then tap on the trailer to make some noise, then click and feed. Only click and feed if your horse stands still. If your horse jumps back, tap lighter on the trailer. We are only clicking and feeding for acceptance of the noise.

Tap again, then click and feed.

Tap again, then click and feed.

Now bang the trailer with your hand, then click and feed.

Bang 2 times, then click and feed.

CLICKER TRAINING: COLT STARTING THE NATURAL HORSE

Walk to a different location, and repeat the same.

Do this all over the outside of the trailer.

When your horse is used to the trailer noises, you can ask them to go in the trailer.

LOADING INTO THE TRAILER WITH ALL FOUR FEET

For this task you will need trailer, halter, lead, and pouch of food.

Put the halter on your horse, if you don't already have one on.

Now you can go in the trailer with your horse, if the trailer is large enough for you to go in. If you have a straight load 2 horse, you can walk into the other stall. Remember this is the learning process, and we are trying to make this as comfortable as we can for your horse. You being with them is important, but you must stay safe. If you have a stock trailer, you can go in with them, but you have to remember to stay out of their way. You are not going to stop your horse from going back outside if they want to. If you have an escape door, you can use that to escape out of, if you need to.

If you have an escape door, unlatch it, but keep the door shut. You don't want your horse to see a big opening. They just might jump through it trying to get out of the trailer if they panic.

My horse, Jack, decided that he was going to jump out of the trailer, and put his two front feet through the small hay opening while we were driving down the highway. I looked back in the rear view mirror and saw two feet hanging out of the window. A 16-hand horse doesn't fit through a hole about 1 foot in diameter. He ended up sitting down with his front feet in the trailer feeder compartment. He was pinned in the corner. Because he was so athletic, he managed to get up and bring his feet back through the hole. I think we forgot to close the door, so Jack said, "I'm out of here." He just didn't know he couldn't fit. I have no idea why he tried to do that. He was not hurt, and we were lucky for that. He never did that again.

The cue for going into the trailer is walking up to the back of it. Your horse should smell the trailer, think, and walk in the trailer. My goal is for my horse to know what a trailer is. If the door is open, they should understand that going in is what I want. I want my horses to say to me, "I see the trailer, I want to go in."

Since your horse has had both front feet in the trailer before, all you have to do is withhold the click until they put at least one front foot back in the trailer. If they are having problems, you can click for a good try.

Step up into the trailer with your horse. Click for them putting both front feet into the trailer. Make sure, if you have a stock trailer, to not be straight in front of them or in their way if they decide to turn and come out. Click when your horse tries to move forward into the trailer. Some horses just walk right in before you're ready. If they are afraid, keep clicking and feeding for their little efforts. Some horses have problems picking their back feet up. If they just lean and not pick up their back feet, wait for them to move their back feet before you click. Backing them up can readjust their feet, then try again. If your horse is scared they will back up and come forward all on their own. They are trying to figure it out. Some horses are afraid to back out, so they go in, turn around, and come back out. That is fine.

Click and feed when they move one of their back feet into or next to the trailer. Some horses get their feet in and back out, and try again. That is just fine. It is what your horse needs to do. This is how they learn. When you get all four feet in the trailer, click and feed a jackpot.

Whatever trailer you have, you need to have a good routine with your horse for loading. This teaches patience, and is safer. I have a routine that I use with all of my horses since I use a stock trailer. My routine would be to go into the trailer with my horse, turn my horse around by disengaging their hindquarters, back them up into the front stall. They must stand still while I go unhook the middle gate. Slowly close the gate, unhook the lead or take off the halter. Then click and feed for the whole process. I usually let my horse go free inside the front stall. If I am loading two horses in a stock trailer, I will load my first horse. The second horse I will ask them to go in on their own. They usually will stand facing the other horse while I close the door. I make sure that I stay out of their way if they have to come out. This process is not rushed. I always close the door slowly. I leave the lead and halter on just in case they run out before I have a chance to shut the door. I never trap my horse in the trailer. We will work loading until they feel comfortable about the trailer. I will then take the lead off after I have shut the door. If I am going to leave the halter on the horse for trailering, I do not use a rope halter. I always use a web halter, preferably leather or a breakaway halter. This means that the halter will break if they get a foot through it or if they get it hung up on something. Rope halters don't break, and it is very easy for them to get their foot caught up in it, especially if they are not tied.

If you have a slant load trailer and you need to lock them into their compartment, you would have your horse step up into the trailer, move their hindquarters over, have them stand still and slowly latch the partition. Then tie your horse when you walk outside the trailer. Tying your horse is only so they cannot turn around. The lead should be long enough so their rump hits the back of the trailer wall if they back up. If you need to tie them before you exit the trailer, just loop the lead, but do not tie it solid. If your horse all of a sudden starts to pull and you have not latched the latch yet, they might get scared and stomp you trying to get loose. Some people allow their horses loose in a slant load compartment, which is too small for a horse to turn around. I am not a big fan of this for a young horse, because some horses want to turn around, and if there is not enough room they might try to go over the slant partition.

EXAMPLE OF LOADING IN A STOCK TRAILER

Lead your horse into the trailer. Click and feed for them getting all four feet into the trailer. Ask them to walk a few steps in, then turn them around by disengaging their hindquarters. Click and feed.

Ask them to back up into position. Click and feed. Ask them to stand still, and walk a few steps away from your horse, then click and feed.

Walk away from your horse and take the middle partition and move to close it. Click while you are moving the gate. Repeat but this time close the gate, then click and feed.

When this task is finished, your chain of tasks should be:

Lead your horse into the trailer.
Ask them to turn around.
Back up into position, stand still, and wait for the gate to close.
Then click and feed.

Now that your horse will go into a trailer, it is time to sharpen you and your horse's skills. At some point your horse will say to you, "I am not going in that trailer." For whatever reason, some horses just don't want to go in.

SCARED TO LOAD

I was taking English pleasure lessons, getting ready to take Natchez, my Arabian gelding, to his first show. We were doing very well, and I had great anticipation for the show. I took Natchez previously to the show grounds just to get him used to the arena. I went with my friend Karie. Karie brought her horse Dillon another Arabian gelding. Both of the horses did great for our first practice run.

On the day of the show, Dillon and Natchez both loaded into the trailer with ease. I was so grateful that Natchez was a good loading horse. When I purchased Natchez his owner said he couldn't do anything but load into a trailer. It was the only thing he was good at. Natchez was sold to me as an untrainable horse. I was so proud that I was able to show him. When we arrived at the show, Natchez was calm and cool. Both of the horses showed very well.

When we were ready to go home, Dillon loaded in the trailer right away. When it was Natchez's turn, he refused to load. I thought to my self, "Not a problem. We will work this out." I didn't have good trailering skills back then. I felt lost and confused. Natchez refused to go into the trailer. Nothing worked. I could not figure out why he didn't want to load. It was a slant load trailer that he was not used to, but he had been in it before. The only thing I could figure out was Natchez knew something we didn't about this trailer.

I had to get Natchez loaded so we could get home. After two hours of trying to get Natchez loaded, a man walked up and said he was watching us, and he had a solution. I told him, "You are not going to hurt my horse." He said he was not going to hurt Natchez in any way. He commented that he had never seen a more stubborn horse in his life, but he could get him in the trailer. So I let him help. We took the lunge line, draped it over his rump just above his hocks. The one thing that Natchez would do is stand with his front feet right next to the back of the trailer, but wouldn't step up. It took 2 people on one side and 2 people on the other. We pulled. The pull knocked Natchez off his feet, and he fell to his knees into the trailer. When he stood up, he was in, so we shut the door and went home. I was certainly not proud of what we had done. I will never load a horse that way again. I never had any trouble with Natchez loading in the trailer until that day. Natchez was a difficult trailer loading horse from that day on. We tried many different horse training books and trailer loading videos, and some training tips worked. I could get him in the trailer, but it was not solid. We had to trailer him from Portland Oregon to Pagosa Springs Colorado, because I had moved. I was so nervous about loading him. I would think, "How long was it going to take this time, and how many people are going to watch the show." My skills did get better, and it was getting easier, but I still had that feeling of not really being in control. When I started Natural Horsemanship it was much better, and I had the feeling of having more control, but Natchez would refuse to load into the trailer, no matter what kind of trailer I used. I could get him in after a lot of work, but he sure hated it, and he was so nervous. We were missing something. When we started Clicker Training everything changed. He had a chance to think about the whole process instead of panicking, and because of the way Clicker Training is set up, I could relax also. Natchez loads in a trailer much better and more willing now.

DOMINANCE ISSUE

I sold a young mare named Dahlia to a nice lady named Cindy. Dahlia and Cindy were getting along great, until they bought a new horse, named Scarlet. Dahlia was the only horse that they had, and Dahlia was so excited about the new horse, she attached to Scarlet like super glue. Cindy and Dahlia's relationship changed since Dahlia wanted to be with Scarlet all the time. One day Cindy called me to tell me that all of sudden Dahlia wouldn't load into the trailer. I told Cindy I would be right over. When I arrived, Scarlet and her new rider, a friend of Cindy's, were walking in a circle in the pasture, waiting for Cindy to load Dahlia. All Dahlia wanted was to go with Scarlet. Cindy was confused about her perfect loading horse not wanting to go into the trailer. All of the sudden she was very herd bound and wanted to do what she wanted, not what her owner wanted. I told Cindy to get her extension stick. Dahlia took one look at it and loaded immediately. Cindy was trying to get her to load by asking her, not telling her. Dahlia didn't need to be asked. She needed to be told. Dahlia had all of her Clicker Training with trailering, but because Dahlia was such a nice horse, she never refused to load until that one moment came when she told her owner she had something better to do. I wouldn't use Clicker Training at this point to get her loaded because this was not a pain or fear issue. It was a dominance issue. If you click and feed when your horse is trying to dominate you, you are just reinforcing the behavior.

Dahlia had all of the proper training with Clicker Training, and now it was time to use some negative reinforcement. That doesn't mean that I couldn't click for her going into the trailer when asked, if I thought a click was in order, but I don't have to. The only reason I would click for her going into the trailer would be if I could get her mind to stop being dominant. She could load into a trailer physically but her mind was saying, "I don't want to go, but I have to because you are going to make me." I wouldn't want to reward Dahlia for that kind of mind set. The whole point is to have a partner in your horse. When I took one look at Dahlia and her behavior, she was a long way away from a click. She needs to learn to calm down under these situations.

CLICKER TRAINING: COLT STARTING THE NATURAL HORSE

DOMINANCE TRAILER TASK

This task will help you if your horse just said, "not today, I am not going into that trailer!" You might not use it all the time, but it does let your horse know that you are in control, and they will have to load if asked. It also depends on why your horse is not loading. I use Clicker Training for a horse that might have a pain or fear related issue.

When it is a dominance issue, I use this method, but only if they have loaded with Clicker Training first, and it was a very positive experience.

You will need your halter, lead, extension stick, pouch of food, and a trailer.

Lead your horse to the trailer. Do not click. Your horse knows how to lead.

This is the exact same task as walking through the gate. I will change the words a little.

Stand at the back of the trailer. You will not be going into the trailer with your horse. Keep your position the same. Do not move. Your horse has to go first.

Stand on the left side of your horse.

Extend your arm out, and attempt to lead your horse in the direction of the opening of the trailer. If they do not want to go into the trailer, and they just stand there, bring your focus behind your horse's withers. If they do not walk forward, or even try to smell the trailer, lift your extension stick up in the air, and motion towards their withers or just behind. If that does not work, start tapping just behind their withers. Your horse should understand what this is, and take a step forward, or at least try to acknowledge the trailer. If not, keep tapping until they do. If your horse backs up, just keep tapping lightly until your horse takes a step forward or leans forward. Click as soon as your horse gives some effort, release pressure, then feed.

Repeat the same.

Do not keep clicking for the same results over and over. Extend the click once they have leaned forward. Expect a bigger try next time before you click. If they lean and smell the trailer, and that was more effort than the last time you clicked, I would say a click and feed is in order. If your horse gets scared and starts backing up, your horse could be afraid of the trailer and more work at liberty with the trailer might be needed. Your horse should not be scared at this point. Sometimes it is just too much to think about. Make it easy on your horse, get to one thing at a time. You will have to be the judge of what your horse is going through. Our goal is to phase out the click.

Load your horse from their other side. You need to load your horse from both of their sides. This can be difficult. If they are not used to you being on the other side, you will have to back up and do some tasks over again to get them used to the other side.

Now that they are loading successfully you can start clicking for them standing still while you shut the door and standing calm in the trailer.

When this task is finished, your chain of tasks should be:

Walk to the trailer.
Ask your horse to go into the trailer with you remaining outside.
Secure your horse into the trailer.
Close all doors of the trailer.
Then click and feed your horse for successfully loading.

I always have some small treat for my horses waiting when they load. It can make the whole experience much more enjoyable for them. It also calms them down and gives them something to do while you are securing the gates and doors.

CHAPTER 14
FACE MUZZLE AND EARS

It's time to work on your horse's more sensitive parts. The muzzle can be sensitive, and the ears are usually a challenge.

You will need halter, lead, clicker, and pouch of food.

I am sure you can touch your horse's face by now, but have you touched their muzzle or even their ears. You never know when you are going to have to check your horse's teeth or doctor their ears.

Touch your horse's face down to the muzzle, then click and feed.

When I can touch the muzzle, I massage it with my hands for a few seconds, then click and feed. If your horse really doesn't like to be touched on their muzzle, you will have to go very slow, and click and feed for what they will allow you to touch. You might even have to back up to their face.

When I started with Cheyenne, one of my paint mares, the one thing that she hated was her chin touched. It really bothered her. It took a long time for her to get over that.

Make sure you can also touch inside their mouth where your horse's bars are, where the bit will go. Click and feed as you go. Phase out the click by touching parts of the muzzle, then the whole muzzle. You do need to phase it out as soon as your horse will allow you to touch their muzzle without them moving.

TOUCHING THE EARS

You will need, halter, lead, clicker, and pouch of food.

Horses are very sensitive to their ears being touched and you may not be able to just start rubbing a horse's ear. Some will let you touch their ears, and others hate it. The best way to touch the ears is as fast and smooth as possible. You can give your horse a good scratch on the base of the ears, and most of them just love it. Then you can sneak up the ear really fast, then move back to the base of the ear. Some horses are ticklish, and touching quickly will make it less ticklish.

Rub your horse at the base of the ear, then click and feed.

Rub your horse at the base of the ear, then move up about an inch to the bottom of the ear. Click when you move up, then feed.

Rub the base of the ear, then move up 2 inches. Click when you are at the 2nd inch. Then move your hand back to their base of the ear, then feed. You will have to move your hand fast.

Rub the base of the ear, then move up 3 inches. Click when you are at the 3rd inch. Then move your hand back to the base of the ear, then feed.

Rub the base of the ear. Then move over the entire ear. Click when your hand is at the tip of the ear, then move your hand over to their topknot, then feed.

Repeat this several times.

Do this on the other ear. This can take several sessions.

At some point you will have to slow down. Repeat the same steps, but move slower. If your horse is still having problems, keep repeating. They will get used to it.

HAVING YOUR HORSE TOUCH YOUR HAND WITH THEIR EAR

It is up to you if you want to do this. It is very effective, but will take some patience.

CLICKER TRAINING: COLT STARTING THE NATURAL HORSE

I remember one year my stallion, King, came up with a terrible sunburn. Since he is a Cremello, he gets sunburned, but usually only in late summer. But this was spring, and his face was beet red. We took him to the vet and the vet said the combination of the sun, and some pasture grasses, such as clover, can be toxic and this can create sun sensitivity. Our pastures were covered with clover, because of the unusually dry year. I could not get a halter on him. I tried to put some cream on him. I was successful the first day. The next day King was not going to let me put cream on him, and I could tell it just hurt too much. He was trying, it just hurt too much when I touched his head. I loaded the cream in my hand and held my hand out and had him look at it. He knew exactly what I wanted. He closed his eyes, put his head in my hand for one second. I clicked when he put his cheek in my hand, which only put the cream on his face. The next time he put his cheek in my hand, he closed his eyes and pawed. It hurt so much. I stopped putting the cream on. I put him on a supplement that finally worked. I led him around with a rope on his neck for 2 months. Even though touching his face hurt terribly bad, I could still get him to do it with Clicker Training.

You can teach a horse to put their head or ear in your hand. This allows them to think about the task.

Hold your hand up and touch the base of your horse's ear. Click and feed.

Then touch about an inch of your horse's ear, click and feed.

Hold your hand up by his head in the air and wait for your horse to touch his ear to your hand. If not, repeat touching and a few more clicks. Even if they come towards the direction of your hand, you can click and feed for their progress.

Then hold your hand out again until they touch their head or ear to your hand. When they do, click and feed.

Repeat the same on the other ear.

CLIPPING EARS

When you clip a horse, you have to remember that clipping is cosmetic. Usually it's not for any reason other than your horse looking good. I do not put it on my list of 'have to's.' Most of the horses that I work with don't have a clue what a clipper is. If there is something that is not solid on their training, learning about clipping goes to the back burner. But if you must, there is a good way to introduce the clipping process at an early age that won't get into your real training time. It took me some time to add 'Clipping Your Horse' into my program.

I finally decided that my horses needed to learn to be clipped. I started out with Image. I figured since she was Clicker Trained, it would be easy to just mark what I wanted. She was doing just fine with the noise of the clippers, even though she was 6 years old and had never seen or heard clippers. She was just fine with the clippers until I started trimming the actual hair. She jumped back and tossed her head. She was so disturbed by the cutting of the hair that she shook her head for about a week. This was very discouraging. I have had other horses that did this and it took a long time for them to get used to the clippers, and it never really was pleasant. I want my horses to enjoy it. Joe, one of our stallions, hated the clippers on his ears. We worked for about 2 years until he finally was good enough to clip, but we still had to argue about it. He just never got used to it. I don't think that I was doing enough simulations of clipping. A good clip horse can take months, and you have to practice everyday. That is one of the keys to success with clipping.

When I was ready to start working on my other horses, I was not pleased with how Image jumped, and I sure was sick of the whole process. I wanted to make sure that I could learn from Image. If all your horses go along just perfect, you wouldn't learn anything.

I like cordless clippers. They are easier to handle and the cord won't get in the way. You don't need a very powerful clipper to trim the ears, face, and under the chin. They are even inexpensive enough so that anyone can own one. They run about $50. There are even some small clippers that you can find at department stores for about $10. I like these because they don't cut as well and it makes it harder to clip a big chunk of hair out by mistake.

I didn't want to start out the same way with Cheyenne as I did with Image. So I tried to think of things that I could use to simulate the same feeling as a real clipper. A hand held massager would work, but I could not find one. I have a battery-operated toothbrush that I paid about $5 for. I was willing to sacrifice it for the cause. I wanted to use the toothbrush in my daily grooming routine. I introduced it to Cheyenne and she did what was expected of a Clicker Trained horse, she stood still and enjoyed the toothbrush on her face and her ears, even on the first day. Of course, I clicked and fed for the process. I did this for about 7 sessions, about a week, just to make sure. I used the toothbrush on her ears where it itched the most. She liked that. I then brought out my cheap small clippers. I trimmed her face and part of her ears. She did great. I think she was one of the easy ones though. Not a real test.

Image was next to start working on. She was fine with the toothbrush until it twirled the longer hair on her chin and she jumped. That was my answer. The twirling of the hair felt the same as the hair actually being cut. Every horse that I used the toothbrush on, reacted the same, as if it were clippers. I used the toothbrush on Image everyday, and in a few days we had great improvements. I was clicking and feeding the whole way. I would consider Image a difficult horse for clipping. She now accepts clipping very well. I treat all horses as if they would act like Image. I don't want them to tell me they hate it, I just want them to slowly learn to accept it. King, my next horse, was a piece of cake. I clipped him the second day I worked with him. He sure loves his toothbrush. He now expects his tooth brushing everyday. I even taught him to stand really still when the clippers are clipping.

TOOTHBRUSH TASK

You will need clicker, halter, lead, battery operated toothbrush, and pouch of food.

Start this process after you have worked your horse, when they would enjoy a good brushing. I usually brush my horse with a regular brush first to relax them.

Take out your toothbrush, and stand at least 2 feet away from your horse. Turn on the toothbrush to see what the reaction to the toothbrush noise would be. If your horse just stands relaxed, click and feed. Move it about a foot closer and hold the toothbrush up in the air. Click and feed if your horse stands still.

Move even closer, almost touching your horse on their shoulder. Click if they stand still, then feed. If they jump back or get startled, you can ask them to target the toothbrush. It depends on the horse whether you have them target it first, or just start brushing your horse with it. Sometimes it can be easier if they don't target it and get used to it first. Image did much better without targeting it first. She was fine with it on her body, but when she targeted it, she would get upset.

Move the toothbrush enough to touch your horse on their shoulder. When they let you touch them, click then feed.

Repeat, but start moving the toothbrush around and brush them with it for a couple of seconds. Click while you brush them, then feed. Continue this on your horse's sides and belly, clicking and feeding when you feel it is appropriate. This is the same exercise you would use in touching your horse with a plastic bag.

Move up the neck, clicking and feeding.

When you can get close enough to the head, take away the toothbrush and hold it out in front of your horse's nose and see if they smell it or look at it. If they do, click and feed.

Have them target it for 2 more clicks.

Take the toothbrush and hold it about a foot away from their face. Click and feed if they stand still.

Repeat this in different locations around their head, a foot away. Do not touch your horse with the toothbrush on the head. This will startle most horses.

Do this on both sides.

Brush your horses back and on their shoulder with the toothbrush, then click and feed.

Work your way up the neck letting the horse be the judge of what they will accept for clicking and feeding.

When you get to their throat you will have to go very slow inch by inch, and you just might have to spend some extra time twirling the hair over and over until they get used to it.

Progress towards the head, clicking and feeding down the jaw to their muzzle. Do not leave any part UN- brushed or twirled. Soon your horse will just love this.

Do this on both sides.

TOUCHING EARS WITH THE TOOTHBRUSH

I usually work on the ears last. The face has to be completed before attempting the ears. You can go up from their face to the ears, or you can come from their neck to the ears. Your horse will tell you what works best for them.

The first thing I do is brush around the base of the ear where it is usually itching from the halter or bridle, especially if they are a little sweaty. Most horses want the base of their ear rubbed. That is why most horses will rub on you while taking the bridle off.

This should be a very simple task. If your horse is enjoying the brushing, you can slowly sneak up the ear for 1 second, then click when it gets to the bottom of the inside of the ear. Next time you do this, go a little bit higher. Don't make a big deal out of this. If they shake their head, you need to do more work. Progress higher and higher, until you can brush the inside of their ear. Be quick about this, especially in the beginning. I think for some horses, clipping the ears can be very ticklish or the clipper noise bothers them. That is why most horses don't like their ears touched. It would be the same if someone worked on me to keep me from being ticklish. Work quickly and don't make a big deal out of it, or you may cause more problems. If your horse continues to shake their head, go back to where they don't, and keep working on it.

This task can take weeks, even months. Make a routine out of it. Do this everyday to your horse. Phase out the click gradually, as soon as your horse relaxes.

PHASING OUT THE CLICK ON THEIR FACE ON ONE SIDE

Brush 1/2 of the face, then click and feed.

Brush ¾ of the face, then click and feed.

Brush the whole face, including the muzzle, then click and feed.

Do the same on the other side.

Stand in front of your horse.

Brush the top half of the face with the toothbrush on both sides, then click and feed.

Brush ¾ of the face on both sides, then click and feed.

Brush the whole face on both sides, including the muzzle, then click and feed.

WORKING WITH CLIPPERS ON THE FACE

I will use the cheaper set of clippers. Go through the same process with the toothbrush, but turn around the clippers so you will not clip them and they can get used to the sound and vibration. Your horse might notice that it sounds and feels different. They should accept it right away. If not, you might have to go back to the toothbrush. Trim the long hairs around the neck down the jaw. You just might have to click and feed for the whole process. I usually never trim the muzzle, because your horse needs their whiskers for feelers.

I usually do not clip the inside of the ear. Your horse needs that hair for protection. Clip around the base of the ear, clicking and feeding. If you must clip the inside of your horse's ears, try to clip the ear with one fast stroke to avoid the tickling. Click and feed if they stand still.

Do both sides.

CHAPTER 15
HEAD DOWN AND STANDING STILL

HEAD DOWN TASK

One important task is to have your horse put their head down. This has a calming effect and will also help you put the halter on a little easier. When I first started with Clicker Training I taught Cheyenne how to put her head down. When Cheyenne was confused about something she would offer putting her head down. I liked this because she was talking to me. As long as she had her head down everything was going to be OK. When I wasn't asking Cheyenne to do any thing she would stand still and lower her head. I would count in seconds how long she stood still then I would click and feed. Soon she would stand still for about 5 minutes, then 10, then 20, and so on. Then I could start phasing it out the click. Now she knows what to do when I am not asking her to do anything. Then she soon would stand in a position that made her feel comfortable and patiently wait. Head down is a good signal to tell your horse you want them to do nothing. They need something to do when there is nothing for them to do. "Stand still, lower your head, and relax."

You will need halter, lead, target, clicker, and pouch of food.

With halter and lead on, stand on your horses left side.

Take your target and ask your horse to target it, then click and feed.

Bring your target down toward the ground a little and have your horse target, then click and feed.

Repeat 2 more times.

Bring the target to the ground and have your horse target, then click and feed.

Lay the target on the ground and have your horse target, then click and feed.

Repeat 3 more times.

Wait and do nothing to see what your horse offers you.

If they target the ground on their own, click and feed.

Repeat this around 10 more times.

Do the same on both sides of your horse.

Adding a Cue to Head Down Task

Place your hand on your horse's poll and leave it there until your horse's head goes down to the ground. Click and feed.

CLICKER TRAINING: COLT STARTING THE NATURAL HORSE

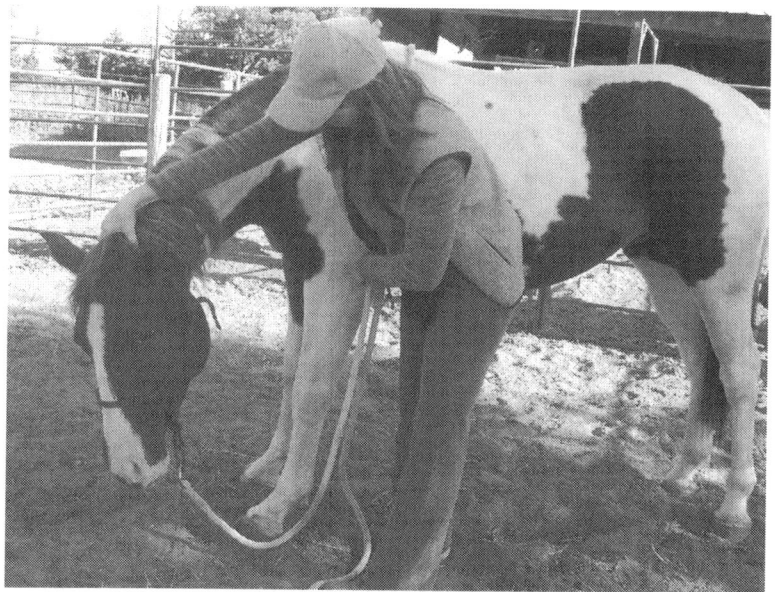

Cherry, putting her head down on cue.

Repeat this for 5 more times.

You can end the session for now.

You might have to repeat the same on your next session. Practice this enough and your horse should lower their head when you use your hand. If they do not, you can use some pressure to get their head to go down. Then click and feed. Make sure your pressure does not cause pain, just discomfort. If their head does not go down, go back to your target and try again.

You can use the same sequence to add other cues to head down. You can place your hand on their halter and give slight pressure and they should follow the pressure down. You can also put your hand on their neck and have their head go down.

Remember to do this on both sides.

STANDING STILL TASK

If your horse is having problems with standing still, the best thing to do is teach your horse that standing still is a desirable thing. If this is not taught, it may not happen. Your horse should be standing still when brushed, saddled, mounting, tied, or when you wish. This should be something that your horse wants to do.

Putting his head down will calm your horse, and this will help him to stand still.

There are several cues or signals for standing still. I will never brush my horse while he is moving. The brush itself is a signal to the horse that they should stand still. When I present the saddle to my horse, it is a signal to stand still while I put the saddle on. When I secure the saddle, this is a signal for standing still. When I bring a winter blanket out to put on my horse, that is also a signal to stand still until the blanket is secured. These signals are learned over time. To get started I teach certain things first.

You will need clicker and pouch.

Have your horse in an area with no other horses. A stall or a round pen would be good.

Ask your horse to drop his head on cue. You should not have to click for this.

Pet your horse on the neck. If your horse stands still, click and feed.

Pet your horse from the neck to their back. Click and feed. If they bring their head up, you can ask them to bring it back down, but do not worry about this too much. If your horse looks relaxed and stays calm, that is your goal.

Continue to pet your horse on their neck to their back. Again, if they stand calm, click and feed.

CLICKER TRAINING: COLT STARTING THE NATURAL HORSE

Repeat the same on the other side.

When this task is finished, your chain of tasks should be:

Pet your horse on their neck to their back on both sides. If your horse stands still, click and feed.

Walking Away from Your Horse while They Stand Still

Now that your horse is working with you and standing still, pet your horse on the neck and take one step back from your horse. If your horse stands there and does not follow you, click come back to your horse, and feed.

Practice:

Take 2 steps away from your horse. If your horse stands still, click, walk back to your horse, then feed.

Take 3 steps away from your horse. If your horse stands still, click, walk back to your horse, then feed.

Take 4 steps away from your horse. If your horse stands still, click, walk back to your horse, then feed.

See how far you can get from your horse. On the first session you should walk away no more than 10 steps. The sessions should be very short. If you do too much too fast, your horse might follow you, and you will be letting your horse fail. We are setting up for success, so take what your horse gives you and work more on it another time. If your horse wants to leave, you need to figure out why. Your food may not be good enough to keep his interest.

Standing away from your horse while they stand still.

Pet your horse softly on the neck, then move to the back of your horse. This is a cue for them to stand still.

Walk 2 steps away and count to 1. Click if they stand still. Walk back to your horse and feed.

Walk 2 steps away and count to 2. Click if they stand still. Walk back to your horse and feed.

Continue this pattern until your horse can stand still with you standing 2 steps away for at least 10 seconds. Then move around your horse to the other side. Take a few steps away and count to 2, then click and feed. Count to 3, click and feed. Count all the way to 10. Get creative.

Soon your horse will be standing still during brushing, saddling, and anything else you would like to do.

WHEN IS THE BEST TIME TO START YOUR HORSE?

Horse's bones are not closed until they are around 5 years old. You can ride them when they are 2, but lightly. I still have yet to see a mature 2-year old. 3 year olds are better, but 4 & 5 year olds seem to be best. I have started 7 and 8 year olds with some of the best results, but they did have some prior ground training.

Some younger horses don't have the confidence to stand still, take a saddle, or a rider. If they are having problems in their training and they are young, it could be because they are immature. I can't tell you how many times I have put young problem horses back out to pasture and had them come back months later a completely different horse. I really do like them older for riding.

With babies you have to be patient, as they are easily scared. You might mistake an immature horse as UN-trainable or wild. Keep in mind that you just might be asking too much of them too soon. It is like asking a 2-year old child to drive a car. Sometimes you have to teach what the horse is capable of learning for their age. Horses can learn what we want to teach them at a young age, but the lack of focus and maturity can slow you down and even get you into trouble.

CLICKER TRAINING: COLT STARTING THE NATURAL HORSE

If you are having problems, stop and rethink the process. They may need more maturing time. I know that many horses have been stamped as bad and, most likely, it was because they just were not mature enough to accept the tasks.

A good example of an immature horse was Bobby Sox. I have talked about this horse before. We brought her in at 6 months old to have her started with the halter. It took me about 6 weeks to get a halter on her without trouble. I gave up on her, and put her out to pasture for 4 years. During that time, we were able to take care of her health, but that was the extent of it. When we finally brought her in for training, I was convinced I would have problems with her, but she was just perfect. She did not spook, and she was very easy to catch. We put a pad and a saddle on her back the first day. She walked on a bridge at liberty the next day. She was a completely different horse. She was very mellow and easy to get along with. The only thing that I contribute this to is the fact that she needed time to grow up. The owners felt guilty about leaving her out to pasture so long, and not starting her sooner, but there was no guilt any more about Bobby Sox. She was ready for her training at 4 ½ years old, and the timing was perfect.

I never recommended selling her, because she was so fearful as a baby. I had no idea what she was going to turn out to be. She grew up and took the personality of her mother, which is very sweet and loves people. It took her some time to grow up. You can't make a 10-year-old child act like a 20-year-old grown person. It is just nature. I have had many young horses sent to me because they were considered UN trainable. What I have found is that they needed a patient trainer and more time to grow up.

I thought Bobby Sox would be the one that I could not help, but it turned out she cured herself. I know I am a much different person now than I was when I was a teenager. If I only knew then what I know now. But I would not be the person that I am if I didn't make mistakes and learn from them. We are all different when time passes.

CHAPTER 16
LATERAL FLEXION

You have to have brakes on your horse. There has to be a way to control your horse just in case the worst happens. *Lateral Flexion* is when you ask your horse to turn their head to the side until they touch their nose to their shoulder or belly. This puts your horse in a position where it would be difficult for them to run off or buck. It takes most of the power out of the horse.

The method that I used to teach a horse lateral flexion before Clicker Training was to release pressure when their head flexed a little. This works, but it can take a long time. This method would be using negative reinforcement as the main teaching tool, so the horse will only do what is necessary. Your horse will have a tendency to lock up a little. Today, I only use Clicker Training for teaching this method, even when I am retraining a horse that has good lateral flexion. It makes the process so much more pleasant for you and your horse.

We have to think about our horse's physical capabilities. The horse's neck might not be as limber in a particular direction. They resist only because it is a physical matter, not because they do not understand. It can take some time to get the horse's neck used to flexing and stretching out those muscles. I see the strain that it can take on them. Forcing it is inconsiderate and may make your horse more hesitant. The most that I have ever seen a horse flex in the pasture is if they have an itch on their side and they try to scratch it, and that only lasts a few seconds.

I teach lateral flexion with the rope halter and lead first, not the bit. If they cannot flex with just a simple rope halter, your chances of good lateral flexion with a bit will be much less, since a bit can be harsh.

For the lateral flexion task you will need clicker, pouch, target, halter, and a lead rope.

Stand on the left side of your horse at their shoulder.

Drape the lead over your horse's neck on their left side. We do not want to use the halter and lead, but have it there for the next set of tasks.

Ask your horse to follow the target to their left belly or shoulder. When their neck is flexed, and they touch the target, click and feed. Do not ask them to hold the flex. As soon as they touch their nose to the target, click so they can straighten their neck out and have a rest.

They might back up or move around you. Ignore them and wait for them to stop, and try again. Click when they touch the target, then feed. Figure out how to move the target where you would like them to touch it. If they are having problems following the target, you can move it where they succeed, then advance from there.

Practice this a few times.

Hold the target at your horse's shoulder or belly. They should come to the target on their own. Practice this a few more times. We are only looking for them to flex their neck to touch the target, belly or shoulder for 1 second.

Repeat this several times.

Your horse will figure out right away what you want and start flexing automatically. When they do, take the target away and see if they can flex on their own without the target. This is important because now you are clicking for the task of flexing, not touching the target. The horse usually gets too focused on the target and is not paying enough attention to the task. When they flex on their own where you would like them to, click, then feed.

Repeat clicking and feeding for them offering you the flex without your help at least 5 times.

ADDING A CUE TO LATERAL FLEXION

The cue for Lateral Flexion will be a light pull with the lead in the direction of the flex. We don't want to pull or cause a strain on your horse. Give them a chance to figure it out with just a light pull.

When your horse offers flexion, place your hand on the lead, as your horse is flexing, pull the lead lightly. Let your horse feel some pressure so they will know what the pressure is. This should be light.

Repeat this several times.

Practice:

Ask your horse to flex with the cue one time click and feed.

Ask your horse to flex with the cue two times then click and feed.

Repeat up to 10 times.

Do the same on the other side.

Now your horse has shown you that they have an understanding of flexion, but only if you are standing on the side of the flexion. When we ride we will be asking our horse to flex from sitting on top of them. Our position will be different. We are not riding yet, but we can get a good simulation of riding from the ground.

It is important that the horse flexes for us standing on the opposite side of the flex. Horses perceive everything in regard to our position. They will think that you standing on their side is the cue. This is not our end goal, but very good progress.

Leave the lead draped over their right shoulder. Walk to the other side of your horse. You will now be standing at your horse's left shoulder. You will still be asking your horse to flex to the right.

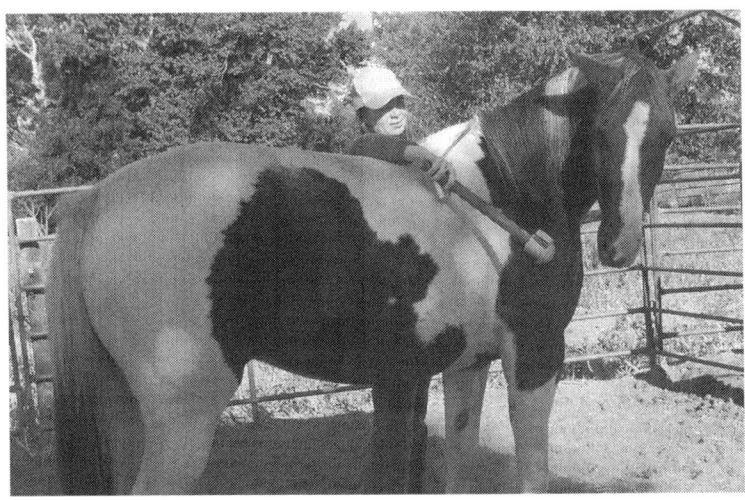

Cherry flexing to the right.

Your horse will automatically think that they should flex towards you. So they will follow you and flex to the left, because they have mistaken the task. Ignore this.

Take your target and place it over your horses back so it will be at the same place where you previously clicked, which would be at their right shoulder. You can reach over your horse's back or take the target around to the front so your horse can see it. Then bring the target around to their right side and have your horse flex, touch the target, click and feed. You might have to do this in small increments at first. This will confuse your horse a little, and it might take some time to get them used to flexing while you are standing on their opposite side.

Take your target again and slowly place it over your horses back to their right shoulder. Wait for your horse to think and make a decision. They should come around and touch the target. If not, you can help them by waving the target to get their attention. When they touch it, click and feed.

When your horse consistently flexes and touches the target on their right side while you are standing on their left side, take the target away and see if your horse can 'show you what they know' by flexing on their own towards their right side. Remain on their left side. Nothing will change other than your horse not seeing the target. Wait, and be patient. They might get a little lost. If you feel that your horse is too lost, go back to the target. Waiting a little longer for them to think might just give them enough time to get the connection. Some horses take to it right away, but some take more time. If it takes more time, and it is a horse that already knows how to flex with negative reinforcement, that tells me that they really didn't understand lateral flexion. This should clear it up for them once the task is finished.

Have them show you what they know on their own, up to 10 times, clicking and feeding for every desired flex. Some will move their neck half way around. If you know your horse can flex all the way to their shoulders or belly, do not click for a half flex. They are trying to do less and get the click. They are trying you out to see if you are a pushover. If they continue to give you less effort, end the session for the day.

When your horse is flexing to the opposite sides with ease and eagerness, their lateral flexion is complete for your 'show me what you know' checklist.

Adding the cue

Make sure the lead is draped on the right side of your horse, while you are still standing on the left side. When your horse is already flexing on their own, pick up the lead and add the cue of pressure on the lead so your horse will recognize the cue for the task. Your horse already knows that flexing is a good thing and teaching him a cue to it will be no problem.

You want to add the cue for lateral flexion at the same time your horse starts to flex. This is very fast work, because horses won't waste time. It might take you a few tries to get organized. Click and feed every time your horse flexes to the position taught, no matter if the cue was there or not. It is up to you to make sure that the cue is there. If you mess up, it is not your horse's fault. If your horse is having a problem with the cue, walk to their right side and use the cue while standing on their right side a few times then go back to the left side and see if there is improvement.

Practice asking your horse to flex to the right with the cue, while standing on their left side, 10 times in a row.

Now you can phase out flexing on their own, and only reward when the cue is given. You don't want to wait too long to give the cue. Your horse will be flexing repeatedly over and over again. Only click when there is a cue. If you can keep up with your horse, that is fine. If you did not ask yet, ignore the offering, but hurry and give the cue so they don't get too frustrated. Keep the pressure very light. If your horse feels too much pressure too fast, this might confuse them. Wait with light pressure for them to make a decision. If your horse resists, you might be pulling too hard. Go back and use your target for help.

Ask your horse with the cue 10 times, clicking and feeding every time they flex. If you feel your horse is too automatic and they are flexing before the cue is given, don't worry. Just you standing in that position can be perceived as a cue to your horse.

Don't wait for them to offer this to you anymore. Use only the cue, and click for only the cue. If they offer it to you that is fine, but you don't click and feed for them offering on their own anymore.

Do the other side.

Repeat the same exact process for the other side. You will need your target to get them to flex to the left. This will get them focused on that side. The left side can take longer than the right because they will be focused on what they have just learned. I like to do one side and leave the other side for another day. Too much information too soon can get them frustrated.

When this task is finished, your chain of tasks should be:

Ask your horse to flex to the right on cue, while standing on the left side of your horse. Then click and feed.

CLICKER TRAINING: COLT STARTING THE NATURAL HORSE

Ask your horse to flex to the left on cue, standing on the right side of your horse. Then click and feed.

This part of lateral flexion is finished. Your horse now has an understanding of it. When we start to ride our horse, the cues will still be the same, but we will maintain it with some pressure. You might think that they flex this easily all the time. When your horse is in a different situation, they may need some help, and if you get into trouble, you will have to use pressure for that help. I don't use pressure for teaching, because it changes how the horse perceives the task. When the horse offers you a behavior, it gets stuck in their mind as something desirable, and it will make the tasks easier under stressful situations.

CHAPTER 17
SADDLING

PREPARING FOR THE SADDLE WITH ROPES

Your horse should be use to ropes around their legs and body prior to this process.

You will need a halter, two 12-foot lead ropes, clicker and pouch.

You can start on either side of your horse.

Stand at your horse's shoulder.

Take your lead rope or a rope and wrap it around your horse's body where the cinch would go. Tighten the rope very slowly around your horse's belly, and then loosen it. Click when the rope is tight, if your horse stands still, then feed.

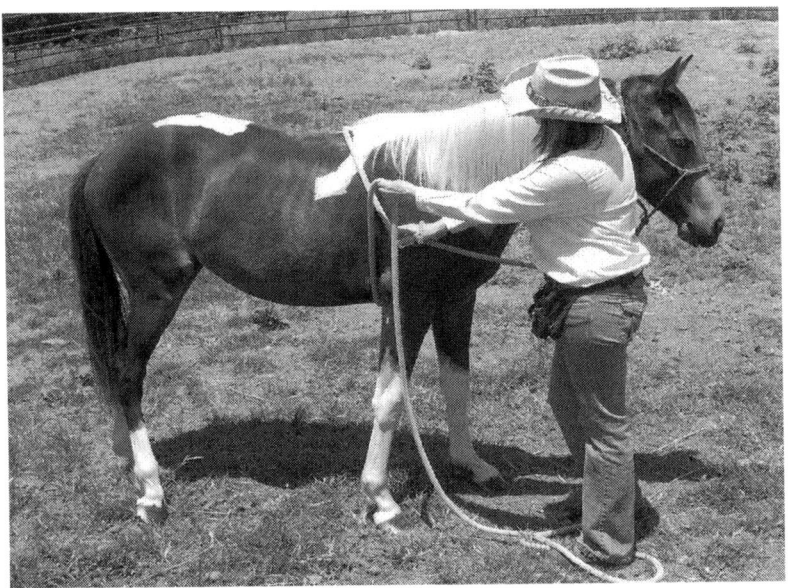

Jasmine is getting used to the rope.

Ask your horse to walk while you are tightening and loosening it. Click when they relax while the rope is tight, then feed.

Take the rope and wrap it around the horses body where the back cinch would be (if you had a western saddle with a back cinch).

Pull on the rope lightly, if your horse stands still while tightening, then click and feed.

Ask your horse to walk around as you tighten and loosen the rope. If they relax and accept it while tightened, click and feed.

Most horses are fine with this. When I have used this without Clicker Training, it did work well but there was always the possibility of bucking. They learn that the only way to get the pressure off is to stand still and not buck. Don't forget to do this on both sides. Do this task until it is solid and they accept it calmly.

I learned my lesson on this, years ago. My every day saddle doesn't have a back cinch. We purchased a new saddle that had one. We tried it on Joe, my father's horse that I had been riding for about 2 years. Thankfully, I always work my horses a little before I get on. Joe bucked so much that he hit the fence and now has a permanent scar on his leg. I then started using the ropes further back on their bellies. It is a much safer way to help a horse get used to cinches.

INTRODUCING THE SADDLE PAD

You will need clicker, pouch, halter, lead, and a saddle pad that can get dirty.

Ask your horse to smell the saddle pad first, then click for them targeting it.

Repeat.

Rub your horse on their neck with the pad, click when the pad touches your horse, then feed.

Move it to the shoulder. Click and feed.

Repeat.

Move it to their back. Click and feed.

Repeat.

Drape it over your horses rump, click and feed.

Repeat.

Do this on both sides.

Lay the pad on the horses back. Click and feed.

Take it off and lay it again on your horses back. Click when the pad is laying on your horses back.

With the pad on your horses back, ask them to go for a walk. Take the pad off while they are walking and let it lay on the ground. Click when it hits the ground.

Repeat a few times on both sides.

Let the pad fall off your horse and land on the ground, click and feed when it falls to the ground, if your horse accepts it quietly.

Repeat several times.

Do this on both sides.

INTRODUCING THE SADDLE WITHOUT THE PAD

You will need halter, lead, saddle, clicker and pouch.

Hold your horses lead with your left hand.

Let your horse target the saddle. Click and feed.

Repeat 3 times.

Stand at your horse's shoulder and brush the saddle on your horse's shoulder. Click and feed if your horse stands still for this. It will be hard to hold the saddle and click so you might use your tongue click. You will have to put the saddle down and feed.

Repeat 2 more times.

Swing the saddle on top of your horse and lay it on their back gently. If you hold the saddle in one hand with the side of the saddle on your hip, it will be easier to swing it onto your horse.

CLICKER TRAINING: COLT STARTING THE NATURAL HORSE

Click when you lay the saddle on your horse, then feed.

Take the saddle off and repeat 2 more times.

Swing the saddle on again and leave the saddle on, wait for 5 seconds, then click and feed. During those 5 seconds pet your horse.

Repeat up to 20 seconds.

Take the saddle off and lay it on the ground and ask your horse to smell the saddle. Remember if this is a nice saddle, your horse might bite it or paw it. Using an older saddle that can get dirty might be better.

Repeat the same 2 more times, putting your saddle on for 20 seconds, then click and feed. Lay the saddle on the ground and have your horse smell the saddle, then click and feed.

Put the saddle back on your horse, walk off and ask your horse to follow you. Walk 5 steps with the saddle on, click and feed.

Walk 5 more steps with the saddle on, click and feed.

Walk 6 steps with the saddle on, click and feed.

Walk 7 steps with the saddle on, click and feed.

Skip to 10 steps, click and feed.

Continue to 12 steps, then click and feed.

Keep going until you can walk 25 steps with the saddle on your horse.

When this task is finished, your chain of tasks should be:

Walk for 25 steps with the saddle laying on their back.

Then click and feed.

Repeat the same on the other side. Your horse should see you put the saddle on from both sides.

I like to put the saddle on for the first time without the pad, because you don't have to cinch it up so tight. The saddle seems to stay on better, just in case the horse gets scared, jumps or bucks. They are less likely to lose the saddle. There are some pads that you can purchase that have a material that sticks to their back and the saddle. They work well also. It is up to you to decide what works best for your horse when the saddle is first put on. Always prepare for the worst. Don't forget your breast collar. This will keep the saddle from slipping back. It also keeps the saddle from slipping under your horse. You don't want this to happen to any horse.

Ebony, a black mare that we had purchased for breeding, had 90 days professional training. The story was that someone put a saddle on her without a breast collar and tied her up. The saddle slipped under Ebony's belly and she kicked like crazy to get the saddle from under her belly. She broke loose and broke the saddle into pieces. She was never the same after that. We would all like to have a horse that just stood still if this ever happened, but that is not reality. You never know what a horse will do under this type of situation.

The saddle can and will loosen easily if your horse bloats. Horses will expand their belly so you don't tighten the cinch too tight. After you have worked a horse for a while on ground, they forget that they have blown up their belly and suddenly the cinch is loose. Horses protect themselves from tight cinches. How would you like to have something around your belly so tight that you felt like you couldn't breathe, or move? I don't like to have a cinch so tight that my horse is uncomfortable. If you have to tighten a cinch too tight, your saddle might not fit your horse. Eventually, your horse will become what we call, "cinchy."

Natchez, my Arabian, is very cinchy. Long ago, when I started him, before I had much experience, I would pull the cinch so tight that it hurt him. I was afraid that the saddle would come off. Over time, he started to bite when the saddle was put on. He didn't just bite a little, he would bite to hurt you. He put many bruises and bite marks on me. He broke the skin many times. I defended myself by blocking his bites. I was hurting him and he let me know about it, then I acted like he was a bad horse. How unfair is that? When I stopped tightening the cinch so tight, he still bit at me, thinking that was what I was going to do. When I started Clicker Training, it took about 10 minutes to fix by clicking when he didn't try to bite me. When I cinched him up and he stood still with a nice look on his face, I would click and feed. Life for Natchez is much better now.

TIGHTEN CINCH OF THE SADDLE

You will need halter, lead, saddle, cinch, breast collar, clicker and pouch

If you have prepared the horse and have gone through all the steps, you should not have any problems. Most horses don't do anything, and they don't get bothered. It becomes something they already know. I have had a few horses buck, only because I chased them around. Before Clicker Training, I used to like to see a horse buck a little when the saddle was put on. It tends to imprint in the horse's mind that they cannot get the saddle off when bucking. The saddle makes different noises when a horse jumps or runs and it can scare them, so they start bucking. Some horses buck, and some never do. Be careful, and listen to your horse. If things are not going according to plan, back up a few steps in your training. There is no time schedule. Your horse should be completely relaxed at all times.

Bobby Sox (this is the same mare that was hard to halter break when she was a weanling) was in training. Bobby Sox was doing very well and she never bucked, not even once, during the 30 days she was with me. It was time for her to go home. I was giving a lesson to her owner. This was the third riding lesson and they were doing great. It was a very cool day. I could tell that Bobby Sox was feeling good. The owner saddled her up and he seemed happy with her. He asked me since she was doing so well, if he should work her on ground first. I told him, "Yes, of course. You always check your horse out when you first put the saddle on, just to see if everything is going to go right." He asked Bobby Sox to move to the right and she started to buck. The buck ended up getting bigger and bigger. The owner looked at me and asked me what to do. I told him to let her go and get out of her way. By that time Bobby Sox was bucking so hard her mouth was open and she was making honking noises. She had never bucked before that day. She soon stopped and it was all over. I told the owner she was through bucking, and he asked how I knew. I didn't have an answer for him, I just knew. I looked at her body language. On that day she felt so good she just wanted to hop a little, and that scared her enough to make her go a little crazy.

He seemed very disappointed in his horse. I told him that this is what horses will do sometimes. That is why we always work them before we ride. I told him that I thought that it was a good thing that he was here to see that. She might never do that again. I took over and worked Bobby Sox for a while, then I rode her all over the pasture and she was perfect. She just had a moment. As far as I know, she has never bucked since.

I put the saddle on for the first time after the end of a ground session.

I usually will use the round pen for putting the saddle on for the first time. If my horse gets away from me they can only go around in a circle.

Let your horse target the saddle, then click and feed.

Place the saddle on your horses back from the right side, then click and feed.

Prepare the cinch to be put around your horse. Click and feed if they stand still.

Walk around to the left side.

CLICKER TRAINING: COLT STARTING THE NATURAL HORSE

Stand at your horse's shoulder, facing the back of your horse.

Wiggle the saddle around. If your horse stands still, click while you are wiggling, then feed.

Put your left hand under your horse's belly and grab the cinch.

Pull up and have it touch your horse's belly. Click and feed when the cinch touches their belly, if they stand calmly.

Repeat, but this time take your tie strap and wrap it around the cinch loop at lease twice until the cinch is slightly tight, click and feed. Do not buckle the saddle yet. If the strap is not tight enough and it is not buckled, it will loosen, and the saddle will just fall off. If you buckle the saddle when it is not tight enough it could slip back to your horse's flanks. You have not put a breast collar on. This is a crucial time. Most horses won't do anything, waiting for the next click, but I have had some jump in the air because it felt different. When I don't use a saddle pad, the saddle will stay on a little tighter. We are not riding the horse yet, so it won't bother them to not have the pad. The most important thing is to make sure that the saddle stays on.

Tighten the cinch a little tighter click when you are tightening it then feed. It should take about three pulls. It doesn't have to be so tight that it chokes the horse. Just snug so they can't buck it off.

Buckle the saddle. Click when you buckle, then feed.

The breast collar needs to go on next. The breast collar should not bother your horse, but if it does, introduce the breast collar without the saddle. Click for your horse standing still while you place the breast collar on. Once that is on, you are ready.

Ask your horse to back up by wiggling the rope, click and feed.

It depends on the horse's history of how they accept the saddle whether I ask for them to walk in a circle or not. Sometimes I will just lead the horse around the pen, clicking and feeding for every step. If you have a calm horse you can ask your horse to lunge at a walk. It does not matter which direction. If they walk half a circle click and feed. It is difficult for a horse to walk with the saddle on for the first time, since it feels different to them when they move.

I just ask them to walk with it, not trot. Trotting can cause a horse to buck. The longer they stay calm, the better. If they buck or hop around, try to keep them from running over you or hitting a fence. They will soon stop. There will be no clicking if they buck or hop around. Sometimes they get so busy trying to figure out that the saddle is on that they cannot think. This means they may not be hearing a click. Bucking is not a bad thing. It is the horse realizing something is stuck on their back and they are just trying to figure it out.

Ask them to walk the other direction.

When you think that your horse is calmly accepting the saddle while moving, click and feed for them being calm.

Make the session short. It is always best to stop when things are going well, instead of waiting for something bad to happen. Doing too much too fast won't get you anywhere.

WALKING YOUR HORSE WITH THE PAD AND SADDLE ON

You will need halter, lead, saddle, saddle pad, breast collar, clicker and pouch.

If your horse is having problems with the cinch and seems a little upset, you can put the saddle on again without the pad, or you can go back a few steps to working with ropes and tarps. Sometimes horses are just not ready yet for a saddle. Do some more groundwork.

Make sure that you drape the lead over your arm, and do not tie your horse for saddling at any time. Make sure that you can control your horse at all times.

CLICKER TRAINING: COLT STARTING THE NATURAL HORSE

Place the pad on your horses back. Click and feed.

Place the saddle on your horses back. Click and feed.

Pull the cinch down and tighten it slightly. Click and feed.

Tighten it again until you can buckle it. Click and feed.

Put the breast collar on, then ask your horse to walk in a circle. Remember how far your horse walked before, then click when they have walked farther.

Walk your horse around the pen. They need to get used to it.

Make sure that the experience with the saddle is a calm one. If they are prepared ahead of time, you will get farther with them in the future. I have had some horses that seem to buck more than some others. Just because they buck a little, doesn't mean they always will. Give them a chance to soak the whole experience in.

I used to let the horse loose in the round pen, until a horse taught me not to do that anymore. Baby Face was a great horse and was doing very well. He seemed so calm. We went through our saddling session with ease and I was very pleased with him. I let him go on the first day of saddling, and he did great until he turned around and looked at the saddle. He scared himself, and took off bucking. He did stop, but this affected him so badly I had to start over. He was terrified of the saddle just being 'stuck' on his back. It took me an extra 30 days to get him over this. He was fine with anything but the saddle. He viewed the saddle as a cougar on his back that would not get off. I should have stayed with him and not left him to face the cougar alone. He taught me a good lesson.

PHASING OUT THE CLICKS FOR SADDLING

You be the judge of when to start phasing out the click for saddling.

Click and feed when the pad is put on.

Click and feed when the saddle is put on.

Click and feed for every pull of the cinch.

Next time you saddle your horse put the pad on. Do not click.

Put the saddle on, then click and feed.

Pull the cinch for 2 pulls, then click and feed. Here's a little tip when cinching your horse up. I find that if you scratch your horse next to the cinch they will like the cinch better. It gives them something pleasant to focus on.

Next time you saddle your horse, put the pad on, then put the saddle on. Do not click. Pull the cinch one time, then click and feed. Don't forget to scratch your horse next to the cinch.

Next time you saddle your horse, put the pad on, then put the saddle on. Pull the cinch one time, then go on ahead and tighten the cinch enough so you can work your horse on ground. Then click and feed.

Continue the same until you can phase out the click for the whole saddling process. It is now learned. No need to click and feed again unless problems develop.

GETTING YOUR HORSE USED TO SADDLE NOISES

Some saddles make a lot of noise, so it is best to let your horse get used to saddle noises before they start to trot or canter. When they start trotting, the stirrups start to sway and the saddle starts to squeak. Some horses will run from these noises or even buck.

Task One

Halter and saddle your horse. Don't forget where you left off on phasing out the click for saddling.

Hold the lead in one hand. Make sure your horse is standing still.

At this point it doesn't matter what side you start on, but you will have to do this on both sides.

Start tapping the saddle seat with your hand. One tap, then two taps. Click when you tap, if your horse stands still.

Repeat, but tap 3 times. Click and feed on the third tap, if your horse stands still.

Repeat, but tap 4 times. Click and feed on the fourth tap, if your horse stands still.

Repeat the same up to 20 taps.

Your horse should have a calm, not scared, look. They can be scared and stand still. Once they get used to it, they should relax. When you can tap for a long amount of time, you can phase out the click for standing still while tapping, and move to clicking for having a relaxed look on their face while tapping. If your horse still doesn't have a relaxed look on their face, keep tapping until their expression relaxes, even if you have to continue tapping for up to 100 times or more. Only click when they look relaxed. If they do not stand still for any taps, take the saddle off and go back to the flag work in the other chapters.

Do the same on the other side.

When this task is finished, your chain of tasks should be:

Tap the saddle seat for at least 20 taps. If your horse stands still with a relaxed look on their face.
Then click and feed.

Do this on both sides.

If this task takes some time, then you have to make the time. It could take many sessions. If they are doing well, you can move on to task two.

Task Two

Halter and saddle your horse.

Hold the lead in one hand. Make sure your horse is standing still.

It doesn't matter what side you start on, but you will have to do this on both sides.

Pick up your stirrup and flap it so it makes some noise. Start with one flap. If your horse stands still, click when you flap, then feed. If a loud flap bothers them, try to soften the noise by picking up the stirrup and laying it back down softly. You can increase the flapping noise as you go. You don't want to flap the stirrup so hard that it harms your horse. You want to simulate what the stirrups would do if your horse were trotting or cantering.

Repeat, but flap 2 times. Click and feed on the third flap, if your horse stands still.

Repeat, but flap 3 times. Click and feed on the fourth flap, if your horse stands still.

Repeat the same up to 20 flaps.

Your horse should still have a calm expression on their face. Only click when they look relaxed then feed. Don't forget to phase out the click for this.

Do the same on the other side.

When this task is finished, your chain of tasks should be:

CLICKER TRAINING: COLT STARTING THE NATURAL HORSE

Flap the stirrup for at least 20 flaps. If your horse stands still with a relaxed expression. Click and feed.

Do this on both sides.

TROTTING IN A ROUND PEN OR SMALL AREA

I have a particular saddle that I use for starting colts. The stirrups will sway differently, depending on the horse's size. Kiowa is a very tall horse, and the stirrups hit his elbows when he trots. I am sure that caused him to buck a little. On another horse, they may hit their belly a little and miss their elbow. I like to take the stirrups off of the saddle before we trot for the first few times. This allows the horse to get used to the feel of the saddle while trotting. When I feel the horse is doing well with the saddle, I will go on ahead and add the stirrups back to the saddle. If there is a need I will pad the stirrups, just in case it hits on their elbows.

You will need saddle on, halter, lead, a rope at least 20 feet long, clicker and pouch.

If your horse has accepted the saddle and seems comfortable with it, you can ask them to trot in a circle.

For some this is easy. For others it can be scary. Ask your horse to trot to the left. If they are hesitant, it could be because they are not sure. You be the judge of how much you click for trotting with the saddle on. If I have a horse that doesn't seem bothered by the saddle, I will ask them to trot a few steps before I click and feed them. The next time I ask them to trot, I will only click if progress was made.

I like my horse to have a lead line on them just in case they get into trouble. If your horse is comfortable, trotting should be easy. If they want to buck, walk them some more. If you only get three trotting steps, that is fine. Some horses even canter the first try.

Asking your horse to trot on-line with the saddle on, out in an open area.

You will need saddle on, halter, lead, a long rope at least 20 feet long, clicker and pouch.

When the saddle doesn't seem to bother your horse, trotting in a pasture or arena will be next.

If your horse is having problems in the new location and is not willing to trot, you can click and feed for what they will give you. You then can expand out the click for at least 4 circles in each direction, then click and feed. You should have already been working on phasing out the click for trotting, but we have to remember that we are in an open space with a saddle on. If they refuse to go around, you just might have to click and feed awhile.

When this task is finished, your chain of tasks should be:

Ask your horse to trot to the right for 4 circles, then stop your horse and ask him to trot to the left for 4 circles, then click and feed. Our goal is to phase out the click all together.

CLICKING FOR YOUR HORSE NOT PULLING ON THE LEAD AT A TROT

For this task you will be asking your horse to lunge around in a circle and you will not be walking around with your horse. You need to try to stand still. You can still turn around with your horse but stay in a small area.

This will help your horse with the line. Some horses get into the habit of pulling on the line. What you are clicking for is when your horse gives to the pressure. This will allow for a better lunging experience.

Ask your horse to trot in a circle to the left. If they don't pull on your rope, click after a few steps then feed.

Ask again to the left. Expect more steps, then click and feed. If they start to pull on you because of the open space, do not click until they take a circle without pulling on you. The moment they give it to you, click and feed.

Repeat this to the right.

When this task is finished, your chain of tasks should be:

Ask your horse to trot to the left for 2 full circles with you standing still.
Then click and feed.
Ask your horse to trot to the right for 2 full circles with you standing still.
Then click and feed.

CANTERING ON-LINE IN AN OPEN SPACE

It is best to do this task first without the saddle on. It is better that your horse understands what to do before we add the saddle.

When you ask for the canter, it should be asked in the same manner as a trot. If your horse is at a trot, use the same cue as for the trot, the only thing they can do is go faster. Keep asking if they are having problems. Some will not want to canter. There may be some confusion and they could stop. Ask again, and continue to ask in the same manner. If they still do not canter, use your stick and start tapping the ground behind you. Tap the ground once. If they still don't canter, tap the ground again a little closer to your horse. If they still do not canter, tap again a little closer. Continue tapping a little closer, even if you have to touch your horse. When your horse canters, click, even for one step, then feed. If your horse doesn't hear the click, continue clicking until they hear you. If that doesn't work, stop your horse and pet them to calm them down. The stick and the continued nagging can cause them to get a little excited. Most Clicker Trained horses are very slow moving horses. They are taught to repeat what they did last, and the last was trotting for a click.

Ask your horse to canter again. If they are continuing to have problems, start walking or even running beside your horse to give them more room, so the lead doesn't pull on their head and discourage them from cantering. Sometimes horses have a hard time cantering in a circle. By walking or running beside them they can move in more of a straight line, which makes it easier for them to canter. You will have plenty of time to work with pressure on-line later on.

Repeat the same for 2 steps at a canter, then click and feed. It doesn't matter if they come to you for the food or stand where they are.

Ask your horse to canter for 3 steps, then click and feed.

Ask your horse to canter for 4 steps, then click and feed.

If you still have to walk with them that is OK. They are beginning to understand what cantering on-line is.

Continue this until your horse can canter a whole circle, then click and feed.

Repeat the other direction.

When this task is finished, your chain of tasks should be:

Ask your horse to canter in a full circle in both directions. You can move with your horse. Then ask your horse to canter without you moving. This task can take some time.

As soon as this task is finished repeat the same with the saddle on.

LEADS ON GROUND

Since we have to work our horse with the saddle on, we might as well start working on our leads and lead changes on ground.

Before we start working on leads and lead changes, your horse needs to have an understanding of lunging at the walk, trot, and canter. One particular mare, named Jody, needed work on her leads. She had a solid routine and she knew that I always lunged her around to check the saddle. She offered me going to the right. This was the side she preferred to use. I usually will take what I am given and keep a mental note of it for later on. I was glad that she was participating in the task on her own. She immediately moved herself up into a canter because she just learned that she got clicked for a canter. I withheld the click up to 2 circles at a canter. She had been consistently taking the incorrect lead. I'm not sure why, but she did this more than I liked. Now that she could canter in two full circles, no matter what lead she was in, I needed to ask her to take the correct lead.

She offered going the right and quickly moved into a canter on the left lead. It made it difficult for her to canter in a circle without pulling on the rope. I encouraged her to move forward a little faster in hopes that she would change to the correct lead. When she did change, I clicked. She stopped, and I fed her. If she took the incorrect lead, I would wait for her to change leads, then I clicked and fed again. When she consistently took the correct lead, I would click for her cantering 2 steps, 3 steps, and so on, until we reached 2 full circles.

She offered me the same direction, which was to the right. I wanted her to go to the left. I allowed her to move in that direction on her own and then stopped her and asked for the other direction. I clicked when she took the correct lead for the direction she was going. If she was having a real problem, I could work on just clicking for her going in that one direction no matter what lead she was in. Then I can phase that out and only click for leads.

This may take some time, but they are learning to take their leads when you ask them. Horses already know their leads. They use them everyday in the pasture. When we put halters on them and put pressure on them, thinking becomes difficult. Cantering in a small circle can be difficult for some horses. They may be more worried about what you are doing than what they are doing. Some horses are really good at their leads and they seem to pick it up fast, and others have a really hard time.

Practice:

When they take the correct lead, click and feed for one step.

Ask again. Click when they canter on the correct lead 2 steps, then feed.

Ask again. Click when they canter on the correct lead 3 steps, then feed.

Ask again. Click when they canter on the correct lead 4 steps, then feed.

Ask your horse to go in the other direction. When they take the correct lead for that direction, click for 1 step.

Ask again. Click when they canter 2 steps, then feed.

Ask again. Click when they canter 3 steps, then feed.

Ask again. Click when they canter 4 steps, then feed. If your horse offers you more cantering in the correct lead, take it. This is good for a session. End this session on a good note.

Get to the point where your horse can canter both directions for 1 full circle. Continue this every session, until your horse will offer you up to 4 full circles in each direction. When your horse consistently takes the correct lead, that is when you know that they understand their leads.

King, my stallion, was awful at his leads on ground. King is very lazy. We have been working on good departures from the trot to the canter in the correct lead. I have been trying to get more circles at a canter. I want King to look relaxed, with head tilted toward me a little, with slack in the rope and on the correct lead. King did very well for 2 circles, so I clicked and fed. My attention was taken away by a large truck coming down the road. King continued to go in a circle, ignoring the truck. After 4 circles offering a perfect circle, he started to change leads continuously trying to get my attention back. King was trying to get me to click for the changes. I guess I could learn a thing or two from my horse about my attention span. He didn't get rewarded for changing his leads, but I will sure pay attention more. **WE MAKE AS MANY MISTAKES OR MORE THAN WE THINK OUR HORSES DO.**

CHAPTER 18
LINE DRIVING YOUR HORSE

Driving is a must task to do. There were a couple of times that I took advantage of a good horse, and started riding them before I drove them. They all had a hard time getting used to riding. There are a few reasons that we drive our horse, before we start riding. One is that your horse has to get used to things behind them, and the other is getting your horse used to ropes around their legs and sides.

GETTING YOUR HORSE USED TO THE ROPES

This task is a checklist before you start driving your horse. You want to make sure your horse can handle the rope being wrapped around their hindquarters, and giving with pressure.

For this task you will need halter, 20-foot lead or longer, saddle, clicker and pouch

Saddle your horse.

Place the rope over your horses back with the lead on the other side of the horse. Slip it over your horse's rump. Allow it to fall and rest just above the hocks.

Hold the lead until your horse spins around and follows the lead. If they don't move, put some light pressure on the lead. Click and feed when they give to the pressure and turn around all the way.

Jasmine is getting ready to spin around.

Do this on the left, then click and feed. Then on the right, click and feed.

Then ask them to spin around on their left side then their right side, then click and feed.

Now that your horse understands ropes a little better, and they will follow the feel, we can start driving.

We drive our horses so that they can get used to seeing things behind them. They have a blind spot directly behind. Driving can be a simulation of someone riding. We are using reins the same as riding. We are not on their back, but we are behind them.

CLICKER TRAINING: COLT STARTING THE NATURAL HORSE

For this task you will need a halter, 12 foot lead, 2 reins at least 24-feet long of the same weight, saddle on, an assistant (if you have one), clicker, and pouch.

Location: Round pen or a small pasture.

Hook the driving reins to your horse on each side of the halter.

Bring the one driving rein on the right side through the right stirrup. Lay the end of the rope around the saddle horn to hold it until you can hook the left lead.

Go to the left side and bring the other driving rein through the left stirrup. Lay the end of the rope over the saddle horn to hold it.

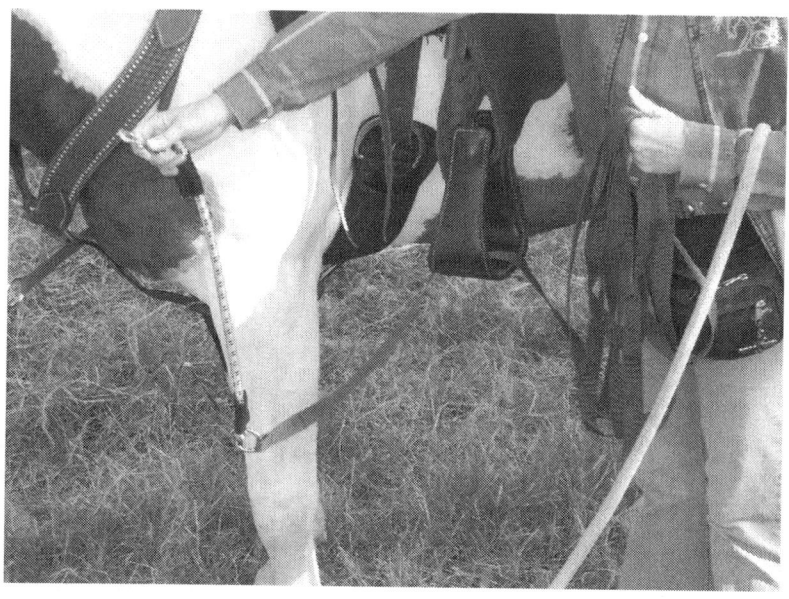

Putting the left driving rein through the left stirrup.

If you have a friend, use them if at all possible. It will make this much easier. I will explain with an assistant and without.

Line Driving with an Assistant

Hook the 12-foot lead to your horse. Ask your assistant to stand next to your horse and hold the lead. Your assistant is going to be a great help getting your horse used to the new cues of driving.

Now that someone is holding your horse, you can now take the <u>left</u> driving rein off your saddle horn, and walk around behind your horse. Have the left rein drape around your horse's rump just above the hock.

Take the <u>right</u> driving rein off your saddle horn and walk to the back of your horse. I like to stand at least 5 feet or more behind my horse out of kicking range. Your horse should not have any problems with this, because you have an assistant.

Have your assistant ask your horse to walk forward. Walk behind your horse on a loose rein.

Walk in a full circle around the pen.

Have your assistant stop your horse and go the other direction. Walk in another full circle. You are getting your horse used to you walking behind them. There is no need to click your horse for this yet.

Have your assistant stop your horse.

Have your assistant ask your horse to walk forward. Click the same time your horse walks forward for 1 step. Have your assistant stop your horse. Your horse will stop all on their own when they hear the click. Your horse might try to come to you for the food, but have your assistant hold your horse where they stopped. Walk up to your horse and feed. While you walk up to your horse, one rope will be draped just above your horse's hocks. You might think it would be easier to have your assistant hold the food, but I want your horse to pay attention to you for the click and feed, not the assistant. The point is to eventually get rid of the assistant.

CLICKER TRAINING: COLT STARTING THE NATURAL HORSE

Repeat the same process by clicking for 2 steps, then 3 steps until you can walk an entire circle around the round pen, then click and feed.

Ask your horse to walk forward with a cluck, not with your assistant. If your horse walks forward, click and feed. Now your assistant will be following your lead. If your horse doesn't walk forward, then your assistant can help.

If your horse is walking forward when you ask, your assistant can unhook the 12-foot lead.

With your assistant standing next to your horse without the lead hooked, ask a few more times for your horse to walk forward. Click and feed when they walk forward a few steps. If they hesitate to walk forward, you might have to go back to clicking for every step again until your horse gets the idea. Always break it down into smaller steps if there is a problem.

Ask your assistant to walk in front of your horse. Your horse should follow your assistant. If they do not, ask them to walk forward by clucking to them to move forward. They will soon hook on to the assistant.

Ask your assistant to turn to the right. At the same time pull lightly on the right 24-foot lead. Click when they turn, then feed.

Repeat this a few times to the right.

Repeat the same process to the left.

Ask your assistant to leave the round pen. You should be able to drive your horse on your own.

Ask your horse to walk forward with a cluck or kissing sound. Make sure that your sound is different than your tongue click. They should walk forward without any problems. When they take 1 step, click and feed. Your horse might try to come to you, but the ropes may get piled up, so stop them with the other rein. This can get a little difficult. They might try to go one direction or the other, not understanding what happened to your assistant and looking for comfort with you. Continue to keep them straight. When they stand still, click, walk up to them, and feed.

Practice:

Ask your horse to walk forward for 2 steps. If they stop and expect a click after one step, kiss or cluck to them with more enthusiasm to get the 2 steps, then click and feed.

Repeat for 3 steps.

Repeat for 4 steps, then more, until you have made a full circle.

Ask your horse to turn to the other direction. Click if they turn nice and light, then feed.

Ask your horse to walk forward for at least 5 steps. Click and feed.

Ask your horse to walk the rest of the circle, then click and feed.

Ask your horse to walk forward and turn to the right. Click and feed.

Repeat to the left.

Now you can start phasing out the click and work on a combination of turning and walking forward.

When you feel your horse has an understanding of driving, and they understand walking and turning without being clicked, you can move on.

Line Driving without an Assistant

Going to the left:

Take the right lead off the horn and drape it over your horses right side, this will make the right rein drape just above your horse's hock around them to the left. Take the left lead off the horn and take the left lead out of the left stirrup. Now you will have a 24-foot lead on the left side of your horse not in the left stirrup. The right lead will be through the right stirrup and draped behind your horse. Ask your horse to walk forward by leading with the left lead. Your horse should walk forward without any problems, if you have taught them to circle correctly. If they are hesitant, clucking or kissing to them can help, or you might have to go back and work more on lunging your horse. The right rein needs to be loose enough not to have contact with the halter. Your horse is just going to carry it in a circle to the left. Click when your horse walks off for a few steps, then feed. It is easy to feed because you are standing at your horse's side.

Cheyenne walking to the left. The left driving rein is not looped through the stirrup and the right driving rein is looped through the stirrup.

Going to the right:

Stop your horse and repeat the other side. You will have to drape the left lead through the stirrups and take the right lead off the right stirrup.

By now your horse should be walking forward in a circle without you having to click. They already know how to go forward in a circle.

Ask your horse to walk forward and kiss to them at the same time, slowly start to walk behind your horse little by little. Keep encouraging your horse to walk forward if they try to stop. When you can walk behind your horse, click and feed.

Practice this same sequence on the other side.

Take the left lead and drape it through the stirrup so that you have both leads draped through the stirrups.

Walk behind your horse and cluck or kiss to your horse to walk forward. They should walk forward. If not, you can tap them with the rope lightly on their rump. Some horses will try to turn and come to you. If they try to come to you, you might get wrapped up in the reins. I direct them with the reins to keep them straight.

Ask your horse to turn to the other direction. Click if they turn nice and light, then feed.

Ask your horse to walk forward for at least 5 steps, click and feed.

Ask your horse to walk the rest of the circle, then click and feed.

Ask your horse to walk forward and turn to the right, click and feed.

Repeat to the left.

Now you can start phasing out the click, and work on combinations of turning and walking forward. When you feel your horse has an understanding of driving, and they walk and turn without being clicked, you can move on.

I now have the driving reins through both stirrups getting ready to walk behind Cheyenne.

BACKING WITH DRIVING REINS

This is a great exercise. It is as if you are backing while in the saddle. This of course is much easier with an assistant, but if you do not have one, we will learn both.

Backing with an Assistant

Have your assistant ask your horse to back up with light pressure on the halter. Make sure that if your horse backs, that the assistant releases the pressure the second they back up. Click and feed the exact moment your horse takes one step back.

Have your assistant ask your horse to back up again. When the back up takes place, put some pressure on both of the reins lightly. This is your cue for backing. When your horse gives to the pressure to back up, click and release the pressure for 1 step, then feed.

Repeat the same sequence.

Ask your horse to take a step back by pulling lightly on both driving lines. If your horse does not step back, have your assistant help your horse. As soon as they take a step back, click, release pressure, and feed.

Ask your horse to back with pressure. When they take one step, click, release pressure, then feed.

When your horse is backing for one step easily and comfortably, you can ask for 2 steps. To ask for 2 steps, take both reins and add light pressure for one step, release as soon as they take one step, ask again with light pressure for the second step, click, release, then feed.

Ask your assistant to leave the round pen. Ask your horse to back with pressure for 1 step, click, release, and feed.

Ask your horse to back with light pressure for 1 step, release pressure. Ask again with light pressure for the 2nd step, click, release pressure, and feed.

Ask your horse to back with light pressure for 1 step, release pressure. Ask again with light pressure for the 2nd step, release pressure. Ask again with light pressure for the 3rd step, click, release pressure, and feed.

Continue up to 5 steps.

When this task is finished, your chain of tasks should be:

Ask your horse to back for 5 steps.
Then click and feed.

Backing without an Assistant

Ask your horse with light pressure to back by pulling on both driving lines. Wait with light pressure until your horse takes a step back. Click, release pressure, and feed.

Repeat the same sequence until your horse backs up with light pressure for one step. Do not ask for 2 steps until your horse shows that they understand the cue.

When your horse is light and responsive to backing 1 step, continue to ask for the second step by asking with light pressure again. Click, release, and feed.

Ask your horse to back with light pressure for 1 step, release pressure. Ask again with light pressure for the 2nd step, release pressure. Ask again with light pressure for the third step, click, release pressure, and feed.

Ask your horse to back with light pressure for 1 step, release pressure. Ask again with light pressure for the 2nd step, release pressure. Ask again with light pressure for the 3rd step, release pressure, Ask again with light pressure for the 4th step, click, release pressure, and feed.

Continue for up to 5 steps.

At the end of this task, your chain of tasks should be:

Ask your horse to back for 5 steps, then click and feed.

CHAPTER 19
RIDING

GETTING READY TO RIDE

Your horse should accept the saddle and, over all, have a calm and happy look. Some horses are very easy to start and others need more time.

Some of you might think that you have to have a bit in your horse's mouth before you ride. I always use a halter. I want to save my horse's mouth as much as I can. I usually won't even introduce the bit to a horse until after our first few rides with the halter. I believe that if they are not going to work well while riding with just a rope halter, they won't get better with a bit, since it is much harsher. With too much pressure too fast, I am setting the wrong example that I would like to teach my horses. I don't want them to think of pain, just learning. If my horse jumps or gets scared and I pull on their mouth, that can be a disaster.

BEFORE YOU START TO RIDE CHECKLIST

Can your horse flex with ease in both directions with the halter? ____

Can your horse lead, lunge at a walk, trot, and canter with saddle on? ____

Have they been through the flag and tarps section in this book? ____

FIRST RIDE BAREBACK

Starting a horse for the first time bareback is much easier for some horses. Bareback helps the horse not to have to worry about the saddle and the rider. If you get into trouble, you can just slide off. I have had more success bareback mounting for the first time than with a saddle.

For this task you will need halter, lead, small step, clicker and pouch. You will be practicing your mounting bareback.

I have a plastic step I bought for about $10 that I use. I can easily pick it up and move it around. Every colt starter has their own way of doing things. You can get very creative.

I place the step next to my horse as if I were going to mount the horse. If my horse keeps moving away from the step when placed, I will pick up the step and place it on the ground again. If your horse is scared of the step you can ask them to target it. If my horse stands still I will click and feed. Even if the horse stands still for 1 or 2 seconds, that is enough time for a click and reward. If they continue to move away, be persistent and keep the same routine of putting the step next to them. This might take a few sessions for some horses. Be persistent. Soon your horse will accept the step, and when they do click and feed.

When your horse stands still, step up on your step and click, walk down off your step and feed.

Repeat this a couple of times.

Step up on your step and start petting your horse on their back. Click and feed when you are petting them. Walk down and feed. Your horse is adjusting to you being above them, just as if you where riding.

Step up on your step and start petting your horse on their back, run your hands down to their rump. Click if they stand still. Walk down from your step and feed.

Repeat this several times.

Step up on your step again and pet your horse, then lean on their back very lightly, click and feed. Make sure that you take any belt buckles

CLICKER TRAINING: COLT STARTING THE NATURAL HORSE

off or any sharp objects off your cloths and empty your pockets. We don't want to poke your horse with anything.

Repeat, and lean a little harder. Click and feed.

Repeat several times.

Walk to the other side and repeat the same process.

Your horse should be very relaxed and enjoy having you lay on their back.

When you lay over your horses back, you need to have them see your hand on the other side of their body. If you were mounting from the left side and you swing your foot over your horses back, your horse's right eye will be seeing your right leg. They might have never seen this before, and this can startle many horses.

Horses see monocular, which is single eyed. They see their surroundings as two pictures, one from each eye. They also have a wide range of vision. They can clearly see you above them. Each eye has to be taught to accept something new. Humans have binocular vision, which means both eyes are placed close together to provide an overlapping field of view. We see in one picture.

You might spook your horse when you place your leg over, so it is best to get them used to it before you get on.

Step up on your step and pet your horses back. Click and feed.

Step up again and pet your horses back. Take your hand out over the other side of their back and straighten your arm out and wave it. Let your horse look at your waving hand. When they do, and if they are calm, click, step down and feed.

Repeat this same process up to 5 times.

Do the same on the other side.

LAYING ON YOUR HORSES BACK

Stand on your step and rub your horse, then lean on your horses back. Do not place all your weight on your horse. Lean on your horse. Click when you lean and put some weight, and only if your horse stands still. Step down off your step and feed. If your horse moves, move your step to get into position again. Stay calm. The first lean might bother them a bit.

Practice:

Lean on your horse with some weight for 2 seconds. Click and feed.

Lean on your horse with some weight for 3 seconds. Click and feed.

Lean on your horse with some weight for 4 seconds. Click and feed.

Continue the same for up to 10 seconds, with the same weight as the first. Click and feed.

Lean on your horse with more weight for 1 to 2 seconds. Click and feed.
If your horse stands still lean with even more weight for 1 to 2 seconds, click and feed.

Lean on your horse with all of your weight. To do this, you will have to lean over your horse's back even more. This is a strange spot to be in, so you need to feel comfortable doing this before you start.

Lean on your horse with all your weight for 2 seconds. Click and feed.

Lean on your horse with all your weight for 3 seconds. Click and feed.

CLICKER TRAINING: COLT STARTING THE NATURAL HORSE

Lean on your horse with all your weight for 4 seconds. Click and feed.

Now lay on your horse for as long as you can or up to 5 seconds. Do not click and feed if they walk off. Just slide off and start over.

Continue laying on your horse up to 10 seconds. They might walk off, and that is just fine. If they stop moving and stand still, you can click and feed. If you feel you need to jump off, that is fine, but do not click. This seems like a long task, but it will go very fast.

I know most of you are saying to yourself, "Why not just get on, this is way too much monkey business. I have started horses without Clicker Training, and when you just try to get your horse used to you with the 'get on and go theory,' they will not be solid in the future. Your horse will have less confidence, and you will achieve less, and your training will go slower. If you explain riding to them from the start, step by step, they seem to be calmer and spook less. Riding will be much safer. The good thing about Clicker Training is that I don't have to repeat this over and over again. I know my horse understands and accepts it. That is worth a little extra time.

TIME TO GET ON

As soon as you feel your horse can stand still and accept your weight, it is time to sit on your horse.

Step up on your step, pet your horse, swing your leg over your horse and slide on. I like to lean on their neck and hang onto their neck with my arms before I sit up. If they accept this mounting, click, slide off and feed. This is when it is good to use an assistant.

Practice:

Slide on your horse again and slowly sit up, click after about 2 seconds, slide off and feed.

Slide on your horse again and slowly sit up, click after about 3 seconds, slide off and feed.

Slide on your horse again and slowly sit up, click after about 4 seconds, slide off and feed.

Continue this for up to 10 seconds or more.

If you have an assistant, you can stay on top of your horse and continue to click and feed every 10 seconds. Soon your horse will accept you sitting on them.

FEEDING WHILE SITTING ON YOUR HORSE

You will need halter, lead, step, clicker and pouch.

You should have flexing with your halter already started. An assistant is a great help, but you do not have to have one.

On ground, ask your horse to flex to the left, click and feed. Go to the other side and ask your horse to flex to the right, click and feed.

Get your step.

Tie your lead to your halter to make reins.

Sit on your horse. Click and take your food out of your pouch. Your horse should automatically flex and try to eat the food from your hand. If not, take the reins and ask your horse to flex, as if you were on ground. Show them the food. They should take it.

CLICKER TRAINING: COLT STARTING THE NATURAL HORSE

Cheyenne flexing for the first time while mounted.

Get off your horse and go to the other side and ask your horse to flex to that side on ground.

Mount your horse (do not click for mounting your horse.)

Ask your horse to flex then, click and feed. If they refuse to flex, hold with light pressure until they do. If this still does not work, you need more flexing on ground with pressure before you start to ride.

Sometimes, if my horse gets stuck, I just wait for them to flex. It doesn't take long. It can be a good thing to have your horse offer you the wrong flex, have them think about it, and then offer you the correct direction, then click.

Practice this for a few clicks, until you feel your horse is more solid to the right.

Ask your horse to flex to the left. They should be able to do this because you have clicked for this before, we just need to channel the cue to the action. If they continue to flex to the right, let them, this will not get them a click. Wait for them to stop flexing to the right. Soon they will do what they know, and that would be flexing to the left. Remember, if you ask with a cue and your horse does not perform for that cue, let them figure it out. There will be plenty of time for the, 'have to' later on in training. It is too early to start using too much pressure.

MOUNTING YOUR HORSE FROM THE GROUND WITH A SADDLE

Your horse should be used to having the saddle on.

Make sure that your cinch is tight enough for you to get on. I test my cinch by placing my foot in the stirrup and putting some weight in it. If my saddle moves, it is too loose.

Stand next to your horse's side and place your foot in the stirrup.

Slowly start hopping up and down. One hop, click and feed. You may be throwing your horse off balance, because they are not used to your weight pulling them over to one side. A horse has to teach themselves to balance your weight on one side. My colt, King, was only 13.2 hands when I started him. It was harder to mount him from the ground than my 16 hand mare. King would lean into me, and it was like climbing on a slanted hillside. It was almost impossible. It took some time, but King started to help me, and little by little we both improved.

Practice:

Continue to hop 2 times. Click and feed.

Hop up and down for a total of 3 hops. Click and feed.

Go to the other side and repeat the same process.

CLICKER TRAINING: COLT STARTING THE NATURAL HORSE

Now it is time to go get your step. I like to use the step to mount, because it is easier on your horse when you first start riding. They have to get used to your weight and, for some, it can take time.

Place your step where you can get on your horse.

This time, place your foot in the stirrup and hop up and down 3 times, click and feed.

Do this on both sides.

Step up on your horse using your stirrups. When you are sitting in the saddle, click and have your horse flex. Feed while mounted in the saddle. You will feel different to your horse with the saddle, rather than bareback.

Since the saddle feels completely different, we still need to click and feed for sitting in the saddle.

WALKING FORWARD WHILE MOUNTED WITH THE SADDLE

Always work your horse on ground at a walk, trot, and canter to make sure the saddle is fitting properly. This will also get out some excess energy that your horse might have.

Remember to check your cinch before you mount.

This section will explain how to ask your horse to walk forward while mounted.

You will need halter, 2 leads, clicker, pouch, and assistant if you have one.

I will explain with an assistant and without an assistant. It is always much easier and faster with an assistant.

Walking Your Horse while Riding with an Assistant

Tie your lead to your halter to make reins.

Ask your assistant to snap a lead to your halter.

Use your step to mount your horse. Do not click.

Ask your assistant to take away the step.

Ask your horse to flex to the left. Click and feed. Make sure your assistant leaves enough lead for your horse to flex.

Ask your horse to flex to the right. Click and feed.

Have your assistant ask your horse to walk forward. At the same time, place your legs against your horse's sides. It should only take very light pressure from your legs. When your horse takes a step, click and feed. Have your assistant give your horse enough line so they can flex and take the food from you. Remember to release your legs when your horse moves forward.

Repeat the same process for 2 steps. Click and feed.

Repeat for 3 steps. Click and feed.

Repeat for 4 steps. Click and feed.

Now you can ask your assistant not to lead your horse, but still have contact with the lead rope.

Ask your assistant to walk off. Cue your horse by squeezing with your legs lightly. Click and release when your horse responds to your cue, then feed.

Repeat this process about 4 more times, then end your session.

CLICKER TRAINING: COLT STARTING THE NATURAL HORSE

When this tasks is finished your chain of tasks should be:

Ask your horse to walk forward with the cue for 10 steps, then phase your click out for walking straight.

Walking Your Horse while Riding without an Assistant

Sometimes you don't have an assistant to help. I usually just hang out and sit on the horse until they get so bored they start to walk forward, then I click and feed. You can make some noise to try to get them to move, but that doesn't work on some horses. If you do too much to get them to move, there is a chance of spooking them and you falling off. The saddle causes all kinds of restrictions to a horse, and squeezing, spanking and making excessive noise might cause them to buck. If you have a horse that will not walk, they are telling you something. They are going to buck forward, instead of walk. Bucking is because they don't understand. If you seem to be having real problems with walking forward, your horse might not be ready to be ridden, and you may need more ground work. A horse will tell you every thing you need to know by their actions.

I had a mare, named Spider, that I sat on for 30 minutes. She would not move no matter what I did. I finally had to go find my brother for help. It took one pull of the lead, I clicked, and that was all she needed. She just followed him around the pen, while I would click for her forward motion. When my brother left the pen, she was walking forward on cue. It was either 30 minutes of frustration, or 2 seconds of "smart" work. She was a calm mare and it was safe for my brother to be in the pen.

Mount your horse.

Ask your horse to flex to the left. Click and feed.

Ask your horse to flex to the right. Click and feed.

Ask your horse to flex to the left, then the right. Click and feed.

Ask your horse to flex to the left and right, again to the left and right, then click and feed. The reason I want you to flex so much is this is your only safety net, in case something happens. Your horse has now learned to flex while standing still. If your horse acts up or spooks for any reason, the best thing to do is remain calm and start asking your horse to flex. They know how to flex standing still, but when they move suddenly, it can make some horses feel too claustrophobic to be pulled on under pressure. We have to start somewhere. You should be in a round pen and slowly ask your horse to stop by flexing to the right or to the left.

Now we are ready to go. I will wait for my horse to do something. Most of the time they will flex, trying to get you to click. At this point, they have no idea what you want and, for most, making noise does nothing but irritate your horse. You can try clucking or voice cues to help your horse walk forward. I am not a fan of voice cues, but there is nothing wrong with teaching your horse on ground to walk forward to the voice first. It can work very well. It is best to teach this ahead of time.

Sit on your horse and wait for the correct movement. They sometimes flex so much that it will move them forward a little. When they walk forward, click and feed.

Wait again for your horse to walk forward. When they do, click and feed. It won't take them but a few clicks to figure out that walking is what you are looking for.

Wait again for your horse to walk forward. When they do, sit up straight in the saddle as if you were going somewhere, and squeeze with your legs just a little. You can even cluck. Click and feed when they walk forward.

Repeat the same process 2 more times.

Sit up straight in the saddle as if you were getting ready to walk somewhere. If that doesn't work, try a little squeeze of your legs. If that doesn't work cluck a little. This should get your horse to walk forward. If not, wait for it to happen, click when they take a step forward, then feed.

At this point you will be stopping when you click and feed. They don't know how to stop on cue. The click helps slow your horse down. Even though you are stopping to feed when clicking, this is not the same as halting. Your horse only remembers what they did when you clicked.

CHAPTER 20
FLEXING WHILE RIDING

TURNING

This is what I teach next. Turning is actually easy when starting out. The problem will arise later on when the horse is under more stress. There are many different ways to teach your horse how to turn. Sometimes I have an assistant lead my horse and I give a cue for turning, then click and feed. Or I can ride my horse in a walk and have them walk straight, and at some point the horse is going to turn, so mark it with a cue, click and feed.

You should have practiced this task earlier with your groundwork.

On ground, place your hand where your leg would go, press lightly until your horse moves away from your pressure, click for one step. You don't want to put too much pressure, just enough to make a change in your horse. They will soon figure out that moving away from the pressure is better than leaning into it. They have to figure out how to stop the pressure. When your horse moves away from the pressure, release, click and feed.

Practice this same sequence 5 times in a row for 1 step, and try to lighten up your pressure as you go. Place your hand where your leg would go and press lightly until your horse takes 2 steps. Remember to release the same time you click, but not until the second step is being taken. Release for one step and ask again for another in sequence.

Repeat the same process for 3 steps and all the way until your horse has completed half of a circle. This should be very easy for your horse if you did your groundwork. Your horse should be participating in the task willingly. If not, go back to the groundwork session.

Mount your horse. You don't have to click for the mount. The only thing that you will be clicking for is turning. Your horse might already be on, 'show me what you know.' This is a good thing, because their mind is going to be on turning and you can just add a cue to what they are already doing. When you mount your horse, they just might start turning on their own. Go with it, and add your cue to it, which would be pressing lightly with your leg and directing with the halter and lead. If you are turning to the right, you would press with your left leg where it is positioned and direct the head with your right rein to help your horse. Remember to look in the direction that you are going, this will set your body up in the proper position. Click and feed when they take a step.

You can try to give the cue again and see what happens. It sometimes doesn't work, because unknown cues confuse your horse. If it falls apart, it is better to wait for your horse to offer you a turn, then add a cue to it, and click while they are turning. Soon your horse will recognize the cue and respond to it. It is that simple. Your horse wants to offer this to you, because this is how they are trained.

Practice:

While mounted, look in the direction you want to turn.

Press with your right leg for a left-turn. If your horse does not turn, pull with the left rein lightly. Your horse should turn a little. Click and feed.

Continue the same process for 2 steps, then click and feed.

Continue the same process for 3 steps, then click and feed.

You can continue this until your horse turns half or a full circle.

Do the same the other direction.

Practice:

Mount your horse.

Ask your horse to walk forward with the cue taught.

Ask your horse to turn to the right for 1 step, then click and feed.

Ask your horse to walk straight again, turn your horse to the left for 1 step, then click and feed.

Ask your horse to walk straight for 10 steps.

Ask for a turn to the left for 2 steps.

Walk straight again, then turn to the right for 3 steps, click and feed.

Ask to walk 10 steps, turn to the right for 1 step, click and feed.

Get creative and work on some combinations. You don't have to work on the task for long. As soon as your horse can walk straight for about 30 steps, I phase out the clicking. It is now learned. I also phase out basic turning. It is time to move on to more complex tasks.

FLEXING TO A STOP USING PRESSURE IN THE ROUND PEN

This task will be one of the most important. Flexing to a stop may save your life. This is how you can regain control of your horse. Flexing takes the power out of a horse's hindquarters, which stops the horse. This task needs to be very good. All horses should go through the ground tasks, even if they are already considered a riding horse.

You will be asking your horse to flex to the right to a stop.

Ask your horse to walk forward.

Stop riding, which means sit on your horse without moving your body.

Lift your right rein up with your left hand to shorten your rein.

Run down the rein with your right hand.

Ask your horse to flex, just as if you were asking to flex from a stand still.

Your horse should flex without any problems. Click when they flex, but only if they stop. If they do not stop and turn into a circle, wait until they stop moving their feet, then click and feed.

Repeat the same process on the other side.

In the pen, ask your horse to flex with a light pull. Some horses will be just fine with this and not cause any problems. If your horse does not flex when asked, you should be increasing the pressure slowly until the flex is given. They need to know that the pressure can be there to achieve what you want. When they do give in to pressure, click, then feed.

For some, the pressure will be light and for others it needs to be more firm. If more pressure is needed, use small increments of pressure and slowly increase the pressure until you get the desired flexion.

WALKING STRAIGHT FOR LONGER PERIODS

Some horses like to turn more than walk straight. They do this because when they turn, they get clicked more often than for walking straight.

Your horse may need some help walking forward. They might walk just fine or they will get stuck turning.

Practice the walking exercise for a few clicks.

Look straight ahead.

Lift your body up tall. (Do not stand up in your stirrups.)

If they don't walk, tighten your thighs.

If they still don't walk, have the tightness go down to your calves. If that still doesn't work, tighten your calves again and squeeze. DO NOT KICK. You horse should move somewhere. Since your horse can turn and will listen to your leg, you can use your legs to keep them straight. You can also use your reins to keep them straight. The only way they should go is forward.

Walk a straight line to the fence and have your horse touch their nose to the fence, then click and feed. This is a good exercise for your horse to go in a straight line. Turn around. Do not click for the turn around, but ask them to turn around with your legs. Ask your horse to walk forward, walk to the fence again, touch it, then click and feed. Do this for a few times. This will get your horse more motivated to walk forward instead of turning all the time.

Now you can start walking in a large circle and using your leg to turn.

USING YOUR LEGS TO TURN

Turning to the Right

When you are ready to turn, look in the direction where you want to turn. This will move your body into a position that your horse can feel.

Tighten your left thigh, don't press downward just tighten it. If your horse still doesn't turn, have the tightness go down to your calf. At the same time relax your right leg completely.

Press lightly with your left calf, and hold the pressure.

If your horse still doesn't turn, use your right rein lightly and direct your horse's head to the right. When you use your right rein, you will have to loosen your left rein so your horse can turn to the right.

Click and feed when your horse turns, no matter if it is with your rein or your leg cue. Our goal is to click when they turn with your leg, but we have to start somewhere.

Repeat several times.

You can concentrate on one side if your horse is having trouble. Repeat the same over and over. Then you can see if your horse is a willing partner in turning. Notice if they just start to turn in the direction you have been practicing. They will 'show you what they know.' When this happens, you know that they understand the task. Then you can start to phase out the click for turning.

Repeat the other direction.

Our end goal is for your horse to turn with your focus and body posture, but if they turn with the calves or tightening of your body, that is good for now. This task may take a very long time, so do not get discouraged. If they turn with the rein, that is fine. It could take many months to complete this. Soon your horse will get so good at it, you only have to look in the direction for a turn.

You can pick what kind of turns you would like to use, 1 step turns, stand still turns, 3, 4, or 5 step turns. Turn while walking. Listen to your horse. If they offer you a good turn, click for this. You need to get a good feel for them. Work together. Practice this for awhile, but don't let your horse get bored.

WALKING AND TURNING UNTIL A STOP

This will help you tremendously later on. Most horses will go faster when you use your legs to turn instead of moving away from the pressure. They think that this means to go faster because most people over use their legs for forward movement. The horse just gets confused. This exercise will help your horse. When you use one leg, this means turn, not go faster.

CLICKER TRAINING: COLT STARTING THE NATURAL HORSE

Start off in a large circle to the right. You body language will be in the walking mode. After our horse has started to walk, we need to walk with our horse letting our hips sway with ease. Keep in-sync with their bodies. If we try to think about the walk and go with it, we will walk in unison with our horse. As soon as our gait changes, so will our horse. If you stop walking so will your horse. Soon your horse will recognize this, and follow what we are trying to do. It is a natural thing to a horse. We have to remember to ride this way and keep it consistent. If we ride stiff all the time, our horse will ignore what we do and be less responsive.

Walk along to the right. The circle should be big enough that you will not have to use your turn cue yet.

Relax and walk.

Start by looking to the right. Then ask your horse to turn with your left leg by tightening your left leg and relaxing your right leg. If your horse ignores you, start to press with your left calf on your horses left side where your leg rests. If that does not work, use your rein to turn your horse.

As soon as your horse turns, click, stop then feed.

Repeat with the exact same sequence in the other direction.

Soon your horse will pick up on it and start turning before you ask. That is what you are looking for, but you would really like them to do it when you ask. It takes some time for your horse to be responsive to a look in that direction.

Start again and ask for another turn, and another turn. Click, stop and feed. If your circle gets too small, start over and make it larger.

When your horse is turning with your leg, ask for two turns with your leg, then click and feed.

Keep working on increasing your turns. Chain your turns together as one task.

You will soon find out that your horse will turn a tighter circle with leg pressure. This will tell you to lighten up with your leg pressure.

Turn to the left and do the same.

CHAPTER 21
TROTTING

TROTTING FOR THE FIRST TIME

As with the walk, your body feels different to a horse at the trot. When you trot, your body needs to trot with your horse also.

Now that your horse can turn and stop and we have brakes, it is time to speed it up.

Your horse knows how to walk forward with light pressure. Trotting is just more pressure, and with more movement from you.

Trotting with an Assistant

I work with my assistant on the lunge line. Make sure that your assistant knows how to ask a horse to trot on ground with lunging. When riding with an assistant and while lunging, you have to be a good rider, because your horse will swing their legs around to face the person lunging them. If you are not sure about your riding skills, being without an assistant might be better.

I hold the clicker, because I know what the horse feels like. I will be riding the horse and my assistant will be working with lunging and will have the food.

Ask your assistant to ask for a trot. Your horse should start trotting immediately. You are a passenger at this point.

Click for a full circle. Your horse will be focused on your assistant, because they have the food.

Go around a few times both ways.

Ask your assistant to have your horse walk around. Bring your energy up, tighten your thighs down to your calves, then continue to squeeze with your legs. If your horse does not trot, ask your assistant to ask for a trot on the ground.

Click as soon as your horse trots one step.

Repeat.

You are looking for your horse to respond to you and not your assistant. As soon as your horse trots for 1 step, click, and have your assistant feed.

Repeat for 2 and 3 steps in a row.

As soon as you can trot a complete circle, have your assistant unhook the snap and give you the reins. Ask your assistant to stand as if they had a lunge line. This will help with reinforcement and give your horse something he already understands.

Continue to ask with your focus, your energy level should be up. Tighten your thighs down to your calves, If they still do not move off squeeze with your calves. If your horse trots with your energy up, you have made progress, so click and feed.

Now that your horse can trot, you can start to phase out the click for the departure. If your horse gets blocked down the road, you can click for a better departure later on. If you use too much pressure with horses, they tend to block it out due to confusion. It should only take bringing your energy level up to get them to trot.

I like to use the phrase "life up" to mean an increase in your energy level that the horse will feel.

Trotting without an Assistant

For the walk, we bring our life up, if they do not walk then, tighten your thighs down to your calves, if still no walk, squeeze your calves, they should walk.

For the trot, we would continue the squeeze with our calves until they trot. We will refine this later on.

Focus in the direction that you want to go.

Bring your life up.

Start tightening your thighs, most likely you will get a faster walk.

Bring your life up more. Continue to tighten your thighs down to your calves. If they still do not trot, continue to squeeze your calve and hold and start clucking. This will get your horse going. If not, continue to hold the light squeeze with your life up, and keep clucking, if they still do not trot bring your hand back and tap your horse on the rump. They should trot. You can repeat this several times until they take a trot. Think about going faster, have your life up and start trotting with your body. If this throws your horse off too much to where they get blocked, you might want to practice trotting on the ground for awhile or find an assistant. You can practice clucking on ground for a trot, or use a voice command for help in the saddle.

As soon as your horse takes a trot for 1 step, click and feed. Continue to repeat and lighten as you go until your horse can trot several steps. Don't ask for too much at first. Your horse should catch on the first session.

EMERGENCY STOP FROM THE TROT

It is very important for your horse to learn how to stop from a faster speed. If your horse spooks, they may be going faster than a walk.

Bring your life up and ask for a trot.

Trot for a few steps.

The first thing that you want to do is stop riding with your body. Then lift your reins up and run your hand down one rein. Use the same cue to stop your horse as if you were asking your horse to flex. Click when your horse gives to the pressure and stops, then feed.

Do this on both sides and practice this often. This is your emergency stop.

UNDER PRESSURE RIDING

We have been working our horse in a safe and comfortable place. We know that our horse understands what we are asking, and we have used Positive Reinforcement to achieve great results. If you feel comfortable enough, you can start taking your horse out and ride in different places. It could be something like the pasture next door or an arena. If your horse is jumping around or seems nervous, don't get on and ride. Do some ground work until your horse feels comfortable. There is no need to ride. If you get hurt or your horse gets hurt, it is all for nothing. This is not a race, and if you don't feel comfortable yet, that's OK. If you spend too much time in the round pen doing the same old thing, your horse can get bored. You can work on ground in a different place until you have the confidence to ride. I would start out with an assistant to help you the first few rides outside. They can lead your horse and you can ride. The first thing you should practice is your emergency stop. Ask your horse to do the same things outside as if you were in the pen. I repeat the same clicking and feeding for different locations.

BACKING WHILE MOUNTED

First we need to work on the ground to get your horse thinking about backing up.

Start asking your horse to back with slight pressure on the halter or pressing on the chest. Click for a step backwards.

CLICKER TRAINING: COLT STARTING THE NATURAL HORSE

Do this several times until your horse starts backing without a cue. Once they are in the mind set for backing, mount your horse.

If your horse just starts to back that's OK, click and feed.

Sit deep in the saddle.

Lean back a little, bring your legs a little forward.

Run your hands down the reins.

Your horse should start to back.

If they do not back, make some contact with the halter lightly.

If they still do not back, get off, and do your groundwork again. You might even have to use your reins on ground, or get an assistant for help.

Your horse should start to back without any problems, if you click and feed often. Remember this is still the beginning of backing, so we go through it slowly.

If you practice this enough you will be able to back your horse through your seat or just by making a fist with your hand on the reins. Horses can feel very soft pressure, and you don't have to pull. Good practice is the key. This task can take a while.

CHAPTER 22
ADVANCING

SIDEPASSING

I was working on a mare that apparently knew how to side pass. For some reason she would not side pass with ease at all. To me, if a horse doesn't side pass when asked with a light touch, there is some retraining in order. She was in training with me for some time and she was offering behaviors with great success. If I asked her to do something and she really understood, she should do what I ask. I asked her to side pass and she was ignoring me with a confused look on her face. I knew that if we could start over again on ground that might help her.

I went to find a fence for her to face that would prevent her from moving forward and she could concentrate on just going sideways. She seemed to understand moving her hindquarters over, but her front was the problem. We fixed the forequarters and she was offering me side passing. When I mounted, I asked her to side pass and she was very confused and blocked out my cues. I left her alone and let her think about it.

She started to side pass on her own, so I added a cue to it. Soon she was side passing very well. It was hard to stop her. I asked with the cue for the other direction. She ignored me and kept on side passing the same direction. She had this in her mind and I was not going to change it. I let her side pass till she got to the corner. I did not click and feed, I just ignored her. She then side passed the other direction, because there was no where else to go. I waited for her and she thought a bit. I asked her to go the other direction with a light press of my leg and she started to side pass the other way. I clicked the moment she took a step. She began side passing with ease. I ended the session for the day.

The next day I repeated where we left off. I walked her out to the arena and asked her to side pass, she was getting upset and confused. I took her back to the fence and she side passed with ease again. I turned around and moved about 5 feet from the fence. I faced the fence again. I asked her to side pass and she side passed with ease in both directions. I ended the session for the day.

The next day I repeated the same. I went to the arena and asked her to side pass and she side passed with ease in both directions. Its not that she didn't want to side pass the first time I asked in the arena, she just needed a focal point to remind her. These tasks are harder than you think, and we take advantage of our horse assuming that they are being disrespectful. When in reality, they just don't understand. She now side passes when I ask her to. I don't have to click anymore. She understands what I want and will do it.

If you did the proper ground training with your horse offering you behaviors by moving forequarters and hindquarters over, you should have no problems with the sideways task. If you have not finished your groundwork, you should go back and finish that up before you do this task.

SIDE PASSING ON-GROUND

You will need halter, lead, clicker, pouch, and extension stick.

This task is best done along a fence. The fence keeps the horse from going forward. When you ask a horse to side pass, they think that you want them to go forward and in the confusion they will automatically walk forward. The fence tells them that forward is not an option. Sideways will be easier.

Have your horse face the fence.

Ask for them to move their forequarter over by tapping them on their shoulder lightly with your stick. Click when they move over, then feed.

Ask for the hindquarters to move over by tapping them on their rump. When they move their hindquarters over, click and feed.

Repeat forequarters, then hindquarters. Click and feed for every time your horse moves over.

Soon you will notice that your horse will start offering this to you. Your horse will be side passing before you ask. That is what you are looking for. When they side pass on their own, click and feed: As soon as you feel your horse is side passing with ease, work on the other side. Then start to add a cue to side passing. Get rid of your stick and press your hand lightly where your leg would be, which is slightly behind your cinch. You are now adding a cue for side passing.

Repeat the same on the other side. Remember, your horse should be 'showing you what they know' to get this task finished.

Do this task for a few sessions.

SIDE PASSING IN THE SADDLE

Repeat the side passing on ground first, just to get the task in your horse's mind.

Mount your horse.

We will be side passing to the left first.

Face the fence.

Look towards the left.

Hold the reins so your horse has to face the fence.

Open up your left rein as if you were going to turn your horse slightly to the left.

Hold the right rein straight but loose enough to not restrict your horse from moving sideways.

Take your left leg off of your horse's body.

Tighten your right thigh. If that does not work, then have the tightening go down your leg to your calf. I like to sit on my horse and wait for them to offer me side passing, then I will add my cue to it. Your horse should be 'showing you what they know' by side passing on their own. If they do not, go back to the ground work, and practice some more.

Repeat the other direction.

When your horse is side passing at the fence under saddle, it will be difficult to walk away from the fence and side pass.

Turn around and walk about 5 feet from the fence.

Face the fence again. Ask your horse to side pass.

This will be much easier on your horse. They will look at the fence, which is an object to remind him what to do. Pressure alone is not enough. Click and feed as soon as your horse goes sideways. You can start asking for more steps as you go, then click and feed.

Repeat the other direction.

By now, you should be able to ask for a side pass anywhere. If not, you need to practice side passing in different locations. Be patient. You can now start phasing out the click for side passing, and save the click for extra side passing effort.

TURNING EXERCISE WITH LEGS

Lets work on a little more turning with our body and legs. This is a fun task and will come in handy later, when you really need your horse to move away from your leg. There is nothing like having a horse move lightly away from your leg, especially if you are trail riding and you need to move in between trees or fences. Your legs should control your horse's body.

I don't like to overdo using my reins for turning. You should not have to be pulling on your horse's head all the time. It is a good back up when you need it for safety, but they should be turning from leg pressure remember, you can always get it lighter and better.

Walk your horse in a straight line for about 10 steps. You can even count out loud. If you horse is zig zagging too much, you can click and feed for walking a straight line for a few times, until they start to straighten up.

Turn your head to the right and look in the direction where you would like to go. Remember that your body is at the walk with your horse. Do not look at your horse. Your shoulders will automatically turn with your head, and your whole body will start to change. Your horse may not turn yet.

Tighten your left thigh.

If still no turn, take that tightening down to your calf.

Press with your calf. If there is still no turn, make sure your right leg is off of your horse. If still no turn, slide your hand down your right rein. Close your hand on the rein and slightly hold. If still no turn, pull with very light pressure only enough for your horse to turn their head. If your horse fights you and you feel like you have to pull too hard, get off and practice flexing on ground. Mount and work on flexing. It could be something as simple as a distraction that has your horse blocked.

Click when your horse turns, even if it is after the pull on the head. You need to give your horse a chance to be lighter. Remember our goal is for your horse to move over with leg only, not with the halter. We have already worked on the halter.

Repeat the exact same steps.

As soon as your horse turns with just your leg, and you do not have to use your reins to turn, click as soon as they make a step with your leg pressure. It does not matter if it is only one step.

Do both sides.

See how light you can get a turn. Then you can do the same with the trot and canter later on. There might not be an end goal to this. You will be working on getting it lighter in all the training of this horse. It can be as subtle as the thought of turning. You can add different elements to it. Can you turn your horse in different places on a trail or in a crowd?

CANTERING

You are ready for a canter. You should be trotting very well with different speeds. Sometimes a horse just starts to canter while you are riding. If this happens, you can click as soon as they take the canter, even if it is one step. If you're not ready yet, you can ignore it and try to slow your horse down to a trot. I usually take advantage of what a horse gives me.

Make sure it is a comfortable place for your horse, and that there is enough room to have your horse feel free to canter. It will be harder if your space is limited. If you are trying to direct your horse too much, they may get confused. You don't want to tell your horse what direction you are going to go. You only want to click for the transition. This is what we are working on.

Focus on where you would like to ride.

Bring your life up.

By this time your horse should be walking. From the walk keep focusing and bring your life up again into a trot.

Bring your life up stronger for a faster trot.

CLICKER TRAINING: COLT STARTING THE NATURAL HORSE

Bring your life up again, extend your arms out towards the front, you will notice that your horse will want to go faster. If you need to start clucking with your mouth, the noise alone should push your horse into a canter. Wait for it, but do not force it. DO NOT USE YOUR LEGS. This could make your horse confused and they will slow down or stop. It will be too much pressure. As soon as you get one step of a canter, click. Be prepared for your horse to stop when you click then feed.

Repeat.

Your horse will automatically start giving you more steps. Take them. Up to 5 steps is good for the first day.

You might say to yourself, "I am only getting five steps. That's not much." Those 5 steps in the positive are far better than 1000 steps of confusion. You will get more very quickly in the near future.

I had a mare that didn't understand what I wanted, but I knew she wanted to head toward the gate every time I would trot around and I could feel her wanting to go faster towards the gate. Since this was her first time cantering, I took what she was willing to give me. I trotted her away from the gate and came around in a large circle and brought my life up and she fell into a canter. She would not canter in any other spot, but I took what she gave me and marked the behavior for success.

Now that you have at least 5 steps, start phasing out the click for 6 steps, then 7 steps until you have completed a whole circle. Keep working on this, but remember not to click and feed for what you have already clicked for. It is now a responsibility and you need to use pressure to keep them going. There is no need to relearn this task over and over again.

I was working a mare named Easter, and it was time for her to take her first canter. She was doing very well. She loved Clicker Training and would do anything for a click. She was very smart and a serious worker. I moved her up into a canter for the first time. I clicked at the first step. She stopped and I fed her. I asked her to move up again into a canter. I waited for 2 steps, then clicked and fed. I repeated the same and she was getting the hang of it. We easily moved up into a canter for 3 steps, I clicked, stopped and fed her. I asked for the canter again, and she gave me 2 steps willingly, then put her ears back. I encouraged her to take 2 more steps. When she did, I clicked and fed her. Now she was upset that I was asking for more and more steps. She would much rather take the 1 step and quit. I didn't want to click when her ears were back but if she took the 5th canter step I had to click, because that is what we were working on. I just couldn't change the sequence because she had an attitude about it. I continued clicking and feeding up to 10 steps, ignoring her bad attitude. I could be clicking and feeding for her putting her ears back, but I was not sure if that would be stuck in her mind or not. We stopped and rested for awhile. I started the sequence up again. I knew that she could canter 10 steps, because I clicked and fed for it, and she was willing to do so by having a good transition to the canter. I asked her to canter again. She put her ears back. She did know how to canter, but she had a sour look on her face. She cantered with ease for one step, but that ugly face was still there. I ignored her and didn't click. Luckily, she put her ears up on the 6th step, so I clicked and fed. I just changed the sequence to her training. Canter, and smile. I asked her to canter again, and she put that ugly face on again. This time she put her ears up on the 3rd stride. We were making progress. I asked again, and this time she took the transition with a smile I clicked right away. Even though it was for only one step, she was cantering with a smile from the get go. She cantered with a smile for up to 6 strides, and I ended the session for the day.

I have had many horses do this. Most of the time, I just ignore them. They just want to get the treat. Or they could be scared of the canter. If there is a real problem, you can do the same task that I did with Easter. Most of the time, they get over it when they become more confident about cantering. It can throw some owners off and they think that their horse is always going to do this. You can shape a behavior to anything you want with Clicker Training. One difference about teaching a horse to canter with Clicker Training is they don't run off. They want to stop more than go. That cuts training time down so much. It is very hard to teach a horse to slow down.

EMERGENCY STOP AT THE CANTER

It is very important to teach your horse to stop from the canter. When a horse spooks, they might run away with you, and chances are, it will be at a canter or a gallop. Don't rely on a click to stop your horse. They only remember what they did at the time of the click. If you click while your horse is running away and they only stop to collect food, you will be teaching your horse how to run away.

Bring your life up and ask for a trot. Bring your life up again and ask for a canter.

Canter for a few steps, but no more than you have clicked for.

The first thing that you want to do is stop riding, then lift your reins up and run your hand down one rein. Use the same cue to stop your horse as if you where asking your horse to flex. Click when you horse gives to the pressure and stops, then feed. It is best to practice a gradual slow down to a stop instead of a bold stop. If your horse is going faster than you expect, turn your horse in a circle and gradually slow down to a stop.

Do this on both sides and practice this often. This is your emergency stop from a canter.

BITS

When your horse seems very comfortable with the halter, you might just choose to ride with the bit. I only use a snaffle bit. The snaffle does not have shanks and applies no leverage. The snaffle is jointed in the middle. The middle of the mouthpiece can be large. The larger the less the severity. I do not use any twisted wire mouthpiece.

I don't think the bit can be taken lightly. We have to remember that it is their mouth and it is very sensitive. I only use the bit for finishing work. I am also very comfortable riding with a halter, even very young horses. I usually don't even think of putting a bit in a young horse's mouth until I have ridden the young horse for up to 30 days. It also depends on the horse.

INTRODUCTION TO THE SNAFFLE BIT, OR RETRAINING FOR THE BIT

You will need halter, lead, snaffle bit, clicker and pouch of food.

When I first started Clicker Training I had to think of the best way to introduce the bit to a horse. I was trying to think of the most positive way and all I could think of was to have the horses do it themselves.

Take your bit off of your headstall. You want to have just the bit. I like to put something on the bit so it tastes good to the horse, and it will make it more interesting. My horses really like Dark Karo Syrup. Pancake syrup works well also. Your horse will tell you what they like. Remember, before we start with the bit, your horse should be used to you touching them in their mouth and their ears. (See Chapter 14)

Place the syrup on the mouthpiece.

Hold the bit in your hand without the headstall on it.

Ask your horse to target the bit. When they target the bit, click and feed.

Repeat this several times.

Your horse will try to bite and lick the syrup on the mouthpiece. Click and feed when they lick the bit.

Repeat this several times.

They will soon try to bite the bit. When they do, click and feed. It will taste good to them, so they will continue to lick and bite it.

Your horse will soon suck it up into their mouth. I still let it be up to them what they want to do. When they bite it, I click and remove the bit, and feed.

When they are used to biting it, I will hold it on the bars of their mouth for a couple of seconds, then click. When they will spit the bit out, I will feed. I will continue this until they can hold it in their mouth about 10 seconds.

Continue this for a couple of days, or a few sessions, before you put the headstall on again.

WORKING WITH THE BIT AND THE HEADSTALL

Usually, the headstall is not a problem for your horse, but I did have one mare that really thought it was a problem. She has a very soft nose and the halter was fine with her, but not that leather thing. I slowly worked with her and she was able to get used to it. I clicked and fed for the headstall being around her face.

Place the bit back on your headstall and add some tasty syrup to the mouthpiece.

Place the headstall on each side of your horse's face with the bit just below their mouth. If they don't like the headstall, click and feed for working with the headstall around their face. You can even take the bit off and have a separate session with just your headstall.

Your horse should take the bit in their own mouth. You can lift it up to the bars of their mouth. Most horses take the bit just fine but some just don't care for it. You can put your fingers on the bars of your horse's mouth to get them to take the bit.

Hold the headstall so the bit rests on the bars of your horse's mouth, for just a few seconds. Click while the bit is in your horse's mouth, and allow your horse to drop the bit out of their mouth. At this point you are not putting the headstall on over their ears. This gives your horse a chance to get used to the bit for a few seconds before you just put it on.

Repeat the same a few times.

You can now stop putting syrup on the bit. Take the headstall with the bit and ask your horse to take it in their mouth. This time place it over their ears politely and put the headstall on. Some horses love the bit and take to it easily. Others think that it is going to gag them. I only allow the bit to stay on for a few seconds at first, then take it off. Click and feed just before you take it off. I have had some horses take a couple of weeks to get used to the bit. You will have to be the judge of how long the bit should be in their mouth before you take it off. It is always best to allow your horse to get used to it.

When my horse accepts the bit I will allow my horse to carry the bit in their mouth for a few sessions. Make sure you don't attach the reins to the bit. You don't want them to catch the reins on something. That could bruise their mouth. Bits need to be handled with care. I don't leave the bit on unattended. I would hate to have my horse catch it on something and rip their mouth.

STARTING TO USE THE BIT ON GROUND

Have the halter on underneath your bridle. You will have two sets of reins. One attached to the halter, and one attached to the bit.

Ask your horse to flex to the left with the halter, click and feed.

Ask your horse to flex to the right with the halter, click and feed.

Ask your horse to flex to the left with the halter again, click and feed.

Repeat this several times.

Wait to see if your horse will offer flexion to the left. Click and feed.

Pick up the rein to the bit and gently pull the rein towards you for the left side. Click and Feed. Your horse is offering you this behavior anyway, so you can make the transition as soft as possible. At this point I will add some pressure to the bit, just to let the horse know that slight pressure means flexing. Repeat several times. Don't "pull" on the bit. Just add some light pressure.

Do the same on the other side.

USING YOUR BIT WHILE MOUNTED

Still have your halter on underneath your bridle.

While mounted, ask your horse to flex to the right with the halter, click and feed.

Ask your horse to flex to the right with slight pressure of the bit. Go very slow and with very slight pressure. If they get confused and pull on you, use your halter for help. You will have to get a little coordinated for this.

Repeat several times, both sides.

When your flexing is working well, you can ask your horse to go for a walk.

Walk straight and focus ahead.

Ask your horse to turn to the right. You are NOT going to turn with the bit. You are still going to use your focus by turning your head to the right, and then your body. If your horse does not turn to the right, tighten your left thigh, if they still do not turn, tighten down to your calf and press with your calf. If they still do not turn, use the bit for help. If they do not respond to that, use your halter for help. If your horse turns with your focus and body position you should be very proud, you did your job. If they turn with the tightening of your thigh or calf, still be very proud, but you still want to get lighter. If you have to go to the bit, it is still a great success, job well done. If you have to use the halter, you will need more practice. Practice this several times.

Repeat the same steps to the left.

Now you can chain some of these tasks together. Ask to go to the right, then to the left, then click and feed. You can even start a figure eight at a walk.

Get your walk secured with the bit before you trot or canter. I usually will keep the halter and the rein on the horse until they get used to the bit. This can take up to 2 weeks or more depending on the horse. I will not take the halter off until my horse responds as lightly to the bit as the halter.

HERD BOUND HORSES

Herd Bound is when a horse wants to go back to the other horses.

Jody, a Paint mare, was ready for training and was allowed out to pasture with the other horses. She was a good mare and tried really hard. I could pull her out of pasture and ride her, and she was fine, but her mind was not 100% with me. Her Clicker Training went well, and she learned how to think, but she had a small magnet in her that pulled her towards the pasture. She would perform great, but I could tell she wanted to be somewhere else. When I would put her in the stall and leave her, she would pace back and forth trying to get out of the stall to see her friends. I left her in the stall for around 2 days and she did nothing but pace. When she stood still, I let her out. She did improve a little after that. When I took her on a trail ride and she couldn't see her pasture mates, she was perfect.

Some horses see you as a pasture mate. Angel, a Paint filly, is perfect when she is with me, but if I left her in a stall with no other horses around she would do nothing but pace. When I would return she would stand next to me quietly. When I took her out on trail on her own she was perfect and really didn't care about the other horses. I am very grateful that she trusts me as much as her pasture mates, but her being in a stall all alone with her pacing back and forth is a problem, not to mention she could not be tied and left alone. I always expected to get the shovel and fill in the large ditch that she dug while pacing.

The first thing to do is prepare to separate your horse from the other horses on a regular basis. Some horses are more extreme than others. Angel is more in the middle. The most extreme would be a horse that is herd bound while under saddle. I was showing one of my paint stallions at a show and met two women who had some nice mares that they were showing. If both of the ladies showed in the same class, the mares were fine, but if they had different classes, the ladies had a hard time controlling their horses. If one had to go in the ring without the other, the lady with her mare had to stand at the gate so the other horse could see her. If the mares could not see each other, they started jumping all around. The ladies placed first in every class. One lady would win her blue ribbon while the other would be standing at the rail jerking her horse around trying to control her. The ladies were so proud of their blue ribbons. They sure thought they were the best at what they did because they won the blue ribbon. Everyone outside the show ring had to accommodate them, because they couldn't control their horses.

The first thing that I always suggest when we start working our horses is to separate them as much as you can. Have a routine for separating your horses on a regular basis. You do have to have a facility so your horse doesn't get out.

As a routine, I bring horses in during the day and put them in stalls with no other horses around and let them out when they stand still. At first, they pace and throw some dirt around. I ignore this and wait for my horse to stand still before I let them out. This can take some time, so be patient. It wouldn't be a bad idea if your horse could stay up in a stall overnight. Soon they calm down and get used to it. Some horses get better if they cannot see the other horses, and others feel better if they can. Most will want to go with the other horses if they can see them leave. This is really good for them to get used to doing. Try doing this with all your horses on a routine basis.

HERD BOUND HORSES WHILE RIDING

Have you heard of the saying, "left brained and right brained." Left brained is when a horse is thinking and he can be taught. Right brained is when a horse is on automatic and is not thinking. They are only reacting. When you are riding a horse that is looking for other horses, you might feel that you cannot control them, no matter what you do. You feel they just might take off, or buck, because they have something better to do. That is a herd bound or right brained horse. You can't get much done with a right brained horse. In Clicker Training, we only want to work with a left brained horse. When they go into right brain mode we have to figure out how to survive the best we can.

HONEY THE HERD BOUND HORSE

Honey was a Shetland Pony that had a history of bucking kids off. She was in great need of some training. Her story is sad, from what I have been told. She is an ex-barrel horse who would buck the kids off when she had enough, and then someone would discipline her through punishment. That didn't work so they sold her. She figured out that bucking someone off was better than letting them ride her. Punishment does nothing to solve the bucking problem. She had no clue what she did wrong. She only looked at the person as harming her, so her attitude was bad.

I was fortunate enough to have her in for training for about 7 days. She did do well for those 7 days and we didn't get into much trouble. I was now able to continue training Honey at her farm, but Boltus, her pasture mate, lived there too, and she relied on him for her comfort. Honey was in love with Boltus.

When I started riding Honey, I found out that she was a real sweet mare and tried to stay out of trouble. She was just fine when Boltus was around, but if Boltus left, she would do anything to be with him. That's when the bucking started. If you have been riding a long time, you usually know when a horse is going to buck. I believed that she would, if I stayed on long enough. I have a saying about horses who act like this, and that is "Don't make me get off." The last thing that Honey wanted was to make me get off, but she didn't know that at the time.

When I say, "Don't make me get off," it means if I dismount, I am going to ask her to move her feet. She did have some good ground work. As soon as Honey said to me "I am going to buck you off," by snorting and shaking her head, I dismounted, hooked the lunge line to her, and asked her politely to go around in a circle. Honey did this well, since she was an ex-barrel pony and fast was her middle name. When I would ask her to leave and go around in a circle, she would run full blast, not wanting to stop. She couldn't wait to run to get away. She lunged with her head away from me. If she felt she needed to run, I allowed her to do what she felt she needed to do. She needed to run until she figured out that she was not being harmed and was running nowhere. She believed I was harming her, even though nothing was happening. She had to figure this out for herself. If she ran for a long time, I would click when she volunteered to stop, and look at me. I would then mount again. If she only ran a little and stopped, I would just pet her and mount again. I mounted and she told me again " I am going to buck you off," by snorting and pawing the ground. I dismounted again, and repeated the same with a smile. She ran for a short time, so I just mounted again. She stood still and rested. I clicked and fed her and I ended for the day.

I continued with this for many sessions. She was getting better and better, and I was feeling much better about riding her. One day she was doing well on ground so I mounted. She started snorting. I know her well enough to know that when she snorts, she's angry, so I was not going give her any room to get angry. I dismounted and we went to work. Soon the anger decreased. I was training her for a 6-year-old boy to ride. I was not sure I could fix this problem. I told the owner if she would separate Honey and Boltus, we just might have a chance of fixing this. The owner separated her from Boltus for about 4 days. When I arrived, I rode Honey unaware that she had been separated from Boltus. Honey rode perfect and she went everywhere I asked her to go, without me having to get off. I thought I was such a good trainer. I fixed her. When the owner told me she had been separated from Boltus for 4 days, I knew it wasn't all me, it was the separation. She didn't have that need for Boltus anymore.

The owner continued to separate her on and off during her time in training with me. The training and the separating paid off. Honey turned out to be a great little horse for a child and the little boy ended up learning how to ride on her. Honey became a good pony after all. She's not perfect, but she has a good heart. If Honey was a mean spirited horse, I would not have much hope. Clicker Training made a huge difference in her. When she calmed down and went where I asked her to go, I would click and feed her so she would know what was right. That helped a tremendous amount. Now Honey runs up to us from the pasture ready for her riding lesson. I was able to tell Honey that she did not have to run anymore. If you walk and stand still and maybe trot, your life will be so easy. She figured that out, and is much happier. I can hardly get her to go around in a circle anymore. All she wants to do is stand still or walk, which allowed her new owner to learn how to ride.

Honey, and her owner Bryn, who is 6 years old, on their first ride together.

Most people never separate their horses. It does have something to do with the horse and rider relationship. Some people say, "Your horse will do better, if you had a better relationship." That might be true, but if you think about it, horses are herd animals. They are with their pasture mates 24 hours a day. They depend on each other to survive. We usually only have the time to be with them 1 hour a day or 2 to 3 hours a week.

That is not enough time to build a good relationship. You would have to be with your horse 24 hours a day, and your horse still might choose to be with their own kind.

I take many of my horses on trail rides on ground. They need to have really good ground working skills for this and it is a must for all riders to have good ground working skills. You never know when you are going to have to dismount and take care of a horse that has gotten too excited. It is much safer to be on ground than trying to ride through the process. Getting bucked off will affect you and your horse for a long time.

RIDING A YOUNG HORSE ON THE TRAIL

It is best to be prepared while riding out in a pasture or trail. Have a rope halter on underneath your bridle and have a rope at least 12 to 24 feet long hooked to your horse or you can loop it or tie it to your saddle.

If you are out riding on the trail and you feel that your horse's attention is not with you, such as not stopping, prancing, or trotting off, don't wait for your horse to get into trouble. A good sign is snorting, bobbing or shaking of the head. If your horse is just not listening to you, it's a good time to get off.

Dismount your horse.

Attach your lead to your horses halter, if not already attached.

Ask your horse to go around in a circle. They do not have to canter, they can trot if they want to. The important thing is that they are moving their feet. What we are doing is making the right thing easy and the wrong thing difficult. When you dismount, they are not getting relief if they have to start moving in a circle. You don't have to hurry when you dismount. The dismount for your horse is only a brief relief and will be easily be overcome with work. It is difficult to go around in a circle and it is easy to stand still and relax. When they relax we will reward them.

If they are excited they should go around you in a circle with ease. Remember, before you go out on the trail, your ground skills have to be perfect at home.

When you feel your horse has calmed down and started to think a little more, stop your horse. Tie your lunge line back to your saddle and mount again.

If your horse relaxes, click and feed.

If not, dismount again, get your lunge line and ask your horse to go around in a circle again. You can now ask your horse to go the other direction when you choose. We are only clicking and feeding if your horse stands still and relaxes while mounted. We are not trying to get your horse tired, we are just trying to get them to think.

When they seem calm again, get back on and try again. I usually only have to dismount 2 or 3 times to correct this. The second time I have to dismount, I will work my horse a little bit more and the third time even more. When my horse calms down, I will click and feed for them calming down. Then I will start to phase out the click for them staying calm. Click when you think your horse made the correct choice. You will not have to click that often. A trail ride usually will keep your horse motivated. I will also click when my horse stays calm in a scary situation and listens to me. With Clicker Training, you can reward your horse for walking home instead of running, or avoiding spooking at a scary object. Later on, you can dismount your horse and click and feed for them allowing you to dismount and staying calm. You can shape any behavior for anything you like.

IN CLOSING

I am glad that I had the opportunity to work with these horses in the way I did. I had no restrictions, no time frame, and no customers to rush me. I let the horses make the choices. I have found that if I take the stress and time restraint out of the training process and stick with the philosophy of Clicker Training, the horses all did better and got farther than ever before and it was even faster. I was able to do things with horses that I had never dreamed of before Clicker Training. I did a full time 5-year study of my training methods and horse's reactions to Clicker Training. I allowed myself to open my mind and heart up to them, and this book is what they taught me.

CLICKER TRAINING: COLT STARTING THE NATURAL HORSE

If you would like to contact Leslie please see her web site at **www.clickhorse.info**.

Made in the USA
Columbia, SC
30 November 2017